YANKEE ELOQUENCE

IN THE

MIDDLE WEST

YANKEE
ELOQUENCE
IN THE
MIDDLE WEST

The Ohio Lyceum 1850–1870

By DAVID MEAD

GREENWOOD PRESS, PUBLISHERS
WESTPORT, CONNECTICUT

Library of Congress Cataloging in Publication Data

Mead, Carl David, 1913-
    Yankee eloquence in the Middle West.

    Reprint of the ed. published by Michigan State College
Press, East Lansing.
    Includes bibliographical references and index.
    1. Lyceums. 2. Lectures and lecturing--Ohio.
I. Title.
[LC6552.04M4 1977]   081   77-5130
ISBN 0-8371-9323-0

COPYRIGHT

MICHIGAN STATE COLLEGE PRESS

1951

Originally published in 1951 by Michigan State College Press,
East Lansing

Reprinted with the permission of Michigan State University Press

Reprinted in 1977 by Greenwood Press, Inc.

Library of Congress catalog card number   77-5130

ISBN 0-8371-9323-0

Printed in the United States of America

PREFACE

The popular lecture system in America was an outgrowth of the earlier lyceum program which Josiah Holbrook established in Massachusetts in 1826. The professional lecturers, who flourished in the East in the 1840's, came westward with the railroads which spread across the Alleghenies in mid-century. By 1850 a rich market was open in Ohio for the Eastern lecturers, and by 1855 Ohio's communities were important stopping points on a vast network of lecture routes extending from the Atlantic seaboard to the Mississippi.

This book attempts to give a history of the popular lecture system in Ohio, to show the development of cultural taste as it was exhibited by public reaction to the Ohio lectures of prominent Easterners, and to give detailed schedules of the Ohio lectures of fifteen Eastern orators. Except for Chapter I, "The Background of Eastern Culture in Ohio," which is not intended as an exhaustive investigation of that subject, but rather as a historical summary of Eastern cultural influences, the study is confined to the years 1850–70, two decades which saw the widespread establishment, growth, and decline of Ohio's lecture system.

The popular lecture system in Ohio has not previously been examined, and the experiences of Eastern lecturers in the state have received but little attention from writers. Studies have been made of Emerson's Cincinnati lectures (Louise Hastings, "Emerson in Cincinnati," *New England Quarterly*, XI, September, 1938, 443–469), and of Melville's three Ohio lectures (George Kummer, "Herman Melville and the Ohio Press," *Ohio State Archaeological and Historical Quarterly*, XLV, January, 1936, 34–36). Other references to the Eastern lecturers in Ohio are confined for the most part to the occasional mention of specific discourses by the lecturers themselves or by their biographers.

The chief source materials are contemporary newspapers, published and manuscript journals and correspondence of the lecturers, and records of lecture sponsors. Guided by Arthur D. Mink's *Union List of Ohio Newspapers Available in Ohio* (1946), I have searched the existing files of newspapers printed between 1850 and 1870 in most

of Ohio's communities. The splendid newspaper collections of the
Ohio State Archaeological and Historical Society, the Western Reserve Historical Society, and the Historical and Philosophical Society
of Ohio have been especially helpful. While I have attempted to
make the lecture schedules in the Appendix as complete as possible,
there are undoubtedly omissions, because, apart from the factor of
human error, there are gaps in the newspaper files of some Ohio
communities.

I am indebted to the *Ohio State Archaeological and Historical
Quarterly*, the *New England Quarterly*, the *Northwest Ohio
Quarterly*, and the *Bulletin of the Historical and Philosophical
Society of Ohio* for permission to reprint parts of the book which
have previously appeared as articles. Emerson's manuscript diaries
are used with the permission of the Harvard College Library and
of Edward W. Forbes, president of the R. W. Emerson Memorial
Association. I should like also to acknowledge my indebtedness to
the Ohio State Archaeological and Historical Society, and particularly
to Robert C. Wheeler of the society's newspaper library, not only
for their rich stores of material, but also for their interest in the uses
of that material. William H. Hildreth of the Ohio State University
has made useful suggestions and has imparted something of his in-
fectious enthusiasm for the study of Ohio's past. My largest debt is to
William Charvat, also of the Ohio State University, who suggested
this investigation and who has contributed generously to its preparation. The pleasure which I have received from making the study has
been heightened by the constant interest and encouragement of my
wife, Lillian Felton Mead.

DAVID MEAD

EAST LANSING, MICHIGAN
March, 1951

CONTENTS

vii

CHAPTER

I

THE BACKGROUND OF EASTERN CULTURE IN OHIO

THE LYCEUM in nineteenth-century America was a romantic, democratic adventure in the growth of a nation's culture. The ideal of the lyceum system—the promotion of a cultured society—fell short of achievement in both East and West, but, like the other romantic ideals of the time, its glory lay in the pursuit of perfection rather than in its achievement. Though essentially a New England institution, the lyceum became an important center of social and cultural life in communities from the seaboard to the Mississippi. It was established as a place of moral and mental progress, where intellectual improvement could be brought about through lectures on literary, scientific, and moral subjects. With adequate support from the public, the lyceums could become a great power for good; they could spread knowledge through the land and elevate the hearts and minds of men.

The real significance of the lyceum in the West, and particularly in Ohio, can be realized only when the institution is viewed as part of a cultural pattern which had been taking shape since pioneer times. The lyceum took root and flourished in the frontier communities of Ohio and other parts of the West because Eastern settlers, especially those from New England, brought with them a passion for education and morality which greatly influenced the native attitude toward cultural progress. But once the lyceum had become established, and down to the late 1850's, Western people, displaying a strong sectional spirit, saw in the lyceum system a means of furthering an independent Western culture. Both these influences, the New England love of moral instruction and the Western aspiration for a distinctive culture, had an important effect on the nature of the Western lyceum and the reception of those Eastern lecturers who spoke from its platforms. The impact of Eastern culture in Ohio is evident in the state's early history, in the efforts of New England people to bring moral stability to the West through the founding of colleges, and in the establishment of lyceum education. The Western dream of an indigenous culture is illustrated by the growth of the publishing industry in Cincinnati, the intellectual capital of Ohio, and by the persistent hope that the lyceum would contribute to the development of great men in the West.

1. *Pioneer Influences*

THE EARLY history of the Ohio country is in part a narrative of New England pioneers who courageously undertook the task of transplanting their civilization to the Western frontier. Before the Ordinance of 1787 opened the way for the orderly settlement of the Northwest Territory, a considerable number of English, Scotch-Irish, and German adventurers had deserted their land holdings in back Pennsylvania and the upland South to stake claims on the fertile soil along the north bank of the Ohio River. But the first important project to induce large-scale immigration to the newly opened West was of New England origin.

In 1787 the Ohio Company, organized the year before in Boston, purchased from the federal government a million and a half acres of land lying north of the Ohio and bounded on the east and west by the seventh and seventeenth ranges of townships surveyed under the Ordinance of 1785. With traditional New England interest in religion and education the promoters of the Ohio Company resolved that in each township one section of land should be allotted for religion and one for schools; from the whole territory two townships were to be set aside for a university.

In 1788 Manasseh Cutler, land agent for the Ohio Company, organized a group of New Englanders to establish a permanent settlement in the Ohio country. They founded Marietta, a New England village on the frontier. In laying out the settlement these homeseekers provided for their familiar village commons, for inlots, or home sites, and for outlots, or agricultural areas. As a result of the Ohio Company's resolution to employ a teacher "eminent for literary accomplishments, and the virtue of his character," the Rev-

erend Daniel Story of Boston arrived in the spring of 1789 and
started a school.[1]

The Marietta pioneers, who were people of unusual education and
character, insisted upon the recognition of cultural values. Thus from
the very beginning the New England schoolhouse and the New
England meetinghouse were centers of social life in the pioneer
community. And it was here that one of Ohio's first lyceums was to
be founded. An English traveler who visited Marietta in 1806 observed that the village had a weekly paper, a courthouse, and a
prison. In addition, the New England regulations of church and
state were enforced "to a point bordering on an arbitrary exaction."
Every family was required to contribute a fixed annual sum for the
support of the public schools and the church. The citizens paid a
rigid respect and strict observance "to the moral and religious ordi-
nances of the sabbath." So "never was a town more orderly or quiet."
There were no mobs, "no fighting, no racing, no *rough and tumbling*,
or any thing to be observed but industry, and a persevering application to *individual* views."[2]

In these early years, when members of Manasseh Cutler's band
left the parent group to establish new settlements in the Ohio wilderness, they carried with them the enthusiasm and ideals of New
England village culture. The influence of the Marietta settlers on
the cultural growth of the upper Ohio Valley was persistent and
strong. Chronologically theirs was "the first coherent and unified
plan for cultural development," however much that plan was to be
altered by native forces and those of the South and East.[3]

The influence of the Middle States upon the cultural development
of the Ohio country grew in importance after the settlement of

[1] Beverley W. Bond, Jr., *The Foundations of Ohio*. Vol. I of *The History of
the State of Ohio*, ed. Carl Wittke (6 vols.; Columbus: Ohio State Archaeological
and Historical Society, 1941), p. 286. The writer is indebted to this volume for
much of the historical information in this chapter.

[2] Thomas Ashe, *Travels in America, Performed in 1806, for the Purpose of
Exploring the Rivers Alleghany, Monongahela, Ohio, and Mississippi, and As-
certaining the Produce and Condition of Their Banks and Vicinity* (London:
William Sawyer and Company, 1808), p. 123.

[3] J. M. Miller, "Genesis of Western Culture: The Upper Ohio Valley, 1800–
25," *Ohio Historical Collections*, IX (Columbus, 1938), 28.

Symmes' Miami Purchase. This tract, extending along the Ohio between the Big and Little Miami Rivers, was bought in 1788 by John
Cleves Symmes with the financial support of a group of New Jersey
land speculators. While Symmes' program for settlement of the
West lacked the careful planning and cultural vision exhibited by the
founders of the Ohio Company, his contract with the federal government provided for the allotment of a college township; this provision
resulted in the establishment of Miami University in 1809.

The Scotch-Irish and English settlers from New Jersey and Pennsylvania split into small groups and founded several villages, the
most important being Losantiville, which Governor St. Clair renamed
Cincinnati. A Presbyterian church was under construction there in
1792, and the following year a school was established. On November 9, 1793, the *Centinel of the North-western Territory*, the first
newspaper in the Ohio country, began publication. New Englanders
in Cincinnati were few, although among them were some of the
community's most prominent citizens, men who were to take an
active part in making Cincinnati a lyceum center in the 1830's.

The pioneers from the Middle States were chiefly commercial
people, maintaining a thriving trade with Kentuckians south of the
river and transporting furs and other goods by flatboat to markets
in Pittsburgh and the East. They were somewhat more complacent
than the austere New Englanders of the Ohio Company's settlements and were less concerned with the perpetuation of a coherent
set of cultural values. Their chief cultural influence was religious;
Methodists and Quakers organized frontier congregations, and the
churches of the Presbyterians soon outnumbered those of the New
England Congregationalists.

During the 1790's there was a steady immigration of Virginians
and Kentuckians to the rich land north of the Ohio. Many of these
settlers, together with pioneers from Pennsylvania and Maryland,
established homes in the Virginia Military District, a tract lying
between the Scioto and Little Miami Rivers. The immigrants to the
Military District produced new influences on the pattern of Western
culture. To Virginians and to Kentuckians born in Virginia, the

tavern and the court were important centers of social life. The reckless, high-spirited pioneers from the area south of the Ohio were
temperamentally in sharp contrast with the reserved, industrious
New Englanders. When Thomas Ashe was in Marietta he noted
that "Virginians who at times visit the town, remain for a short
period, and return to their own shores astonished at the municipal
phenomenon they witnessed and wondering how man could think
of imposing on himself such restraints."[4]

The political agrarianism of these Southerners was to have a
significant effect on the governmental policies of the new territory.
The Chillicothe convention that framed the constitution with which
Ohio became a state in 1803 was controlled by Virginia Jeffer-
sonians.[5] Their influence resulted in the concentration of power in
the state legislature rather than in the hands of the governor.

To the religious life of the Ohio country the settlers from the
upland South added the creeds of the Protestant Episcopal Church
and the Baptist Church. Pioneers from Maryland and Pennsylvania
fostered the growth of the Catholic, Lutheran, Methodist, and
Presbyterian faiths.

The second important migration of New Englanders to the Ohio
country occurred in 1796, when Moses Cleaveland and his followers
surveyed and settled the Connecticut Western Reserve. After this
great area in the northern part of the Ohio territory was ceded to
Connecticut in 1786, its settlement was organized by the Connecticut
Land Company. The Reserve attracted pioneers not only from Connecticut, but also from Connecticut culture areas in Vermont, Massachusetts, New York, and Pennsylvania. Settlers from most of these
states found the northern route along the lakes or over the Mohawk
Trail easier than the arduous journey across the mountains to the
Ohio Company tract. The largest community in the Reserve was

[4] Ashe, *Travels*, p. 123. Early Western travelers frequently observed the
contrast in morality and industry of the Ohio settlers and their Virginia neigh-
bors across the river. See, for example, Thaddeus Mason Harris, *The Journal of
a Tour into the Territory Northwest of the Alleghany Mountains* (Boston:
Manning and Loring, 1805), p. 58.

[5] John D. Barnhart, "The Southern Influence in the Formation of Ohio,"
Journal of Southern History, III (February, 1937), 29.

Cleaveland (later spelled Cleveland); other early villages included Hudson, Warren, Painesville, and Youngstown.

The civilization which was planted in the Reserve was almost entirely of New England origin. As there was no general civil authority over the Reserve before 1800, the institutions established were originated by the local inhabitants, most of whom were New England people. So "townships were organized, ministers appointed, schools established after the manner of New England, and thus were planted the beginnings of institutions of New England origin, centuries old, in the 'far west.' "[6]

Although the Connecticut Land Company made no formal provision for the support of religion in the Reserve, and no public land was set aside for schools until 1803, both churches and schools were soon established. In 1800 the Connecticut Missionary Society, founded in 1798, sent Joseph Badger as a missionary to instill New England ideals into the inhabitants of the Reserve. Badger, preaching the doctrines of Congregationalism, traveled throughout the region, serving as both minister and teacher. In 1801 he established at Hudson the first organized church in the Reserve. Badger was followed by other missionaries who were also pioneers in promoting education in the West.

Migration to the Ohio country increased considerably after 1795, when the Treaty of Greenville, establishing a definite boundary line between the Indians and Americans, made most of the territory safe for settlement. The liberal terms of the land companies, the prospects of gain from rising land prices, and a pioneer spirit of adventure lured thousands of immigrants to transport their families westward down the broad Ohio, or across the Appalachians, or along the northern lakes. Sometimes the stream of population from New England was caught and held for a while in upper New York or Pennsylvania,[7] or pioneers from Virginia and the upper Carolinas settled temporarily in Kentucky, but there were increasing com-

---

[6] Karl F. Geiser, "New England and the Western Reserve," *Proceedings of the Mississippi Valley Historical Association*, VI (1912–1913), 67.

[7] Dixon Ryan Fox (ed.), *Sources of Culture in the Middle West* (New York: Appleton-Century Company, 1934), p. 45.

plaints from both the East and South that the "Ohio fever" was depriving those areas of many of their best citizens.

Between 1800 and 1825 Ohio's cultural growth was slow. New England Puritanism, Middle Eastern Presbyterianism, and Southern political agrarianism persisted as major forces in the cultural pattern, but they were considerably transformed by the shaping influence of the frontier. The development of a coherent culture requires not only sufficient concentration of population to induce social progress, but also economic stability. In Ohio there was neither.

The state was dotted with small communities, many of which had few or no facilities for education or religion except through the occasional visits of the itinerant Presbyterian, Methodist, or Congregational minister. During this period the Methodist circuit rider, preaching and organizing churches in the wilderness settlements, was a familiar figure in the West. There was also a growing number of native "preachers," who made up in zeal what they lacked in formal education, proclaiming a variety of emotional creeds in the frontier communities. Interest in religion was stimulated by the Great Awakening, which rose out of Kentucky about 1800 and swept in a frenzied course across the Western territory.[8] The Awakening produced the Disciples of Christ, or Christian Church, which became very strong in the West.

Despite the increasing commerce in the river communities and the arduous labors of farmers and traders in the inland settlements, there was little money in circulation. No market was available for grain or the simple articles of family manufacture. Yet money was necessary for tools and books and the other implements of civilization which could be obtained only from the East. Moreover, most of Ohio's pioneers had bought their land on credit from the Eastern land companies. Many settlers, unable to meet their payments, defaulted, while some moved on westward in search of cheaper land.

Perhaps the greatest obstacle to the development of culture was the frontier itself. The time and energy of the pioneer were con-

---

[8] Margaret J. Mitchell, "Religion as a Factor in the Early Development of Ohio," *Proceedings of the Mississippi Valley Historical Association*, IX (1915–1916), 85–87.

sumed in clearing the forest, building a home, and providing sustenance for his family. The small farmer who was obliged to transport his few bushels of corn twenty or thirty miles by horseback to the nearest mill found little time for cultural pursuits. Even in the larger communities the practical affairs of commerce and the struggle for profits were necessarily the major interests of most citizens.

The chief evidence of cultural attainment was the founding, by New England groups, of several Ohio colleges, including Ohio University (1804), Miami University (1809), Worthington College (1819), and Western Reserve College (1826). If the hardships of the frontier weakened the New England religious fervor, they did not alter the passion for moral education. It is this enthusiasm which emerges as the most important of the Eastern cultural influences.

2. *Cincinnati: "Athens of the West"*

IN THE years after 1825 Ohio's population increased rapidly, particularly in the cities, and social progress was accelerated. There were visible signs of material prosperity in the commercial activity on the Ohio and on Lake Erie, in the building of canals, in the appearance of diversified and specialized types of agriculture, and in the growth of manufacturing.[9] Newspapers became more numerous in the cities and towns;[10] by means of their exchanges, editors were able to reprint the news from journals in other parts of the West and in the Eastern cities. Ohioans took particular interest in Eastern developments in politics, literature, and religion. Among the state's influential journalists were many Yankee printers who had brought their presses from New England. Other journalists settled temporarily in New York and then moved on westward with the tide of immigration. In some Ohio communities the establishment of literary and debating societies gave promise of cultural growth. The Ohio Mechanics'

---

[9] Fox, *Sources of Culture in the Middle West*, p. 49.
[10] Shortly after 1810 Ohio passed Kentucky as the leading publisher of newspapers in the West; by 1840 Ohio had more newspapers than Kentucky, Missouri, and Michigan combined. Ralph L. Rusk, *The Literature of the Middle Western Frontier* (2 vols.; New York: Columbia University Press, 1926), I, 156–157.

Institute, founded at Cincinnati in 1828, sponsored lectures to promote "the more general diffusion of useful knowledge."

The rapid commercial expansion in the twenties awakened Ohioans
to the potential greatness of the West. Exploitation of the immense
resources in timber, furs, minerals, water power, and agricultural
land gave promise of a vast economic empire beyond the Alleghenies.
The advent of the steamboat, which promoted commerce on the
river and along the shores of Lake Erie, and the completion of the
Erie Canal in 1825, provided new markets for produce. From the
period of settlement, when pioneers were indebted to Eastern
financiers for their land holdings, through the early decades of the
nineteenth century, when Westerners were dependent on the seaboard cities for finished goods, the people of Ohio had been held in
economic bondage by the East. With the expansion of commerce and
manufacturing and with more money in circulation, the West happily
envisioned economic self-sufficiency.

A spirit of growth pervaded not only the sphere of economic life,
but of cultural life as well. From about 1825 until the fifties, when
the building of the railroads tended to break down East-West sectional barriers, the West strove valiantly for cultural self-sufficiency.
The leading center of cultural, as well as economic, progress was
Cincinnati. Because of its central location in the Ohio Valley, its
splendid port on the Ohio, and its easy access to the state's canal
system, Cincinnati rapidly became the commercial and transportation
center of the West. But Cincinnati was more than "Porkopolis"; in
the thirties the city became the "Literary Emporium of the West," a
title earned by her reputation as a book-publishing center.[11]

Cincinnati publishing houses produced not merely standard handbooks on religion, education, and law, but they poured forth a stream
of novels, histories, biographies, and poetry. Many of these volumes
were written by Western authors with the avowed purpose of develop-

---

[11] The marvel of Cincinnati's rapid rise to prominence provoked many such
laudatory titles. A traveler in the West reported in 1834 that "Cincinnati was
never mentioned in America without the addition of such surnames as 'The
Wonderful,' 'The Western Queen,' &c." C. D. Arfwedson, *The United States
and Canada, in 1832, 1833, and 1834* (2 vols.; London: Richard Bentley,
1834), II, 126.

ing a Western literature. Rapid development of the technical skills of stereotyping, binding, engraving, lithographing, and steam paper milling enabled publishers to produce a yearly average of about 350,000 volumes in 1830–31 and between one and two million volumes in 1840.[12] The absence of an international copyright law until 1891 and the inadequacy of the national law enacted in 1790 provided publishers with the opportunity to produce thousands of cheap reprints of the works of Scott, Bulwer, Dickens, and other English writers and to issue, with a Western imprint, the often-unprotected writings of Eastern authors.

While the expanding facilities of Cincinnati's publishing industry tended to curtail the Western market for Eastern publications, Eastern books continued to arrive in great numbers in Ohio. Frequently they appeared as the result of a legitimate sale to a Western bookseller or of a fair exchange between publishers or booksellers in the two sections. Sometimes, however, Eastern books were marketed under more unsavory circumstances. Since independent-spirited Westerners were eager to foster the growth of the section's literary output, and since they were inclined to be jealous of the cultural attainments of the East, the very fact that a book was a Western publication gave it an advantage on the open market. In order to increase the sale of Eastern books in the West, some Eastern publishers, as well as Western booksellers, connived to label Eastern volumes with a Western publisher's imprint, thus creating the impression that they were selling genuine Western goods.

The struggle for supremacy in the Western book market is illustrated by the plagiarism case involving the famous author of eclectic school readers, William Holmes McGuffey. A large part of Cincinnati's publishing output consisted of schoolbooks, particularly after the appearance of McGuffey's first series of eclectic readers in 1836. Previously, Eastern publishers had had little competition in the sale of schoolbooks to the West. By 1838 between two and three hundred thousand of McGuffey's school texts had been issued by Truman and Smith of Cincinnati, and in that year the Boston publisher of Wor-

---

[12] Walter E. Sutton, "Cincinnati as a Publishing and Book Trade Center" (Unpublished dissertation, Ohio State University, 1946), p. 81.

cester's readers threatened a plagiarism suit in an attempt to discredit McGuffey and force his books from the market.[13] While the suit was apparently unwarranted, McGuffey prudently settled out of court and issued a new edition of his readers.

The expansion of Cincinnati's publishing industry, an important development in Ohio's cultural coming-of-age, continued down to the period of the Civil War. Ultimately, supremacy in the industry passed to Chicago, and Cincinnati became a distribution center for Eastern books.

Cincinnati's aspiration to become the "Athens of the West" is further revealed by the interest in magazine publishing between the thirties and fifties. As early as 1831 the city had six weeklies, two semimonthlies, one monthly, and one quarterly; and, in 1848, twenty-five weeklies and six monthlies were in circulation.[14] The editors of many of these periodicals, sharing the contemporary enthusiasm for development of Western literature and culture, devoted their pages to the productions of Western authors and materials dealing with the history and potential greatness of the West.

Among the important early magazines were Timothy Flint's *Western Monthly Review* (1827–30), which undertook to interpret the "natural, moral, and civil history" of the West; James Hall's *Western Monthly Magazine* (1832–37), "devoted chiefly to elegant literature," the most successful of the Cincinnati publications;[15] the *Western Monthly Magazine, and Literary Journal* (1837), which attempted to promote Western literature; and the *Hesperian*, established in Columbus in 1838 and removed to Cincinnati the following year.

Although these magazines emphasized Western materials, the *Western Messenger* (1835–41), which derived its chief inspiration

---

[13] *Ibid.*, p. 207. As part of the plot, the Boston publisher anticipated offering Worcester's readers with the imprint of a Western publisher.

[14] Frank Luther Mott, *A History of American Magazines, 1741–1850* (New York: D. Appleton and Company, 1930), p. 387.

[15] An unflattering contemporary opinion of this magazine and of Judge Hall, "the *censor morum* and *arbiter elegantiarum* of Cincinnati," is given in E. S. Abdy, *Journal of a Residence and Tour of the United States of North America from April, 1833, to October, 1834* (3 vols.; London: John Murray, 1835), II, 387 ff.

from New England, was, perhaps, "the highest point in the literary achievement of early Western magazines."[16] This publication, which has been called "A Boston Flower blooming in the Ohio Valley,"[17] was established by the Western Unitarian Association and received contributions from such notable New England authors as Ralph Waldo Emerson,[18] Jones Very, and Margaret Fuller. The *Western Messenger* was "the organ of New England liberalism in the Valley of the Ohio." It was a magazine devoted to religion and literature, "and both its theology and its literature were tinctured with transcendentalism."[19]

A succession of magazines devoted to literature, education, medicine, and agriculture appeared during the thirties and forties. In 1840 there were twenty such periodicals in Ohio. Although most of these publishing ventures were short-lived, particularly because of the scarcity of able contributors and because of the competition from the established literary journals of the East, and although few of the Western magazines achieved literary excellence, they represent a significant stride in Ohio's cultural progress.

3. Colleges and Western Morality

OHIO's cultural pattern was considerably complicated in the 1830's by a rapid increase in immigration to the West. Since many of the new settlers came from European countries, they brought with them strange social customs, religious beliefs, and political attitudes. The Protestant churches, having charged themselves with the responsibility of fostering Christian education and moral stability in the West, viewed with alarm the growth of Catholicism. In 1835 Lyman

---

[16] Rusk, *Literature of the Middle Western Frontier*, I, 178.

[17] Fox, *Sources of Culture in the Middle West*, p. 63.

[18] Four of Emerson's early published poems appeared in the *Messenger* in 1839; they were "Each and All," "To the Humble-bee," "Good-bye, Proud World," and "The Rhodora."

[19] W. H. Venable, *Beginnings of Literary Culture in the Ohio Valley* (Cincinnati: Robert Clarke and Company, 1891), p. 72. See also Mott, *op. cit.*, pp. 658–663; Rusk, *op. cit.*, pp. 178–185; C. L. F. Gohdes, *The Periodicals of American Transcendentalism* (Durham: Duke University Press, 1931), pp. 17–37.

Beecher, the prominent Cincinnati churchman and father of Henry
Ward Beecher, warned his Protestant brethren of the necessity of
prompt action to thwart the dangers to Western morality:

But the population of the great West . . . is assembled from all
the states of the Union, and from all the nations of Europe, and is
rushing in like the waters of the flood, demanding for its moral preservation the immediate and universal action of those institutions which
discipline the mind, and arm the conscience and the heart.[20]

As for the spread of Catholicism, Beecher observed that

American travelers at Rome and Vienna, assure us, that in the upper
circles the enterprise of reducing our western states to spiritual sub-
serviency to the see of Rome is a subject of avowed expectation, and
high hope, and sanguine confidence, while the correspondence of the
Catholic bishops and priests in this country to their noble and royal
patrons in Europe are full of the same predictions and high hopes, as
motives to their immediate and copious charities to establish Catholic
institutions at the West.[21]

Since the Protestant denominations believed that moral instability
in the West could be prevented only by the efforts of college-bred
churchmen and teachers, these denominations, with aid from New
England, "competed with one another in establishing colleges."[22]
From the beginning these institutions were troubled with financial
problems, their small faculties spending nearly as much time soliciting
funds as teaching. In 1842 representatives from the Western colleges
met at Cincinnati to discuss their common problems. There soon followed, through the united efforts of the Congregational and New
School Presbyterian Churches, the Society for the Promotion of Collegiate and Theological Education at the West.[23] The avowed object
of the society, which was managed in the East, was "to afford assistance to Collegiate and Theological Institutions at the West, in such

[20] Lyman Beecher, *A Plea for the West* (Cincinnati: Truman and Smith, 1835), p. 16.
[21] *Ibid.*, p. 119.
[22] E. Kidd Lockard, "The Influence of New England in Denominational Colleges in the Northwest, 1830–1860," *Ohio State Archaeological and Historical Quarterly*, LIII (January, 1944), 1.
[23] The writer is indebted to John A. Heide of the Wisconsin State Teachers College, Whitewater, Wisconsin, for information about this society.

manner, and so long only, as in the judgment of the Directors of the
Society, the exigencies of the Institutions may demand."[24]

The society, undertaking its responsibilities with true missionary
zeal, concluded at its first annual meeting in New York in 1844 that

It is in its *nature* just as truly a missionary work to educate youth
in the valley of the Mississippi for the Gospel ministry, or for teaching
common schools, or to rescue children from ignorance and from Papal
and other delusions, as it is to do the same work in the Sandwich
Islands or on the banks of the Ganges.[25]

Besides being concerned over the scarcity of ministers and teachers,
the society was determined to inculcate New England moral principles
in the people of the West. A speaker at the society's third annual
meeting in Springfield, Massachusetts, in 1846 declared:

What more benign or blessed work could we project or accomplish,
than to plant another New England, or raise up such a population as
New England has furnished in some other portions of our country, beyond the mountains? If we do our duty to the West, that smiling valley,
while the world stands, will reap the benefits of our well-timed labors.[26]

None of the society's objectives was given more attention in the
annual reports than the resolve to check the spread of Catholicism
in the Western states. Indeed this determination was often expressed
in language more charged with bitterness than Christian love.
Catholicism was associated with European despotism and was inter-
preted as a constant threat to the growth of "intellectual or moral
culture." The Western colleges were frequently reminded that "the
crafty Jesuit is laying deep and strong the foundations of his educational structure."

Between its inception in 1843 and its merger with the American
Education Society in 1874, the society gave financial aid to twenty-six
colleges in the Western states. Seven of these were Ohio institutions:
Western Reserve College, Lane Theological Seminary, Marietta
College, Wittenberg College, Heidelberg College, Oberlin College,
and Wilberforce University. And in every case, assistance was rendered

[24] *First Annual Report of the Society for the Promotion of Collegiate and
Theological Education at the West* (New York: J. F. Trow, 1844), Preface.
[25] *Ibid.*, p. 10.
[26] Rev. Nathan S. Beman, "Collegiate and Theological Education at the
West," *Third Annual Report of the Society for the Promotion of Collegiate
and Theological Education at the West* (New York: J. F. Trow, 1847), p. 23.

only when the moral teachings of these colleges met with the approval
of the society; emphasis was invariably given to a New England
curriculum stressing cultural and classical studies rather than practical
or controversial subjects.

By 1830 the American Education Society, founded in the East in
1815, was operating in the West. This organization helped individuals
rather than schools. Its chief function was to provide clothing, books,
and small financial aid to ministerial students. The New England
influence on Western schools was also furthered by the Ladies' Society
for the Promotion of Education at the West, which endeavored to
send into the section "competent female teachers, of unquestionable
piety, belonging to Congregational churches in New England."

4. *The New England Lyceum in the West*

IN MAKING his plea for the moral preservation of the West, Lyman
Beecher contended that "There must be permanent, powerful,
literary and moral institutions, which, like the great orbs of attraction
and light, shall send forth their power and their illumination, and
without them all else will be inconstant and ephemeral." Among the
"literary and moral institutions" which were developing in the West
was the lyceum, which Josiah Holbrook, a Yale graduate, had founded
in 1826 as a means to promote "the universal diffusion of knowledge."
Envisioned as an international scheme of education with member
societies in every progressive community, the lyceum was immediately
popular in New England, and by 1830 the movement had spread to
New York, Pennsylvania, and some parts of the West.

In 1831 the American Lyceum Association was founded to provide
centralized control of the system, and for eight years the association
encouraged a chain of lyceums ascending through the community,
the county, and the state to the national organization. Annual membership fees were two dollars for adults and one dollar for subscribers under eighteen years of age; life memberships cost twenty
dollars. Local lyceums held weekly lectures and debates; in addition
to diffusing knowledge and Christian morality, they attempted to
combat unwholesome amusements, to aid the common schools, to
exchange "specimens of nature and art," and to establish museums
and seminaries. The entire lyceum movement was faithfully publicized

by the *American Journal of Education* and the *American Annals of Education*.

Cincinnati was a center of lyceum activity as early as 1830. The Marietta Lyceum, founded in 1831, sent two delegates to the second annual meeting of the American Lyceum Association, held in New York in May, 1832.[27] These delegates informed the convention that the Marietta Lyceum, with a membership of one hundred, had given scientific lectures "with happy effect," had successfully counteracted vice, and had advanced the interest of education, morality, and religion.[28] It is not surprising that Marietta, with its New England culture, avidly embraced the lyceum idea as a means of promoting moral education. With an enthusiasm that pleased the convention, the Marietta delegates declared that arrangements were being made to correspond "with all parts of the state," and that "hopes are entertained that similar societies will be established in all the counties of Ohio."

During the thirties and forties, lyceums were established in many Ohio communities, and the weekly debates and lectures on scientific, literary, and moral topics stimulated cultural growth. The Dayton and Cleveland Lyceums were founded in 1832, the Akron Lyceum and Library Association in 1834, the Toledo Lyceum and the Cleveland Polemics Association in 1837, the Marietta Mechanics' Lyceum in 1838, the Springfield Lyceum in 1841, and the Columbus Franklin Lyceum in 1846.

An unusual project "to assist in spreading knowledge and holiness over our globe" was the establishment at Berea in 1837 of America's first lyceum village. The promoters of this scheme were Josiah Holbrook; Henry O. Sheldon,[29] an itinerant preacher; John Baldwin of Connecticut; and James Gilruth.[30] The village consisted

---

[27] Cecil Branner Hayes, *The American Lyceum, Its History and Contribution to Education* (Washington: U. S. Government Printing Office, 1932), p. 66.

[28] "American Lyceum," *American Annals of Education*, II (July 1, 1832), 339.

[29] Sheldon, an early lyceum enthusiast and friend of Holbrook, is listed as a guest at the fifth annual meeting of the American Lyceum Association in New York in May, 1835. "Transactions of the American Lyceum," *American Annals of Education*, V (June, 1835), 267. During the period of the lyceum village, Holbrook lived in Berea, where he manufactured light globes.

[30] *Historical Facts Concerning Berea and Middleburgh Township* (Berea: Mohler Printing Company, 1936), p. 23.

of a tract of five hundred acres, all property of the corporation being held in the form of stocks which were sold, at fifty dollars per share, "to young persons of good moral character; families who desire to remove there; influential friends of science and the moral enterprises of the age; to Lyceums and institutes."[31]

The founders proposed "to make this first Lyceum Village and school a model—the village, a scientific village; its school, to a considerable extent, a Normal school." Here, where discordant sects could meet in harmony and the asperity of party politics could be forgotten, the people were to be educated "by lectures and recitations, with scientific apparatus." The light of moral truth was to be given to those men who would "tear up a manuscript leaf of Homer to light their cigars" or "throw their purses on the stage, in *rapture*, and shout 'encore, encore' to see a foreign dancer teach modesty! morality! and science! by making a pair of compasses of herself."[32]

By 1842 Berea was a transplanted New England community with a dozen buildings and a school of about fifty people. In that year the experiment of the lyceum village came to an end; financially, it had not prospered, though it had admirably pursued its objectives "to redeem man from ignorance and vice" and "to engraft education upon business, and not business upon education."

Lyceums as cultural agents were encouraged by prominent thinkers and educators in both the East and West. Ralph Waldo Emerson likened them to a pulpit. "Lyceums—so that people will let you say what you think—are as good a pulpit as any other."[33] "Here is a pulpit that makes other pulpits tame and ineffectual—with their cold, mechanical preparations for a delivery the most decorous,—fine things, pretty things, wise things, but no arrows, no axes, no nectar, no growling, no transpiercing, no enchantment."[34]

In the middle years of the century the lyceum developed into

---

[31] Henry O. Sheldon, *The Lyceum System of Education* (Cincinnati: Ephraim Morgan and Company, 1842), p. 4.

[32] *Ibid.*, p. 12.

[33] E. W. Emerson, *Emerson in Concord* (Boston and New York: Houghton, Mifflin and Company, 1888), p. 73.

[34] E. W. Emerson and W. E. Forbes (editors), *The Journals of Ralph Waldo Emerson* (10 vols.; Boston and New York: Houghton, Mifflin and Company, 1909–1914), V, 281.

the popular lecture system. The local orator who enlightened his townsmen with a course of scientific, literary, or moral lectures made room on the platform for the celebrity, the professional lecturer whose discourse might be a cultural essay, a frothy political harangue, or a collection of jokes. The advent of the railroad brought a horde of Eastern professional orators to the West. The experiences of those lecturers in Ohio are narrated in the chapters that follow.

Most of Ohio's "lecturers from abroad" came from New England, where the lyceum system had been founded, and where the profession of lecturing flourished. In the South, where a patrician culture persisted, the democratic popular lecture system did not thrive.

While New England cultural values persisted merely as influences in the West and were often absorbed or modified by the multiplicity of forces which composed the culture of the North, the enthusiasm for moral education, which stimulated the establishment of schools and lyceums and gave impetus to the popular lecture system, was still an important and coherent element of Ohio's civilization in the years between 1850 and 1870. When a cultural discourse was given in an Ohio community, the lecturer would surely find a goodly number of truth-loving, transplanted New Englanders in his audience. When the announcement was made that John G. Saxe, the Vermont poet, would deliver his poem on "Yankee Land," Ohio's Yankee lecture-goers would crowd the hall to hear the vivid descriptions of New England and her famous sons, and to applaud good-naturedly the poet's gentle satire of the Yankee institutions which their fathers had brought to Ohio's frontier settlements. And in 1866, when Emerson was making a lecture tour among the growing communities of the West, he observed that "In every one of these expanding towns is a knot of loving New Englanders who cherish the Lyceum out of love to the Charles & the Merrimac & the Connecticut rivers."[35]

The most successful lyceum lecturers in the West were more than mere purveyors of facts. Indeed many a speaker was reminded by the Western press that the materials of his lecture could be read

---

[35] Ralph L. Rusk (ed.), *The Letters of Ralph Waldo Emerson* (6 vols.; New York: Columbia University Press, 1939), V, 455.

in any good encyclopedia. For his factual education the nineteenth-century American relied upon newspapers, periodicals, and books. Although popular orators were expected to be "learned in the arts, sciences and all the higher and more laborious studies of the times," their chief responsibility was to stimulate men to individual effort, to induce thought and discussion. This quality of provocativeness was the principal element in Emerson's success on the platform; he was not an accomplished orator, and the factual content of his lectures was less impressive than their suggestiveness. Moreover, the lecturer was required to do more than instruct; he must entertain as well. Like the novelist, he must captivate and impress. If his discussion was arid and uninspiring, no amount of wisdom, learning, or genius could save him from ridicule.

Although the Western lyceum shared the ideals of the lecture system in other parts of America, it also had some special purposes of its own. From its inception down to the late fifties it was part of the movement to develop an important and distinctive culture in the West. This sectional pride of Western citizens was most apparent in the early and middle fifties, when the new railroads brought the Eastern lecturers across the Alleghenies, and before the cultural impulse of the lyceum had surrendered to commercialism, humor, and political agitation. This is not to say that Western people were opposed to the importation of Eastern lecturers, if those lecturers were celebrities. Westerners were naturally eager to see great men, regardless of their geographical origin, and hundreds of audiences in the West crowded their local lecture halls to hear Emerson, Henry Ward Beecher, Bayard Taylor, and other famous people from the East. But in the mid-fifties, when Eastern lecturers almost monopolized the lyceum programs, the sectional attitude of the West became coherent and outspoken.

Once the novelty of seeing the famous "lecturers from abroad" had worn away, their lectures were criticized by Western audiences in terms of their social profit. Eastern lecturers were an expensive commodity, paid for with Western dollars, and audiences had a right to expect much valuable information. It was here, in the area of subject matter, that many of the Eastern lecturers aroused the indignation of their audiences. Westerners were a practical, mercantile people who stoutly resisted the efforts of learned lecturers to instill in them a taste for philosophy. Lecture audiences were composed of a few intellectuals and a large body of plain citizens— farmers, mechanics, and shopkeepers to whom "culture" meant useful knowledge and practical, provocative ideas. Such people did not take kindly to the philosophical materials of the "intellectual feast" in which the listener was compelled to feed "on the frost work and syllabub that garnishes the feast to which he has been invited." So the Easterners' "pretty conceits" and "heavy mass of mannerisms" were often lost upon a gloomy array of empty seats. Western listeners were critical and independent, and, if a lecture was dull or otherwise unpleasing, they were not averse to stamping out of the lecture hall. Sometimes they were willing to pay a quarter just to look at a famous man, but most imported lecturers were obligated to demonstrate to their audiences that they were superior to local speakers.

The sectional aspirations of the Western lyceum were especially evident in the frequent newspaper complaints against the neglect of Western orators. Sentiment was often strong to break up the "system of foreign lectures." The exclusive patronage of Eastern men hindered the development of those Western scholars, poets, and divines who possessed the talent that could place them among the great men of the nation. If the West was to have a cultural tradition of its own, the lyceums would have to offer inducements to home productions and hold out premiums to native genius. It was bad enough for Western citizens to build their homes after the pattern of Eastern architecture or take their "style of boots and coats and shirt collars from Atlantic dandies" without surrendering their cultural taste and literary judgment.[36]

The lyceums sometimes tried to balance their lecture programs by

---

[36] The influence of Eastern architecture in Ohio is expertly discussed in Frank John Roos, Jr., "An Investigation of Early Architectural Design in Ohio" (Unpublished dissertation, Ohio State University, 1937). According to this writer, "the history of early New England architecture may be read in Ohio." Western carpenters and contractors made extensive use of the Eastern builders' handbooks. The steady migration of Eastern pioneers made these architectural guidebooks available in the West soon after they were published in the East.

offering an equal number of Eastern and Western lecturers. Such an arrangement gratified the sight-seeing public who wished to have a glimpse at Eastern celebrities, and showed a proper respect for the quality of home talent. And in advertising Western lecturers, lyceums pointed out proudly that men like Cassius M. Clay of Kentucky and James E. Murdoch of Ohio had been acclaimed by large audiences in the East.

Eastern orators discovered that the proper way to begin a lecture was to make a few remarks about the rapid economic development and cultural progress of the West. An introduction of this kind put the audience in the right frame of mind to absorb culture. There were some who dared to criticize Western society, to elaborate the advantages of Eastern life and deplore the cultural backwardness of the West. Such famous Easterners as Parke Godwin, George William Curtis, and Theodore Tilton learned the humiliating lesson that sensitive Westerners would not tolerate any unfavorable comparisons with the East or any unsavory comments about their backwoods tradition. The West was no respecter of persons and did not hesitate to attack savagely the efforts of the famous cleric Henry Ward Beecher to make a quick fortune from his Western lectures.

As long as the Western lyceum retained its serious cultural purpose, the chief types of lectures were those dealing with literature, morality, and science. Travelogues and historical lectures were also popular. Humorous and satirical discourses were approved, provided that the lecturer aimed his witty shafts at the common foibles of mankind and drew a moral lesson which would "instruct" his audience; coarse or vulgar humor was not countenanced. Political subjects were taboo, as the lyceum was intended to lift men's interests above the realm of partisan controversy. Reform lectures were enjoyed if they pointed out means of greater achievement in the nation, but adverse criticisms of the "mighty West" were unwelcome and offensive, particularly when they were made by orators from the East.

As audiences were intolerant of dull or incompetent men, the responsibilities of the lecturer who undertook a Western journey were heavy indeed. When Emerson or Theodore Parker lectured in

Boston or New York, he could expect a select, educated audience, but when a lecturer appeared on the lyceum platform of some Western village he was subjected to the criticism of people from all ranks of society. Outside, at the hitching rail, were the horses of the rich and the poor, the educated and the unlettered, the minister, the local editor, the liveryman, the tradesman. These citizens came together naturally and congenially in the democratic atmosphere of the lyceum. They shared a common concern for culture, and, until the next weekly discourse gave them something new to think about, they would discuss the lecture and the lecturer with interest and spirit.

The Western lyceum remained socially and culturally important as long as it held the enthusiasm and support of all classes of society. The first serious defection occurred in the mid-fifties, when mechanics and tradesmen rebelled against the surfeit of "attractive humbug" displayed by the Eastern lecturers. Although lyceum managers provided more practical and scientific lectures in the late years of the decade, their real interest was turning toward commercialism. Thus profit-making became the main motive of the lyceums and remained so until the decline of the whole system. The plain citizens of Western communities no longer felt a strong civic and moral responsibility to support their local lyceums. Lecture attendance became a fashion, a diversion of the sight-seers.

The rage for speakers who would draw served to increase, rather than reduce, the demand for Eastern lecturers, as a large proportion of the nation's famous men lived along the Atlantic seaboard. The growing economic interdependence of the East and West and the advances in transportation and communication slowly broke down the sectional rivalry of the two regions. As the Civil War approached, antislavery agitation and political lectures expressed the common feelings of both East and West and furthered the unity of the North. Finally, the war fired the West with bright hopes of a united nation dominated by Northern economy, government, and culture.

The cultural contribution of the Western lyceum was great, though it became less important during the sixties and after, when profit-making and entertainment superseded instruction as major aims of the system. The lyceum awakened the West to the need for cultural growth. By stimulating thought and the intelligent discussion of diverse topics, it encouraged reading and the founding of libraries. It promoted community interest in intellectual and moral problems and focused attention on the necessity for education of all men in a democracy. It provided pleasure and inspiration for thousands of Western people who were eager for useful, intelligent participation in the progress of America.

CHAPTER
II

I

IN THE spring of 1850, when the members of the newly organized
Literary Club of Cincinnati determined to have a course of lectures
by an Eastern celebrity, their first choice for a speaker was Emerson.[1]
His reputation as a thinker was already established in the West; his
essays were familiar to the intelligent reading public, and their author's reputation had steadily grown since their publication in 1841
and 1844. Ohio's newspapers frequently printed selections from his
essays and Eastern lectures, occasionally to censure his religious
opinions, but more often to admire the originality of his thinking.
"We want some of Emerson's bold thought-strokes in this city,"
wrote a correspondent of the *Cincinnati Gazette* (April 29, 1850).
"He has never been west on a lecturing tour, and our people have a
curiosity to see and hear him."

The Western opinion of Emerson as a lecturer was summarized
by the editor of the *Cincinnati Columbian and Great West*, who observed that while Emerson was a preacher, poet, philosopher, and
traveler,

his distinctive employment is that of writing and delivering, before
promiscuous public assemblages, series of miscellaneous discourses. He
is now *Emerson, the Lecturer*: one of a small class, as yet, in the
United States, who travel from city to city, and State to State, addressing people from incomplete notes or finished manuscripts, on topics of
temporary or permanent interest, presenting, elaborating and sustain-
ing, doctrines and opinions which they indulge for the time, or hold
"for good." Mr. Emerson is perhaps at the head of this class, *in reputation*, if not in ability, and by seniority, and next to him stands Henry

---

[1] Emerson's Cincinnati lectures are discussed in Louise Hastings, "Emerson
in Cincinnati," *New England Quarterly*, XI (September, 1938), 443–469.

Giles, after whom come E. P. Whipple, Park Benjamin, "Shakespeare" Hudson, and one or two others.[2]

Noting that Hudson seldom lectured outside New Hampshire and that Whipple "has hardly strayed farther from Boston than New York and Philadelphia," this critic concluded that

the knights who are regularly in the field, with harness on and visor down, number but three: Emerson, Giles, and Benjamin. Of these, Mr. Emerson is the most philosophical, original and humorous; Mr. Giles the most profound, earnest and comprehensible; Mr. Benjamin the most satirical, practical and poetical.

The details of Emerson's invitation to lecture in the West are preserved in a published address by Ainsworth R. Spofford, one of the founders of the Cincinnati Literary Club:

During the first year of the Club we had a visit from Ralph Waldo Emerson. It came about in this way: His fame as an original thinker and lecturer was well established in the East, but he had never yet visited the West. Many of us read with delight his early essays, books which I am fond of recommending as one of the finest intellectual tonics in all literature. So I took around a subscription paper among our Club members, and to some of the solid men of Cincinnati . . . and soon had $150 pledged for a course of lectures from Mr. Emerson. I wrote him asking him to accept our invitation, with a guarantee of this sum for travelling expenses, and as much more as the receipts of the

---

[2] June 1, 1850. Since the publication of his essay on T. B. Macaulay by the *Boston Miscellany* in 1843, Whipple had achieved a growing reputation in America as a literary critic. The extravagant opinion which Whipple's contemporaries held of his criticism has suffered much at the hands of modern historians of American literature. During the 1850's and 1860's his literary lectures were greatly admired by both Eastern and Western lecture-goers. Whipple's *Essays and Reviews* (1848–49) and *Lectures on Subjects Connected with Literature and Life* (1850) were known to many Ohioans. See pp. 70–73 of this study.

Benjamin was known chiefly for his editorship (1839–45) of *New World*, a sensational New York journal which often reprinted British writings without remuneration to their authors. Possessed of a quarrelsome nature and given to abusive criticism, Benjamin was the target of many libel suits. After trying his hand as a literary agent in Baltimore, Benjamin turned to lecturing. Many of his lectures consisted of original poems written in octosyllabic couplets. See pp. 154–165, below.

Henry Norman Hudson, an Episcopal minister and student of Shakespeare, was a popular lecturer in the East during the 1840's. His Shakespearean lectures were printed in two volumes (New York, 1848), and his edition of Shakespeare's works was published in eleven volumes (Boston, 1850–57).

lectures might bring, less the expense of the hall. He replied that he had just settled down to his spring gardening (it was the month of May, 1850,) but that my letter had awakened a long-cherished desire to see the Ohio River and all that lay between it and his home.[3]

On May 14 Emerson left Buffalo on the steamer "America," bound for Sandusky. He expected to lecture in Cincinnati on May 17, as the entire journey from Buffalo to Cincinnati normally required about thirty hours.[4] Provision was made by the Buffalo and Cincinnati Railroad for passengers of the "America" and other Lake Line steamboats to travel from Sandusky to Cincinnati, a distance of two hundred and eighteen miles, in the cars of the Sandusky and Cincinnati Railroad.

When the "America" was about ten miles from Cleveland, fire was discovered in her boiler room. What might have been a disaster, had the steamer been farther from shore, was averted when the "America" was able to make port at Cleveland. The fire was extinguished after two hours of exertion by firemen and citizens, and the boat was only slightly damaged.[5]

Although arrangements were made for the passengers on the "America" to continue on to Sandusky aboard the "Southerner," Emerson remained, at the invitation of the Cleveland Library Association, to deliver a lecture in the city. He was announced to read "England" on May 16, and the *Plain Dealer* informed the public

---

[3] *The Literary Club of Cincinnati, 1849–1903* (Cincinnati: n.p., 1903), p. 15. Spofford, a young Cincinnati bookseller and later a librarian of Congress, made his invitation an impressive one. In a letter to Thomas Carlyle (August 5, 1850), Emerson wrote that his invitation to lecture in Cincinnati was signed by a hundred men. Rusk, *Letters*, IV, 224. The decision to visit Ohio was apparently not an easy one; in a letter to his brother William (May 6, 1850), Emerson commented: "I am now debating whether to accept an invitation to go, this month, to Cincinnati. I incline to refuse, as my garden wants me, & my library more." *Ibid.*, p. 201.

[4] Daily advertisements of the Buffalo and Cincinnati Railroad appeared in the *Cleveland Herald* in 1850 with the slogan "Through from Buffalo to Cincinnati in thirty hours." The "America" left Buffalo every Tuesday and Friday for Sandusky.

[5] Accounts of the fire appeared in the *Cleveland Herald*, May 16, 1850; in the *Cleveland Daily Plain Dealer*, May 16, 1850; and in the *Cleveland Weekly Plain Dealer*, May 22, 1850.

that this lecture was "the most popular and applauded" of the recent series delivered by Emerson in New York.[6]

Cleveland lecture-goers were well pleased with Emerson; the *True Democrat* commented that the lecturer "delighted a crowded hall—collected together at a few hours notice—with his brilliant discourse." Clevelanders had "rarely heard any lecturer more captivating." His manner was plain yet earnest; his eloquent thoughts and observations were presented "in compact, nervous English."

After traveling to Sandusky on the "Saratoga," Emerson journeyed southward on the Mad River and Lake Erie Railroad. This line took him through the settlements of Tiffin, Kenton, Bellefontaine, and Springfield. At Springfield he transferred to the Little Miami Railroad, which had been opened between that city and Cincinnati in 1848. Emerson described Ohio's flowering countryside in a letter to his wife, Lidian Emerson:

Beautiful road, grand old forest, beeches, immense black walnuts, oaks, rock maples, buckeyes (horse chestnuts) in bloom, cornels in white flower, & red buds—a forest tree whose bloom is precisely the colour of the peach-blossom,—made all the miles rich with beauty; enormous grapevines I saw too: Most of the houses were log-huts, with log-barns. Cities are everywhere much the same thing, but this forest is very unlike ours. The land was all heavy with wood, and, of course, the poor Germans buy it with confidence that it will bear wheat & corn. I saw the land that is never manured, and they say that when the manure heap has grown too big, they move the barn to another place. As we drew nigh Cincinnati, the wheat was from a foot to 18 inches high, & the corn 5 & six inches. Yet the season here, they tell me, is very backward.[7]

After he arrived in Cincinnati on May 18, Emerson's course of "Lectures on the Nineteenth Century" was announced as follows:

---

[6] May 16, 1850. "England" was delivered at Hope Chapel in New York on March 26. Though the lecture had been heard in New York before, "there was a strong demand that it be repeated." Other lectures in the course at Hope Chapel were "Natural Aristocracy," "The Superlative in Literature, Manners, and Races," "Eloquence," "Books," "The Spirit of the Age," and "Instinct and Inspiration." Rusk, *Letters*, IV, 183. All of these lectures, with the exception of "The Superlative in Literature, Manners, and Races," were to be delivered in Cincinnati.

[7] May 20, 1850. Rusk, *Letters*, IV, 203.

May 20   "Natural Aristocracy"
May 22   "Eloquence"
May 24   "The Spirit of the Times"
May 27   "England"
May 28   "Books"

Course tickets admitting one person sold for $1.00, while the entire lecture series could be heard by "a gentlemen and Ladies" for $1.50. Admission to a single performance for one person was 25 cents; for a gentleman and ladies, 50 cents.

The chapel of the First Universalist Church was filled with an "appreciating and discriminating" audience on the evening of Emerson's first Cincinnati lecture. The *Chronicle and Atlas* reported that Emerson spoke "in a plain, easy, but impressive manner," while his thoughts were "rich, varied, striking—true to nature, and eminently suggestive." The editor of the *Gazette* was agreeably surprised by the appearance of Emerson and by the materials of his lecture. He had read numerous journalistic descriptions of the lecturer, but "in the simple dignity and clear, well-knit, impressive common sense of his exposition of Natural Aristocracy," he was so far, "in his intellectual and oratorical lineaments," from resembling his newspaper portraits "that we half incline to think the wrong man has come along, and attempted to play off a hoax upon us backwoods people." The impact of Emerson's "thought-strokes" quite overcame the correspondent of the *Commercial*, who "remained long enough to hear him utter one unmistakable absurdity and left.—We hope he has no idea of *imposing* upon the Western people, by means of his truly singular statements."

After hearing "Eloquence," the second lecture in Emerson's course, the editor of the *Gazette* (May 24, 1850) was "perfectly satisfied" that "Mr. Emerson was Mr. Emerson." His style of reading, though "quite peculiar," was "exceedingly pleasing, and as unpretending as that of a good old grandfather over his Bible." Especially commendable were his joyous spirit, his far-reaching view, and his keen "perception of the ludicrous." Added to these were "a vocabulary every word of which comes down with the force of a sledgehammer" and "a poetical fervor that spreads from the speaker to his audience till the whole becomes one mass of light and warmth."

The members of the Literary Club were generous in their attentions to Emerson during his Cincinnati visit. On the afternoon of May 24 Emerson was visited in his rooms at the new and luxurious Burnet House by Spofford, Rutherford B. Hayes, and Isaac C. Collins, "a committee to invite Mr. Emerson to meet the Literary Club on some evening convenient to himself for the purpose of a free confab on literary men and matters." Hayes, an ambitious young lawyer of twenty-eight, had not yet begun his political career. At this meeting he was much impressed by Emerson's appearance and later made the following entry in his diary:

Mr. Emerson is above the middle height, a tolerable figure, but rather awkward; dresses in the *plainly genteel style*—black surtout and pants, black satin vest and cravat, common shoes. His head is not large, forehead low and narrow, hair cut short—a brown color, eyes grayish blue, a rather large nose with deep lines from the nostrils on either side arching around the mouth, but not so as to give an unpleasant expression. Is agreeable in his manners and first address. Talks, as he speaks, freely, and in a somewhat quaint way.[8]

On the evening of May 24 Emerson read "The Spirit of the Times," which was the least successful lecture of the course. The audience anticipated pointed, specific comments on American life of the time; instead, Emerson's remarks were vague and provided little analysis of the state of national affairs. His manner, declared the *Columbian and Great West*, did not rise "to the full dignity of his theme." Here was a subject "in the handling of which it was within his power to set men to thinking; as it was, he thought proper to do little more than make them laugh."

Most of Emerson's hearers were pleased with the common sense displayed in his lectures. There was another group, however, who wanted to "revel in a higher philosophy," who ardently hoped that Emerson would reveal the secrets of that transcendental metaphysic of which they had read so much and understood so little. The atti-

---

[8] Charles R. Williams (ed.), *Diary and Letters of Rutherford Birchard Hayes* (5 vols.; Columbus: Ohio State Archaeological and Historical Society, 1922), I, 301.

tude of this group was expressed in the *Columbian and Great West* (June 1, 1850). Emerson's reputation was "that of being the chief of American transcendentalists." In recent years the West had heard a great deal about transcendentalism, but there was little agreement about the philosophy which was "characterized in so long a word." People "knew something about Mr. Emerson" and "had heard something" about Bronson Alcott; they had subscribed to the magazine of the New England transcendentalists, *The Dial*, and had "read its 'Orphic Sayings' regularly." But the philosophy of the Eastern thinkers remained a mystery. When Emerson was announced to lecture, Westerners felt confident that at last "the scales were to drop from our eyes." Longingly as they looked for it, however, the transcendentalism did not come. Instead, Emerson's Cincinnati lectures were marked by "common sense, humor, and truth." But perhaps Emerson could be prevailed upon to deliver a second course, and in this the transcendentalism would "be served up, as succeeding courses are at the Burnet House, in the shape of ginger preserves, cold custard, rhubarb pie, or cranberry tarts."

As May 25, 1850, was Emerson's forty-seventh birthday, the members of the Literary Club celebrated the event by taking him for an excursion to Fort Ancient, in Warren County, to see the primitive earthworks which are preserved there. Many years later, Spofford, a member of the party, recalled that

we sat under the trees on the grassy mounds, on one of those delicious June days when the earth puts on her choicest array to stir the senses to gladness. As we chatted over our modest refection, moistened by sundry bottles of Ohio's choicest vintage, Emerson told a story. It was of a Harvard professor of German, himself a German, who went to a Cambridge livery stable one fine winter day for a horse and sleigh to take a lady out sleigh-riding. The weather was very mild, and on broaching the question of the most suitable lap robes, the liveryman inquired: "Professor, shall I put in a buffalo?" "My God, no! put in a horse!" cried the alarmed professor.[9]

On Sunday, May 26, Emerson visited the rooms of the Literary Club. After being introduced to the members whom he had not already met, Emerson "sat down and began a free and easy con-

[9] *The Literary Club of Cincinnati, 1849–1903*, pp. 15–16.

versation on literary men and things in England. Talked two and a half hours on all matters from letters to raising corn and pigs."[10] He described the transcendentalists as "Men who are self-trusting, self-relying, earnest." Emerson was apparently somewhat annoyed by the efforts of his hosts to probe him on the subject of transcendentalism, as Hayes recorded in his diary that "Mr Emerson seemed quite puzzled, not to say vexed, when speaking of this subject. It was forced upon him by questions and suggestions."

Emerson concluded his course before the Literary Club with lectures on "England" and "Books." "England," which contained much material that later went into Emerson's *English Traits* (1856), was the most popular lecture of the course. The *Gazette* (May 30, 1850) termed this discourse, "devoted almost wholly to the personal traits of the people from the middle classes upwards," a "most graphic and interesting" piece of description. It revealed "a profound view of the genius of England, a skilful analysis of the events and qualities that have given that nation its proud position as the leading power of the world, and a fair, independent, comprehensive estimate of the English people."

The final lecture, "Books," though well attended like the others, was not altogether pleasing, as it contained many allusions which the audience could not follow. The *Gazette* (May 30, 1850) found it to be "interesting chiefly to scholars" and "above the range and without the beat of the great majority of the auditory." In one respect, however, it was interesting to all: it showed "the sources at which the now affluent mind of Mr. Emerson had imbibed the materials of its development and richness."

After concluding his course before the Literary Club, Emerson agreed, "at the solicitation of numerous friends," to deliver three private lectures on "The Natural History of Intellect." In this series Emerson departed from his emphasis on the practical and material, which had characterized his previous course, and attempted to satisfy those curious hearers who wished to embrace the higher truths of transcendental philosophy. The result was not altogether satisfying to the curious, and it was quite bewildering to the uncurious. Com-

---

[10] *Diary and Letters of Rutherford Birchard Hayes,* I, 303–305.

menting on the first private lecture, "The Natural History of Intellect," given on May 30, the *Times* reported that a "change from
the material and practical to the metaphysical does not seem to have
increased public attention to this gentleman." While Emerson was
in many ways "a pleasant and delightful talker," it appeared that he
could "be read with more advantage than listened to." A few people
enjoyed his lecture, but it would be well-nigh impossible "for any
person who heard it for the first time to give the point and pith of
it in the form of a syllogism, an aphorism, or any moderately brief
exposition which could be generally comprehended by the average
mind of the city."

Emerson's "The Identity of Thought with Nature" did not cause
the scales to drop from Western eyes. In reviewing this lecture and
its predecessor, the editor of the *Gazette* (June 3, 1850) declared
that the "two lectures have been listened to with great attention by
good audiences, but they are of too abstruse a nature, and altogether
too comprehensive in their method, to be characterised in a newspaper paragraph or two, at all events from a single hearing."

In announcing Emerson's final lecture, "Instinct and Inspiration,"
this correspondent commented hopefully, "We shall in this get the
keynote, we presume, to the whole of the second course, and to some
parts of the first." If the final lecture did supply the keynote to the
others, the reviewer did not detect it; his notice merely observed that
the lecture "evinced the same close reasoning, peculiarity of thought
and nicety of expression which made his first lectures attractive to our
thinking citizens, but was a discourse, which, to abstract clearly, we
should wish to have before us."

On June 4, 1850, Emerson left Cincinnati, with a company of
friends, aboard the mail boat bound for Louisville.[11] Financially, his
first visit to Ohio had been a profitable one. In addition to the re-

---

[11] Emerson's route homeward is described in a letter to William Emerson
(July 1, 1850). Rusk, *Letters*, IV, 216–217. After visiting Mammoth Cave,
Kentucky, he traveled from Louisville down the Ohio to St. Louis. Proceeding
by stage to Elgin, Illinois, he "found the 'two parallel bars of iron,' & came
easily to Chicago." After crossing Lake Michigan to New Buffalo, he took the
railroad to Detroit. From Detroit he traveled the Lake route back to Buffalo,
"& got home an hour before my letter to Lidian dated St. Louis." He arrived
in Concord on June 28.

ceipts of his private lectures, he had received a handsome sum for his course before the Literary Club. Spofford recalled that the lectures were so well attended that

when I came to tender the net proceeds to him there were some $560. Said Mr. Emerson, with that quaint, wise, and radiant smile of his: "What shall I do, Mr. Spofford, with these gifts of the good Providence which you bring me?" "Well, Mr. Emerson," said I, "I think, perhaps, that you had better invest them." "An excellent idea," he replied; "I will write to my brother William, a lawyer in Brooklyn, who knows about such things, and get him to find me an investment. So, will you kindly get me some kind of a draft for $500 and give me the rest in money?"[12]

During his Cincinnati visit, Emerson acquired many Ohio friends who had found beneath the dignity of his manner and appearance a warm, cheerful spirit. "I have seen this city & its people with some thoroughness, & find a deal of kind welcome," wrote Emerson to his brother William.[13] From 1850 until his final visit in 1867, Emerson was to remain for Cincinnatians the first in importance of the cultural lecturers. There were times to come when his lectures would be received with qualified enthusiasm by the public, and with adverse criticism by the press; but, whatever the fate of his lectures, Emerson himself was always to be met by his Cincinnati friends with "a deal of kind welcome."

In response to another invitation of his friend Ainsworth R. Spofford, Emerson returned to Cincinnati in December, 1852, to deliver a private course of six lectures on "The Conduct of Life."[14] After his arrival in the city on December 6, Emerson was immediately engaged by the Young Men's Mercantile Library Association to fill a deferred lecture appointment of the noted Methodist Protestant clergyman Thomas H. Stockton. In announcing this lecture, the *Commercial* predicted that because of Emerson's "distinguished reputation as an author and lecturer," there would be "a *furor* for admission." The *Gazette* added that the hall would be filled long before the hour of

---

[12] *The Literary Club of Cincinnati, 1849–1903,* p. 16.

[13] May 29, 1850. Rusk, *Letters,* IV, 207.

[14] Revisions of these lectures were published in Emerson's *The Conduct of Life* (1860).

opening, "and those who delay going until 7 o'clock will do well to provide themselves with a good stock of patience and portable chairs."

These predictions were justified, as the hall was crowded an hour before the lecture began, "the people, in the meantime entertaining themselves with Harper for December, or Thackeray's 'Harry Esmond.' " The *Times* (December 8, 1852) observed that many of the ladies occupied themselves by knitting or by reading *Gleason's Pictorial*, while "in the rear of the hall, without the view of the audience, some ladies were not allowed seats by the surrounding boors, who lolled at their ease, unmindful of the high chivalric American character they were tarnishing." However, if some of these unfortunates were "women's rights feminines," they were to be doubly pitied, and it was hoped that before long "they may see from their elevated position, the folly of their doctrines in their practical results."

"The Anglo-Saxon," which was rather like a summary of Emerson's *English Traits* (1856),[15] was "listened to with much attention and interest." The *Enquirer* (December 9, 1852) commented that the lecture "was handled in a manner peculiar to the distinguished lecturer." Emerson did "not possess the graces of elocution in any eminent degree—owes nothing to *manner*, and is indebted to his *matter* for his great reputation in the literary world."

The schedule of lectures in Emerson's private course on "The Conduct of Life" was as follows:

December 9	"Power"
December 11	"Wealth"
December 13	"Economy"
December 16	"Fate"
December 17	"Culture"
December 20	"Worship"

There was "a large audience at the new Concert Hall" to hear the first lecture of the series. Doubtless the audience would "have been

---

[15] In a letter to his brother William (December 17, 1852), Emerson wrote that "my English notes have now assumed the size of a pretty book, which I am eager to complete." Rusk, *Letters*, IV, 332. The *Gazette* and the *Times* both mention that Emerson requested the journalists to "forbear making a sketch of his discourse."

larger than could have found seats, but for a provoking defect in the arrangements of the Gas Company," by which the hall remained dark long after the lecture was scheduled to begin. The *Gazette* felt that the "legalized extortion of two or three prices for an inferior quality of gas, ought to ensure to consumers at least a constant supply." In his prefatory remarks, Emerson declared that he was glad to see the signs of culture indicated by the success of Cincinnati's Mercantile Library Association, by the erection of the city's elegant lecture halls, and by the welcome in the faces of his audience. He was pleased that the people were beginning to find their "best excitement" in intellectual exercises; in giving his discourse on "Power," he "would assume that the Ladies and Gentlemen before him came to think, not to be entertained." For Emerson the lecture was never a mere form of entertainment, but rather "a few reasonable words to keep us in mind of truth amidst our nonsense."[16]

Although the daily newspapers commented favorably upon the "rich intellectual feast" served up to the "large audiences" attending Emerson's reading of "Wealth" and "Economy," it is apparent that Cincinnatians greeted these lectures with dwindling enthusiasm. On December 16 a correspondent complained "that the local department of the Gazette, states that the Lectures of Mr. Emerson 'attract immense audiences,' whereas in truth they are but thinly attended." Moreover, in a letter to his wife, Emerson wrote that "Spofford is heroically endeavoring to make the lectures to which he invited me, pay; which Cincinnati is stoutly resisting. But he has made new negociations about details, which will save us, it is hoped."[17]

On the evening of December 15 Emerson delivered "The Anglo-Saxon" at Clegg's Hall in Dayton.[18] The lecture was announced as

---

[16] *The Journals of Ralph Waldo Emerson*, VII, 82.

[17] December 15, 1852. Rusk, *Letters*, IV, 330. The shifting of the fifth and sixth lectures of the course from Smith and Nixon's Hall to the Unitarian Church was probably an economy measure. The arrangement of a lecture in Dayton on December 15 may also have been one of Spofford's "negociations."

[18] The date of this lecture is mistakenly given as December 16 in Rusk, *Letters*, IV, 328. The complication of dates arises from a statement in the *Gazette* of December 17 that Emerson "lectured to the Daytonians last evening on the Anglo-Saxon." This newspaper item was doubtless printed a day late, as the *Daily Dayton Journal*, December 17, and the *Dayton Daily Empire*,

"one of great interest to all who speak the English language, and is at present exciting a great deal of discussion." The *Empire* declared that the lecture "contained a vast amount of profitable information upon a subject of peculiar interest to us as Americans, and yet one that is but imperfectly understood." The manners and national characteristics of the English were portrayed "with a master's hand, and with a degree of minuteness and accuracy that evinced great research and close study on the part of the author." The audience, "though not so large as it should have been," received the lecture with "unqualified approbation."

Emerson's remaining Cincinnati lectures, "Fate" and "Worship," were not reviewed by the city's journals, although the reading of "Fate" inspired a letter to the *Gazette* (December 18, 1852) from "A German." This correspondent objected that "the sturdy lecturer did not take particular pain to reconcile" some of his ideas, and that he introduced many thoughts "which have no bearance upon the subject." The writer concluded that, despite Emerson's pride in America's Saxon origin, the lecturer himself was "entirely Celtic in his philosophy and mode of thinking."

On December 21, 1852, Emerson left Cincinnati on the mail boat bound for Louisville. Arriving in St. Louis on Christmas Day, he wrote to Lidian Emerson: "I had the most pleasant acquaintance & last days at Cincinnati and shall almost feel compelled to go thither again, if the same parties should summon me though it costs me a hundred times as much to go & be there as it would almost any other."[19]

In his future visits to Cincinnati, Emerson only once attempted the reading of a full course of lectures. In 1852 the public was already acquiring a taste for variety; once the people had seen and heard a celebrity on the platform, their curiosity was satisfied, and they rarely showed any sustained interest in a series of appearances by a single

---

December 17, give the date of the lecture as Wednesday, December 15. The lecture on "Fate" was not "delayed till the 17th" (Rusk, *loc. cit.*) but was delivered in Cincinnati on December 16. "Culture," announced for December 17, was not given.

[19] Rusk, *Letters*, IV, 337. At St. Louis, Emerson delivered "The Anglo-Saxon" and the course on "The Conduct of Life" before the St. Louis Mercantile Library Association.

lecturer. The people thus unwittingly encouraged the advent of the traveling lecturer who carried one manuscript across the land, reading it night after night in different communities.[20] And when this custom became widespread in the early fifties, the public and the newspapers joined in cries of "Humbug!" and reverently recalled the time when men like Emerson and Benjamin Silliman read their lecture courses for the high purpose of spreading truth and knowledge.

2

IN JANUARY, 1856, Emerson read his lecture on "Beauty" before large audiences in Cleveland, Columbus, and Akron. At Cleveland his delivery was acknowledged to be "most pleasing" and the more commendable because it attempted "no theatrical flourishes, no pulpit affectations, no oratorical displays." "There is something very attractive in his delivery," wrote the editor of the *Leader* (January 24, 1856). "Every sentence is a finished one, and rolls out as if it intended to mean just what it says; there is nothing like hesitation in it."

The familiar guarded attitude toward Emerson's transcendental thought and abstruse reasoning is present in the reviews. "The lecture, perhaps, was not suited to the popular mind," said the *Leader*. "If some of his ideas were transcendental," added the *Herald*, "there was so much of appreciable elegance and chasteness in their expression, and so much that did please, aside from them, that they were excusable by any hearer, however matter-of-fact he or she might be." The editor of the *Ohio Farmer* (February 2, 1856), who did not "sympathize with the strange liberties which this lecturer takes with sacred and hallowed associations," concluded that "order is not one of the lecturer's merits." Emerson's materials lacked sequence, and "this inarticulateness, more than any inherent profoundness, or novelty in his thoughts, makes him unintelligible as a whole, however brilliant he may shine on the edges of parts." However, despite these specific objections to Emerson's "Beauty," the general impression of the Cleveland audience was that it had "felt the presence of

---

[20] "You write a discourse, and, for the next weeks and months, you are carted about the country at the tail of that discourse simply to read it over and over." *The Journals of Ralph Waldo Emerson*, VIII, 210–211.

an intellectual giant, grand and sublime in power of intellect and range of thought, one who had dived into the most abstruse questions of metaphysics, into the most intricate mysteries of mental research."[21]

The same admiration for Emerson's beauty of phraseology and the same reserved attitude toward the practicability of his transcendental thought are evident in the Columbus reviews. Commenting on the introduction of the lecture, the *Ohio State Journal* (January 25, 1856) observed that "as we watched the canvass, much we feared that the warp was of so fine a texture, that, though priceless, it might be valueless." But after hearing the entire lecture this critic concluded that it was not often that Columbus citizens heard "an entertainment so transcendental, and yet with so much of the practical." Indeed, "in the West the field for the former has not been very inviting, as our battle has been with the forests and the sterner realities of life." Perhaps it was time for Westerners to "ascend into the higher spheres." Emerson showed little skill as an orator. With so many graces of mind he ought to "study somewhat the graces of attitude." His delivery, which appeared to have "the affectation of carelessness," displayed "neither the grace or the beauty so wonderfully revealed from the pages before him." Nevertheless, his discourse would "long be remembered as the finest lecture ever delivered at the Atheneum."

Emerson's lecture at Akron was received with mild enthusiasm. Once again the audience sought practical truth and wondered at the meaning of the transcendental metaphysic. The *Summit Beacon* (January 30, 1856) found it "useless to conceal the fact that a large proportion of those who were present, left with a feeling of disappointment." The audience was "impressed by the scholar-like refinement and brilliant genius of the speaker, but the practical aim of his discourse most were left to guess at."

Ohio audiences rarely greeted Emerson's lectures with anything like unmixed approval. Usually he was badly praised. The hardships of the forest and the field had taught generations of Ohioans the value of the hard fact. There was perhaps a transitory pleasure in attempting to follow the mercurial intuitions of the lecturer's mind, but the return to a practical world would cause the memory of the

[21] *Cleveland Daily Plain Dealer*, January 24, 1856.

experience to fade. The persistent criticism of Emerson was that he left his audience with only a meager fund of immediately useful knowledge. Yet year after year Emerson returned to the West, and Ohio audiences regularly laid aside their mechanics' tools and their mercantile account books and went to hear him. Many lecturers rose to greater popularity in the West, and most of them, after a few years, were cheered off to oblivion. Emerson was one of the few important literary figures from the East whose popularity in Ohio continued for more than a brief time, and he was a lyceum attraction for nearly two decades.

Josiah G. Holland has pointed out that, among the hundreds of lecturers who occupied the platform, only a small number were lasting favorites, and these were almost invariably individual thinkers.[22] They were not the purveyors of commonplace morality or the idle entertainers of an hour; they were men who spoke for themselves, men who challenged their hearers with sharp truths, men who were warmly applauded and then "abused for a year." So far as Ohio's lecture public was concerned, Emerson was such a man.

3

IN LATE January and early February, 1857, Emerson delivered nine lectures before Ohio audiences. Since his Western journey in 1856 he had enhanced his literary reputation by the publication of *English Traits*, embodying much material from his popular lectures on the British people. The first lecture of the 1857 series was read on January 19 in response to an invitation from the Columbus Atheneum. The editor of the *Ohio State Journal* found "The Conduct of Life" to be "interesting and suggestive. It contained many things that will excite thought. It was original and eminently Emersonian."[23] But this critic received a lengthier comment from a correspondent who signed himself "S. Phynx." A friend of "S. Phynx" had been inspired by "The Conduct of Life" to write an essay which, it was hoped, the proprietors of the *Journal* would "not willingly let die." Although

[22] "The Popular Lecture," *Atlantic Monthly*, XV (March, 1865), 364.
[23] January 20, 1857. In Emerson's *The Conduct of Life* (1860) this lecture appears as an essay entitled "Considerations by the Way."

"S. Phynx" declared that his friend had, "with the utmost care," perused Emerson's *Essays*, *Representative Men*, and *English Traits*, "yet it has been utterly impossible to catch the secret of that wonderful style which stands so entirely alone in its capacity for obscuring thought." The "essay," which gave special attention to Emerson's interest in the Bhagavad-Gita and other philosophical writings of the Orient, was as follows:

HOW TO LIVE PROPERLY

Mankind are like oysters—of little value till rightly seasoned. Pepper comes from India, salt from the Hockhocking, mustard and vinegar are cheap and homebred. He who uses only mustard on his natives, will water at the eyes, and perhaps be choked. He whose intellectual powers know only common and indigenous culture, will wear stoga boots, and go to church twice on Sunday.

It is one of the maxims of Burram pooter Bog, the Hindoo Mounshee, that truth is frequently the opposite of falsehood,—and Lord Bacon says "if you wish to make me angry, don't strike my nose with a brickbat, but tweak it gently with thumb and forefinger." And Schiller says that the invention of gunpowder is hidden in the silence of the Dark Ages—yet nothing has made more noise in the world. Two and two make four, and a right angle may be produced as well by a perpendicular and horizontal, as by a horizontal and perpendicular.

France is finished with a blacking-brush. The empire, the monarchy, the republic, the noble, the bourgeois, the peasant. Louis Le Grand, Tallyrand, Jean Baptiste, Sansculotte, all bear the same polish. Thus a Frenchman implies your ability to ride in his every day salutation, and will never kick you before your face.

A wise man has no more ears than a fool; and in those of both are the same parts;—tympanum, auricle, mucous membrane, clavicle, and pax-wax; yet where the one hears only the discourse of many geese or the pandemonium cries of swine, the other discerns heavenly harmonies. For nature is a *maquignon*—a horse jockey, who often sells splints and spavins for health and strength and bottom. Yet it was Al. Bowler, the idiot, says the Zandavesta, who puts heads on both ends of his pins, that he might not prick himself.

Life is a wheel within a wheel. Thought, feeling, sensation, emotion, desire, are all necessary to him who would enjoy a buttered parsnip;—how much more to him who would feast on stars and sunsets. Zoroaster says that when the gods created man, they gave him an arm on each side, instead of two on his back, which they might have done. Zoroaster was right.

Great men can better afford to be small, than small to be great. The fact that Alfred once burnt cakes in a neat-herd's cottage, is fixed in history forever. How often the neat-herd himself burnt cakes, we know not, nor would know, if for a single day he had ruled Essex, Sussex and Wessex.

The Bhagoat Veda says—All men are tarred with the same stick, yet it does not follow, that if you burn the stick, the tar will necessarily have come from North Carolina. It is easier to say one thing twice at different times than two things once at the same time. Hence, if a man is wise, he will not run his head against a gatepost, unless it is a dark night and the post stands right before him, when he will strike it if he goes forward, unless he passes round it, or escapes it in some other way. Even the tenth commandment and the rule of three are not inseparable.

If a man has three friends, he will have four by counting himself one, and the same rule of addition would hold good if he had half a dozen. I called on a distinguished chemist the other day, and found him in the act of converting chicken salad into oyster patties. He told me it may easily be done by means of a leather retort and a guttapercha grid-iron. Yet there are not more than sixty men in a century, or may-be sixty-five, who are seven feet nine, and half of those live in Boston.

The true test of a great woman is the speed with which she will run from a bull in a meadow, yet how few there are who have done more than scream at a spider in a cupboard. "Various and changeable," said the poet, and well does the Shaster say, because a woman with fine teeth is always laughing, it does not follow that one with beautiful eyes will lay awake o'nights.

"Allah il Allah," says the Arabic philosopher, Mohammed Ben Frangelin. Carlyle is Carlyle, and Emerson is his most discouraging symptom.[24]

On January 20 Emerson read his lecture on "Poetry" in Columbus. As the weather was bitterly cold, there was "a very slim audience." According to the *Ohio State Journal*, Emerson "took a comprehensive view of his subject" and though the lecture "did not abound in so many bright flashes and startling paradoxes as the one on 'The Conduct of Life,' it gave the hearer a wide view of the purpose and functions of Poetry."

During the last ten days of January the columns of the *Journal*

---

[24] January 21, 1857. The members of the Cincinnati Literary Club also wrote a burlesque of Emerson's abstruse writing. The appearance of Emerson in Cincinnati usually occasioned the hilarious reading of the parody at the Club's meetings. Hastings, "Emerson in Cincinnati," *New England Quarterly*, XI, 443–469.

were enlivened by a newspaper quarrel between correspondents "G." and "J." over Emerson's religious views. The dispute centered in Emerson's supposed assertion, in "The Conduct of Life," that "good is a good teacher, but bad is a better." If this be true, declared "G.," "it would probably be advisable for us to send our children to the sinks of iniquity for their education, instead of to the Sunday schools and churches for moral instruction." "J." contended that "G." argued from what he thought Emerson meant, not from what the lecturer said. Moreover, "J." thought himself in a proper objective position to examine the matter, since he had never read anything that Emerson wrote. The dispute ultimately degenerated into quibbling, with "G." admitting that "in the multiplicity of paradoxes which abounded in the lecture, it was hard to tell what Mr. E. said or what he meant." But "G." maintained his assertion: "The teaching of Mr. Emerson may be Philosophy but it is not Christianity; it is pernicious, and tends to evil. His propositions should be examined with great care before being received by a popular audience."

From Columbus, Emerson went to Chicago, where he read "The Conduct of Life" on January 22. On January 27, he returned to Ohio and delivered the same lecture before the Cincinnati Young Men's Mercantile Library Association. The *Enquirer* reported that the lecture "was listened to with profound attention," but because of Emerson's "epigrammatic and somewhat disconnected style," it was "a matter of extreme difficulty to follow the thread of the discourse." The *Gazette* gave this careful description of Emerson the lecturer:

Mr. Emerson is a tall man, full six feet high, but slender and bony, and in his plain suit of ill-fitting black, looked not unlike a New England country schoolmaster. His face is thin and strongly marked, his nose large, and his eye-brows highly arched and meeting. He rarely looks his hearers full in the face, but at emphatic expressions has a habit of turning his eyes backward as though he desired to look in at himself. His voice is like his sentences—not smooth nor even, yet occasionally giving a tone of considerable sweetness, and he has an auracular [*sic*] way of delivering himself that is calculated to impress the audience.

When introduced to the audience he stood straight up, exhibiting his tall form—then looked down bashfully at the manuscript in his hand—then advanced rather ungracefully to the stand, and with an appearance of embarrassment, and in a half apologetic, introductory tone, began . . . Gentleman and Ladies.[25]

The *Times* portrayed Emerson as

tall, angular, loose-limbed, with an olive complexion, large features, especially the nose, and a blue or grey eye that has a mysterious and undefinable blight in its depth. He looks and dresses soberly, and has a quaint look, bearing and manner that reminds us more, though not much, of pictures we have seen of Anatomy-of-Melancholy Burton, than any thing else we can recall. He appears to have altered in person since we met him last, two years ago; he is less delicate and intellectual-looking.

His elocution, like his diction and himself, is peculiar, emphatic, abrupt, sharp, impressive and oracular. He is not graceful, but he carries a weight grace and culture alone never could supply. He stands at an acute angle toward his audience, and limberly, and has barely a gesture beyond the motion of the left hand at his side, as if the intensity of his thought were escaping, like the electricity of a battery, at that point.

He has not that fixed though plastic, that culture-obtained mien one would be led to expect who has read his admirable essay on "Manners." His voice is full, strong and rich, but he speaks with a sort of hesitation, not unpleasant but, the contrary, as if he were struggling with a thought too great for immediate utterance.

His lecture is not to be reported—without his own language, his manner, his delivery it would be little—to essay to reproduce it, would be like carrying soda-water to a friend the morning after it was drawn, and asking him how he relished it.

From Cincinnati, Emerson went to Sandusky, where he delivered "Beauty" at the annual distribution of the art holdings of the Cosmopolitan Art Association. The program consisted of an address by the president of the association, the reading of a poem written by Metta V. Victor, a local poetess and early author of the dime novel, the lecture by Emerson, and the lottery by which subscribers to the

[25] January 28, 1857. Emerson's unchivalric habit of addressing his audience as "Gentlemen and Ladies" aroused no comment from Ohio journalists, but when he read "Culture" in Detroit on January 30, 1854, a correspondent of the *Detroit Daily Advertiser* was much annoyed because Emerson "prefaced his talk most ungallantly with 'gentlemen and ladies,' a breach of western good manners, of which he was more than once guilty." C. J. Wasung, "Emerson Comes to Detroit," *Michigan History Magazine*, XXIX (January, 1945), 59–72.

association received such prizes as paintings, engravings, and pieces of sculpture.[26]

Emerson was enthusiastically welcomed, and his lecture, "delivered in a quiet, unimpassioned manner," was "greeted with frequent expressions of approval and delight." It was "full of suggestions for after-thought, garnished by an almost endless variety of illustrative facts, culled from the hoarded treasures of the speaker's scholarly lore."[27]

On January 29 Emerson read "The Conduct of Life" in Cleveland. In announcing this performance the *Herald* cautioned the public that "The hour of the lecture is eight o'clock, on or before which time it is expected that men with heavy boots, or 'creaky' ones, will have located themselves." The Melodeon was so crowded for the performance that some persons "were compelled to stand in the lobbies, or wings of the stage, and a great many went away unable to get even such mean accommodations." The editor of the *Herald*, who was offended by some of Emerson's views, declared that the subject "was treated in the transcendental, sweeping, dry and orderless manner which characterizes the emanations of his mind." Mingled and clothed in "concise and expressive language," there were "brilliant thoughts, caustic wit, correct ideas, sour, bitter expressions of contempt for the 'Masses,' and words of advice, originating in a disordered taste." To Emerson's mind it seemed that "a mechanic is but a bit of machinery, only to be considered as a bit of iron, a nail, or a screw in the general machinery of the world." From such a doctrine, "worthy only of a darker age, may the All Good deliver us!" This critic had heard Emerson "express his hatred to travelers before" and could not understand why he advanced such ideas, "which can only please some green country bumpkin who has never been away from home but once, and then had his pockets picked." There was much in "The Conduct of Life" that was "worthy to be treasured in the memory, as of superior good, but by far the greater

---

[26] This widely publicized distribution by the Cosmopolitan Art Association aroused great interest in the state. Thousands of people in the West paid the annual fee of three dollars which entitled them to a ticket in the lottery and a chance to win such coveted prizes as an engraving of Kossuth or a bust of Daniel Webster.

[27] *Sandusky Daily Commercial Register*, January 29, 1857.

portion was an insult to humanity, and productive of nothing but
wrong sentiments."

The editor of the *Ohio Farmer*, who contended that "Emerson's
philosophy has in it too much of man, and too little of God, to be
a popular, or a working philosophy,"[28] believed that Emerson lectured
under serious handicaps. "His well known philosophical and religious peculiarities, his disjointed style of thought and expression,
his limber elocution, with a sort of St. Vitus-dance accompaniment—
all these, together with a positive personality that repels one, are
against him." But the lecturer also had much in his favor. He was
strikingly original in thought and language; he was "provokingly
suggestive." Emerson pricked and inculcated his ideas into his
audience "with the sharpest wit, and the most pungent satire." In
this lecture there was an abundance of "withering, Mephistophelean
sneers." Emerson "gave it clearly to be known that ignorance, blunder,
weakness and sickness were generally a rascally brood."

On January 31 the *Cincinnati Gazette* announced that Emerson
would deliver a series of four lectures in the city's Unitarian Church.
The arrangements for this course, which was managed by Moncure
D. Conway, are given in Emerson's correspondence. Writing from
Syracuse, New York, on January 16, Emerson told Conway:

I fear I was inconsiderate in not reckoning my means more exactly
in the hasty conversation in Concord about lectures, & that I counted
eggs hatched & not quite hatched, for what seemed to me so improbable
a contingency as a *course* in Cincinnati. My chapter on "Memory,"
the most matured in my studies of "Intellect," is not yet presentable.
An essay which I call "Days," which may yet deserve the Hesiodic
title of "Works & Days," is not yet presentable. At this moment, after
I shall have read my lecture on "Life" to the Mercantile Library, I
shall only have two more with me which I care to read at C., one on
"Beauty," & one on "Poetry." A third, "the Scholar," which was an
address at Amherst, did very well at Boston, last spring, & might pass
at C. and "France."; but I think, that, unless the project can be postponed until April, so that I can go home & prepare for it, it had better be dropped.[29]

---

[28] Emerson's religious opinions were also censured by a correspondent to the
Herald (January 31, 1857), who asserted that "One verse from the Blessed
Book was worth more than all that lecture to strengthen and guide the soul."
[29] Rusk, *Letters*, V, 53–54.

On January 24 Emerson wrote from Chicago's Tremont House to Lidian Emerson:

The winter is nearly as savage in the West as was the last to the great annoyance of me & of all travellers & of the people themselves who have heretofore found this climate milder much than ours. I go hence tomorrow night to Cincinnati, where it seems, I am expected to give a course after my lecture to the Mercantile Library. If I consent, I shall either have to return home first or else set Ellen on a rummaging in the lower regions of the library to find certain MSS. to be sent thither by Express.[30]

From Cleveland, on January 29, Emerson again wrote to his wife:

From Cincinnati I sent you my telegraph to send the Amherst-Williamstown Discourse, "the Scholar"—which message I hope arrived, & is in act of being performed on your part, since it ought to reach me by next Wednesday to be of good use. I very reluctantly decided to stay at Cincinnati, having many times in heart turned my face homeward not wishing to trust the prairie any more. But Conway had worked so hard for me, & filled the papers with paragraphs & persuaded so many people that they ought to be glad to listen, that it seemed perverse, when the days were really at my disposal, not to stay.[31]

The *Gazette* (February 2, 1857) could not give a "connected report" of the lecture on "Beauty" because Emerson "hopped about from theme to theme as a bird hops from branch to branch of a tree—the limbs could all be traced to the trunk of the discourse, but seemed to have no connection with each other." The *Times* explained

[30] *Ibid.*, p. 58.
[31] *Ibid.*, p. 60. Emerson's course was thoroughly publicized in the Cincinnati papers. The *Commercial* of January 19 reprinted a favorable review of *English Traits* from the *New York Independent*. The *Gazette* of January 27 published a letter from a correspondent, probably Conway, giving a long sketch of Emerson's life.
Conway relates that while Emerson was in Cincinnati "Every interval of time he could spare was seized on by leading citizens for luncheons and dinners." On Sunday morning Emerson spoke to the children in Conway's church. "He told them about his neighbor Henry Thoreau, his love and knowledge of nature, in intimate friendship with the flowers, and with the birds he sometimes coaxed to his shoulder, and with the fishes that swam into his hand." Moncure Daniel Conway, *Autobiography, Memories and Experiences* (2 vols.; Boston and New York: Houghton, Mifflin and Company, 1905), I, 283–285.

that Emerson's essays were "most elaborately written, and for publication, which does not take place until they have been given as
lectures in the principal cities." Some of these essays, such as the
one on "Beauty," were too long to be suitable for lectures, "and
therefore he is compelled to skip and omit, which, of course, makes
his very disconnected manner more than ever sensible."

The *Times* (February 3, 1857) described the lecture on "Poetry"
as "a great effort, full of philosophy, lore and keen-edged thought,
dividing the theme into beautiful proportions, to those who could
see them, and at the same time the quaintest and most curious
figures." Emerson had compressed so much material into the discourse that "to retain it almost made the head ache." But Cincinnati
people had rarely heard "an abler, a profounder, or a more elaborate
lecture."

"Works and Days," delivered on February 4, "was full of Thought,
though less abstruse than usual, and fraught with interest." The
Times discerned that "the purest veins of Poesy ran through its
deepness, and an apparent spirit of prophesy was in its utterances, so
solemn and so beautiful."

Emerson read the final lecture of his Cincinnati series on February
6.[32] "The Scholar," said the *Times*, was "less elaborate in diction
than Emerson's compositions generally, but gave true satisfaction to
his excellent audience during an hour and a half." At the conclusion
of this lecture Emerson's Cincinnati friends requested that he give
another course, but he declined to do so.

On January 20, 1859, Emerson read "The Law of Success" in
Cleveland. The city's journalists had not forgotten the abstruseness
of "The Conduct of Life," delivered two years previously. The
Plain Dealer announced Emerson as a man who was "chock full of
scholarship. He is stuffed with knowledge on all sorts of subjects.
He is an immense man, and we hope those who hear him to-night
will understand him."

This writer was evidently one of those hearers who did not under-

---

[32] Emerson was announced to lecture in Yellow Springs on February 5, but
the lecture was not delivered. The details of Emerson's correspondence with
Horace Mann of Antioch College are given in Hastings, "Emerson in Cincinnati," *New England Quarterly*, XI, 443–469.

stand, for he complained that Emerson, though "a great and profound thinker," was nevertheless "illy adapted to the lecture room,"
and his lecture was "a rather sleepy affair." He would "quite as lief
see a perpendicular coffin behind a lecture-desk as Mr. Emerson."
One would be quite as amusing as the other. No, Emerson was "not
the man to talk to the people of the West about the 'Law of Success.' "
He was a learned man, but, like many other great scholars, he was
"impracticable and visionary." If mankind were to adopt his ideas
(provided, of course, that mankind could understand exactly what
his ideas were) "they would live a strange, weird life—the chaotic
dream of a lunatic!" The *Leader* felt that Emerson's "dry, sententious manner" conveyed the idea that "the speaker was addressing
a class of college students," while the *Ohio Farmer* objected to
Emerson's emphasis on individualism. If Emerson were asked to give
the three laws of success he would undoubtedly answer: "Every man
for himself, every man for himself, every man for himself."
Originality and resourcefulness were all very well, but it was hard
to see "how success can be simply a result of individualism."

Emerson's 1860 series of Ohio lectures began on January 30 at
Toledo with the delivery of "Manners." The *Blade* offered familiar
criticisms. No newspaper report could do justice to "a lecture in which
almost every sentence is a living thought, having all the suggestive
powers inseparable from such thoughts." Moreover the listener who
concentrated intensely on following Emerson's thoughts seemed
"not merely led but commanded to think, and sometimes this sub-
jection is so perfect, that his power, freely exercised, becomes
absolutely painful."

The announcement that Emerson would lecture in Cincinnati on
February 2 provoked a quarrel among the city's journalists. Political
feelings were tense at the time; the outbreak of the Civil War was a
little more than a year away, and there was considerable proslavery
sentiment in the southern Ohio community. On January 27 there
had been a great Union celebration in the city, and the people congratulated themselves that the problems of slavery could be solved
and friendly relations maintained between the North and South. A
special train from Columbus had brought 550 guests, including such

dignitaries as the governors of Ohio and Kentucky and the lieutenant
governor of Tennessee. All Cincinnati had turned out to see the
procession as these celebrities were escorted to the Opera House. In
the elaborate program of complimentary speeches and responses
that followed, the assurance of harmony among the states had been
repeated again and again.

The appearance of Emerson, whose antislavery sentiments were
well known, was looked upon by the editor of the *Enquirer*
(February 1, 1860) as a catastrophe calculated to stir up sectional
strife and undo the work of the Union celebrants:

His appearance upon the stand will be a public scandal. It is but a
few weeks since he declared in a speech that John Brown, the hero of
the Harper's Ferry insurrection, "HAS MADE THE GALLOWS
GLORIOUS LIKE THE CROSS!" The utterance of this blasphemous
and traitorous sentiment; this applauding of robbery and murder, of
rapine and insurrection; this insult to every thing which men hold
sacred, ought to debar its author from the recognition of any community which has a proper respect for moral and patriotic feelings. It
is a declaration of opinion which involves moral guilt and turpitude of
a high character. Only think of the atrocious sentiment, that John
Brown has made his gallows as the cross upon which the Saviour of mankind had expiated, by his sufferings, the sins of a guilty world!

The man who cherishes this nefarious belief is to appear before us to
instruct our youth in moral ethics. He comes right upon the heels of
the late patriotic and Union demonstration, in which our citizens welcomed their Southern brethren of Tennessee and Kentucky to our
shores in words of the warmest and kindliest spirit. Before our guests
are hardly out of sight, comes this Emerson, who declared that those
men who invaded their homes from the North, with the purpose of
stirring up their slaves to rise and cut their throats, and to expose them
to all the horrors of a domestic insurrection, did that which renders
them as glorious as JESUS CHRIST!

Emerson was defended by the editor of the *Gazette* (February 2,
1860), who contended that Emerson "likes a strong, startling expression, and is wont to talk, on rare occasions, too irreverently of
what the generality of men regard as sacred." The expression which
the *Enquirer* deprecated as irreverent "was profane in outward seeming rather than in the speaker's mind." Emerson meant simply that
the heroic bearing of John Brown, who died a victim of his own
unselfish zeal, "would give the gallows a higher meaning than as

a mere symbol of retribution for common felony." It was easy to understand how "a mere scholar, not at all a man of the world, might, under the excitement of the time, have conceived and altered such a notion, and with no irreverence of feeling."

The *Commercial* joined in the dispute with an editorial entitled "The Enquirer's Moral Hue and Cry." There were undoubtedly "plenty of Southern orators in and out of Congress, who believe in their hearts that every Republican ought to be hung to the first tree." But this was no reason why "the Mercantile Library Association should refuse to invite any such gentleman to deliver a lecture." The idea that personal opinions are incriminating "or that a man's sincere belief involves guilt, is long since abandoned, except by partizans and bigots." It was unlikely that there would be "any immediate danger to society from the toleration of opinion" or that the revenues of the Library Association would suffer extensively from the malicious endeavors of the *Enquirer* "to excite political odium" against Emerson.

The *Commercial* (February 4, 1860) noted with satisfaction that Emerson's lecture "was attended by the largest audience of the season, comprising a very full representation of the intellect and taste of the city." The subject "was one in which all cultivated society is interested," and the desire to hear Emerson "was considerably stimulated" by the *Enquirer's* antagonistic attitude and effort to "induce people to stay away." Although Emerson's voice had "no marked power or melody," he had converted it "into an impressive and effective organ of speech." Without any of the art of the elocutionist "and with a gesture which, if not positively awkward, has all the qualities of Yankee stiffness about it, the lecturer produces effects with those moderate low tones, which excel those of the practised orator." The *Enquirer* merely remarked that Emerson's manner of delivery was already "familiar to the lecture-going public" and so required no further description.

On February 3 Emerson "held his audience in delighted attention for more than an hour" in the delivery of "Success" at Cincinnati's Unitarian Church. The *Enquirer* found the lecture "terse, pithy, epigrammatic, sententious, subtle, vigorous, bold and sparkling with quaint comparisons and gems of thought." But "its connection with the subject" was not very obvious. The lecture could just as well "be labeled something else, and pass for the genuine article." It was "more abstruse, more irrelevant, more disconnected" than "Manners" and "its leading ideas less easy to point out."

On July 4, 1860, Emerson returned to Ohio to deliver an address before the Literary, Erodelphian, and Ecritean Societies at the thirty-fifth commencement of Miami University. Edward L. Taylor of Columbus, a student at the university and member of the committee that invited Emerson to speak, recalled many years later that during Emerson's stay in Oxford the lecturer was the guest of Professor David Swing. On commencement day Emerson, Swing, and Taylor, at Emerson's suggestion, took an hour's walk through the college grounds. Emerson especially enjoyed the locust grove of several acres on the southwest corner of the campus and just in front of Swing's house. As they rambled through the forest area in the eastern part of the campus, Emerson's companions noticed with delight his remarkable power of observation.[33]

A great deal of "expectation and curiosity had been manifested regarding Mr. Emerson's appearance before a Western university audience." A special train was run from Hamilton, while many interested people "came in carriages from the surrounding country." By eight o'clock the spacious grove in which Emerson spoke was "more than filled by an audience numbering fully 1,500 persons, about half of whom were ladies." Emerson was suffering from a severe cold, and though his hearers "were hushed and intent to a remarkable degree," nothing "could conquer the harshness of tone, which sounded painfully like the rasping of a file." Under such conditions, speaking in the open air would have been an ordeal to "the most hardened habitue of the stump," but to one "of the sensitive temperament of Mr. Emerson, it seemed a crucial test of endurance." However, he went through it "with heroic determination, speaking for more than an hour, and retaining the fixed and apparently delighted attention of the audience."[34]

Emerson's subject was "Thought and Originality," "a plea for

[33] Edward L. Taylor, "Ralph Waldo Emerson," *Ohio Indians and Other Writings* (Columbus: F. J. Heer, 1909), pp. 303–304.
[34] Letter from "Sigma," *Cincinnati Daily Commercial*, July 6, 1860.

thought, addressed to thinkers." He began by expressing the pleasure he felt at meeting such an audience, "under the most delightful auspices, in that fair grove, in that beautiful village, amid temples consecrated to learning." He had come to Oxford entirely a stranger, but the love of learning and the muses had quickly made him acquainted. At one time it had been announced that because of his severe cold, Emerson would not consent to lecture in the open air, "but it was doubted whether a man entertaining such liberal views concerning future punishment would compel an audience to take a foretaste of purgatory, by crowding them into a small and close space, when Fahrenheit indicated 95 degrees."[35] Despite the opinion that "the style of this celebrated man is anything but attractive," and "he confines himself closely to the manuscript all the time," the people of this Ohio village were profoundly impressed by the famous man from the East.

4

EMERSON read only three lectures in Ohio during the period of the Civil War.[36] In those years the platform belonged to the political orators who stirred the emotions of their audiences with frenzied attacks upon the Confederacy or with patriotic appeals for support of the Union army. There was little demand for the learned, philosophical discourses of the cultural lecturers. Nevertheless, when Emerson arrived in Cleveland from Buffalo on January 13, 1863, to deliver "The Third Estate in Literature," the *Plain Dealer* announced that in "these times of war and turmoil" it would be "a relief to listen to a calm and dispassionate, a pure and elevated thinker." In contrast to the political orators, here was a lecturer "whose eloquence is not in mere dazzling rhetoric, but in the natural-ness and beauty of his thought, and the grandeur and sublimity of his ideas."

After hearing the lecture, "replete with beautiful thoughts," and "expressed in the most elegant language," this writer reported that

---

[35] Letter from "McC.," *Cincinnati Daily Gazette*, July 6, 1860.

[36] A fourth lecture, scheduled for Medina on January 17, 1861, was can-celed when Emerson was unable to meet the appointment.

Emerson's large audience was "thoroughly charmed from first to last." It was "a truly delightful effort," added the *Herald* (January 15, 1863), and clearly showed that Emerson was "one of the intellectual giants of the country and the age." The lecture drew the fire of a correspondent to the *Leader* (January 17, 1863), who felt that Emerson had poisoned "The Third Estate in Literature" with "his first-proof Infidelity." This critic wondered if there was such a thing in Boston as "courtesy or propriety capable of restraining a man from calling in the people to hear a lecture on 'Literature,' the most striking parts of which are a disingeneous assault upon their accepted religion."

In January, 1865, Emerson, en route to Pittsburgh, delivered "Social Aims in America" in Warren and Cleveland. Although the subject was a timely one, the performances were not received with much ardor. The Warren *Western Reserve Chronicle* objected to Emerson's oratory, or rather to his lack of it, and concluded that he "satisfied the most of his hearers that he is more attractive on the printed page than on the rostrum." While the lecture was in many ways "entertaining and instructive," much of its force and beauty "was lost from certain defects which marked its delivery, and which would be intolerable in a lecturer of less standing and acknowledged ability than Mr. Emerson." His "mild, moderate elocution" ought to make him very popular "with that class who occasionally pay a quarter for the privilege of sleeping in good company." It was doubtful that more than half the audience could hear the speaker.[37]

On January 19 Emerson, "that ripe scholar and pioneer of popular lectures," delivered "Social Aims in America" before "a throng of

---

[37] January 25, 1865. Emerson suffered an embarrassing experience at this lecture. "The chairman escorted the distinguished lecturer upon the platform, rose and announced that 'it gave him great pleasure to introduce to them Walph Raldo Emerson,'—when it occurred to him that the name was slightly mixed, and so he tried again, and a third time, but with no better success than on the first trial; it was still 'Walph Raldo Emerson,' whereupon universal tittering over the house ensued, with the exception of the martyr (whose stoical doctrine stood him in good service) and his self-exasperated executioner. The latter's chagrin was deepened, and the merriment of the audience was heightened by a voice piping up in the crowd, 'Try it again!' " *Cleveland Morning Leader*, January 21, 1865.

well-mannered people" in Cleveland. The *Herald* reported that the lecture "was superlatively Emersonian, embracing many fine thoughts and much good advice, delivered in the style peculiar to this lecturer, and clothed in pure and simple language." The *Leader* observed that Clevelanders were well pleased with "the pithy sentences of Mr. Emerson," but "the stately and faultless proportions of the address" were marred by "the studied omission of all consideration and estimate of the influence of this civil war upon the social conditions of American life."[38]

5

IN EARLY 1866 Emerson undertook an extensive lecture trip into Indiana, Illinois, Michigan, Minnesota, and Iowa.[39] On January 12 he interrupted his journey westward from Buffalo to read "Social Manners" (i.e., "Social Aims in America") before the College Societies Library Association at Oberlin College. "There will be a general interest to hear one of whom so much good and ill is spoken," predicted the *Lorain County News*. "There will be no trick of anecdote or stage effect in delivery, but the lecture will be one to hold the attention of thinking people." Emerson "had the compliment of a fine audience" for his performance, but if his newspaper critic reflected the common reaction of Oberlin's staid lecture-goers, there was considerable disagreement with the speaker's religious opinions. The lecture was read in Emerson's "peculiar, concise, suggestive style, introducing more of anecdote and liveliness than is the wont of his essays." Yet there was nothing new or striking in thought. It was just the old, old art of "putting things." Emerson, it seemed,

---

[38] January 21, 1856. Emerson's audience was perhaps swelled by the rumor resulting in this journal's report that "This is Mr. Emerson's last lecture-tour. His thousands of admirers regret that this is the last course of public lectures to be given by him." Emerson lectured again in Cleveland in 1866 and 1867.

[39] Emerson's Western trips in 1866 and 1867 are discussed in Hubert H. Hoeltje, "Ralph Waldo Emerson in Iowa," *Iowa Journal of History and Politics*, XXV (April, 1927), 236–276; and "Ralph Waldo Emerson in Minnesota," *Minnesota History*, XI (June, 1930), 145–159; C. J. Wasung, "Emerson Comes to Detroit," *Michigan History Magazine*, XXIX (January, 1945), 59–72; Russel B. Nye, "Emerson in Michigan and the Northwest," *Michigan History Magazine*, XXVI (Spring, 1942), 159–172; Louise Hastings, "Emerson in Cincinnati," *New England Quarterly*, XI (September, 1938), 443–469.

had little sympathy "with the faith that is dearest to us of Oberlin." To him, Jesus was "no more divine than Plato, the Bible no more authoritative than the words of Epictetus." And so by magnifying "self poise, self centre, self culture," he seemed to have failed of apprehending "the most wonderful idea of Christianity," the maxim of "self-sacrifice, self-forgetfulness." "A man of wondrous mind, of most lovable nature, his philosophy fails beside the faith of thousands of illiterate believing souls who would not know the meaning of half the words he utters."[40]

While traveling back to Concord in early February, Emerson stopped in Ohio to fulfill engagements at Toledo and Cleveland. The *Toledo Commercial* (February 5, 1866) informed its readers that Emerson's discourse on "Table Talk" would contain none "of the loose garbage with which many of our writers clothe their thoughts, and none of the buffoonery of a great many lecturers." In reviewing the lecture this writer made the conventional comment about Emerson's inadequacies as an orator. Emerson was "not so attractive a speaker as his splendid reputation would lead one to expect." His merit was entirely in his matter. He appeared "to much better advantage" in the pages of the *Atlantic* than on the lyceum platform.

At Cleveland the *Leader* predicted that Emerson's lecture on "Resources" would be heard "by every man and woman of culture, thought and worthy aim in the city." The "rarest intellectual banquet of the year" was listened to by "a large audience who sat with commendable heroism an hour and a half in a deathly cold room." The *Herald* (February 7, 1866) commented that Emerson's language was "pure and plain, and his sentences made up of the simplest and most forcible Anglo-Saxon words." No lecturer before the American public was "more a favorite with the intellectual portion of the community than Mr. Emerson." His lecture "attempted to convey the idea of the inexhaustible resources of individuals and nations, and that as the wants of either increase so do the inventive genius

[40] Oberlin *Lorain County News*, January 17, 1866. See also Robert Samuel Fletcher, *A History of Oberlin College from Its Foundation Through the Civil War* (2 vols.; Oberlin: Oberlin College, 1943), II, 813–814.

and natural resources of the people." The performance gave abundant evidence of "that deep-thinking mind that is accorded on all hands to this lecturer, poet and philosopher." The editor of the *Plain Dealer*, who was no admirer of Emerson, fastened on the lecturer's deficiencies as a reader. Though Emerson occupied "an exalted position" as a poet and essayist, he was "a decided failure" as a lecturer. "Resources" did contain much of beauty, but "the wretched delivery of the speaker caused the fine points of the discourse to be lost upon his audience." Once or twice he lost his place, and his "clumsy efforts" to "catch the thread" again were amusing to the audience. In the hands of a more skilful reader the lecture would doubtless have been a charming one.

Emerson returned to Cleveland on January 10, 1867, to read "The Man of the World" before the Cleveland Library Association. Although it was "a carefully prepared paper, replete with ideas pertinent to passing events," the *Herald* maintained that "more spirit in the manner of delivery would have added to the pleasure of the occasion." The audience, "composed of people from *elite* circles, . . . smiled approvingly" on some of Emerson's "well timed and quaint sayings relative to the present state of the country."

During his stay in Cleveland, Emerson enjoyed a visit with James E. Murdoch. The actor entertained Emerson by reading Thomas Buchanan Read's poem "Sheridan's Ride," which was then very popular. In a letter to his daughter Ellen, Emerson said of Murdoch: "I had heard wonders of his reading, & he reads with great skill & force, but, as usual, with the *surplusage* of actors. Probably it would sound far better in a hall."[41]

In late January, and in February and March, 1867, Emerson lectured at Detroit, Chicago, St. Paul, and other cities of the Northwest, as well as in Iowa and Missouri. He returned to Ohio in mid-March for lectures at Cincinnati and Marietta. "Social Life in America," read in Cincinnati on March 14, was advertised as Emerson's "only and last lecture in Cincinnati," and the city's journalists stated further that Emerson was making "his last appearance as a lecturer in the West, as he is going to retire from the lecture field."

---

[41] Rusk, *Letters*, V, 489.

At this final performance in the city, Emerson was cordially received by his many Cincinnati friends and by the journalists; even the editor of the *Enquirer* reported that the lecture was "the most attractive" discourse heard during the season and that "regret is felt that it can not be repeated." The *Commercial* declared that Emerson's style was as free as ever "from logical rules and conventional restraints"; he uttered his thoughts as they occurred, but they were "none the less pertinent because expressed at random." Emerson, possessed of "perfect repose" and "a voice of exceeding sweetness," gave an interesting and instructive lecture, though he left for his hearers "the task of arrangement."

On the next evening Emerson delivered "Social Life in America" to "a large and fashionable audience" in Marietta. He prefaced his remarks by saying that it was with pleasure he found himself "in the ancient city of Marietta, whose name and geographical relations were fixed among his earlier recollections as being then laid down on the map as the Capitol of Ohio." And in the surrounding country-side were "towns laid and laying out which will grow to cities in the lifetime of a man."

The correspondent of the *Register* (March 21, 1867) was convinced that the lecture's originality consisted in "Emerson's literary 'manners,' not in the thinking up of ideas—except insidiously to undermine that which is the foundation of social economy." The audience, "for the larger part," was disappointed. Emerson's voice, "though pleasant, was not used in force to reach many in the house." It was apparent that Emerson was a scholar, "although by no means critical in the grammatical use of language or its pronunciation." Moreover, he was extraordinarily well read in polite literature and was "a first-class culler of the notable sayings of others." But the chief defect of the discourse was its lack of unity; indeed, "what nine-tenths of the Lecture had to do with our 'social life,' might puzzle a sharp-brained critic to discover." Emerson talked about "manners, character, conversation, sentimentalism, aristocracy, social spirit, but it was in the abstract." As for consistency in the subject matter, "the Lecturer could begin in the middle, and work forward or backward; or go to the end first, and take his beginning last; or strike this paragraph or that one, this or that sentence—go through or between, above or below—and the Lecture be as complete in any case, even though the half were left out, or more patched on."

In December, 1867, Emerson made another speaking tour in the West. His lecture schedule, which was arranged by George L. Torbert, corresponding secretary of the Associated Western Literary Societies, took him into Ohio, Illinois, Iowa, and Missouri. The first of his four Ohio appearances was made at Cleveland, where "Eloquence," a new essay bearing the same title as one which Emerson had delivered on his first Ohio journey in 1850, was read on December 4. The discourse, which was advertised to be "such a treat as is only afforded once in an entire course of lectures," was attended by a very large audience. Realizing his limitations as an orator, Emerson, in his introductory remarks, "expressed himself as being fully aware of the imprudence of venturing upon a topic which, to do it justice, required the very power it described." The *Herald* found that Emerson's manner had not changed; here were "the same quiet, confident power" and the "intense nervous force" which he seemed to hold in check "by an occasional closing of the fingers upon the hand." Emerson's habit of turning simultaneously several pages of his manuscript evoked the following comment from this critic:

Ralph Waldo Emerson's lecture on Eloquence reminded us of the way it is said vessels are built on the St. Lawrence—by the mile, and then cut off to suit orders. Mr. Emerson turns over about six sheets where he reads one, and it is of no consequence where his turning over stops; one place to splice on, or to leave off, is just as good as another. His lecture, called "On Eloquence," or by any other name, would pass as well, while, no doubt, from that cord of manuscript before him, he could extract any required number of lectures, on any required subjects, just as a magician can draw all sorts of liquors, on demand, from the same bottle. Lectures now-a-days are like ready-made doors and windows—made by machinery, and adapted to any kind of a frame; if they rattle in the frame, it is not to be wondered at.

At Painesville, where Emerson delivered "American Culture," the *Telegraph* (December 12, 1867) was not altogether pleased with the combination of thoughts which the lecturer selected from his "cord of manuscript." Many in the audience were "thoroughly dis-

appointed, in the man, in his manner, and most of all, in his matter."
It was nearly impossible "to trace any legitimate connection between
the theme and the discussion." Now and then Emerson culled "a
pithy sentence or quaint illustration" from a "mass of manuscript
that seemed quite embarrassing to him, judging from the frequency
with which he turned his pile of paper first one way and then the
other, with an air which seemed to say, 'I don't know where to find
my thought.'" Though he said a few excellent things in the best
possible manner, "he utterly failed to interest his audience and
realize in their thought and feeling their beautiful ideal of the
transcendental lecturer—Ralph Waldo Emerson."

On December 28, when Emerson made his first appearance in
Steubenville, the hall was filled to capacity "with the beauty, wit
and intelligence of the city" to hear "Social Life in America." The
Herald (January 3, 1868) observed that Emerson's appearance and
manner were "decidedly against him." Ungainly in form and "exceedingly awkward" in his "postures and gesturing," Emerson
produced not "the slightest effort at oratorical effect." His calm,
deliberate, and at times inaudible voice was "entirely wanting in
the indescribable magnetism which some men possess to penetrate
and arouse."

Emerson's last Ohio lecture was delivered at Columbus on December 30, 1867, when he read "Manners" before the Young Men's
Christian Association. The story of Emerson's Columbus visit is
narrated by Edward L. Taylor.[42] In the seven years since 1860 the
young Miami University student had become a prominent Columbus
attorney and local historian. During his Columbus visit Emerson
was a guest at Taylor's home. As the day of the lecture was a pleasant
one, Emerson "expressed a desire to have a walk about the city."
Consequently, the two friends took a leisurely stroll down High
Street. At the intersection of Broad and High Streets, Emerson
stopped for some moments to admire the architecture of the State
House. Taylor led him inside the building, where they "made a call
on Governor Hayes." Since Emerson's first meeting with Rutherford
B. Hayes in Cincinnati seventeen years before, the Ohio lawyer had

---

[42] "Ralph Waldo Emerson," *Ohio Indians and Other Writings* (Columbus:
F. J. Heer, 1909), pp. 303–309.

pursued a political career which was to result, in 1876, in his election to the Presidency. On this occasion Emerson and Hayes "talked perhaps near half an hour, during which Mr. Emerson again expressed his admiration of the building."

At dinner that evening Taylor entertained Emerson, Hayes, and several prominent Columbus citizens. Taylor's guests "all came early and so had an hour or more conversation before dinner. Mr. Emerson was in fine spirits and seemed to me to be at his best." The entire party then proceeded to the First Presbyterian Church, on the corner of State and Third Streets, to hear Emerson's lecture. Taylor recalled that the discourse was very well received, and at its conclusion many admiring Columbus people crowded around Emerson with the hope of being introduced to him. Taylor's guests returned to his home, where they engaged Emerson in a long and pleasant discussion of Carlyle, Thoreau, Phillips, and Beecher.

The next day Emerson left Columbus for his home in Concord. Taylor wrote that, as Emerson prepared to go, "He took my hand and in the kindliest tones of voice said, 'Come to Concord; come and see me at Concord and we will take a walk to Walden Pond and see where Thoreau lived.' "

According to Taylor a rather unpleasant aftermath of Emerson's visit occurred on the next Sunday, when a Presbyterian minister in the city delivered "a terrific discourse against Mr. Emerson, and said, 'That he had not expected to live to see the time when a Presbyterian pulpit would be disgraced by Ralph Waldo Emerson lecturing from it'; and then went on to censure those of his congregation who had 'so far forgotten their religious duties as to attend the lecture.' " Taylor was pleased to recall that the pastor's congregation vigorously defended Emerson and that the minister "soon resigned his charge and faded away into oblivion through the medium of an obscure country church."[43]

---

[43] The manuscript "Records of the Columbus Presbytery" provide no clue to the identity of this minister. None of the city's Presbyterian pastors "soon resigned" or accepted rural charges. The minister who attacked Emerson may have belonged to some other sect, or perhaps Taylor exaggerated his fate. Taylor's account of Emerson's Columbus visit contains several curious factual errors; he declared, for example, that Emerson had never visited Columbus prior to 1867 and that Hayes and Emerson had not met before the State House call.

During the years from 1850 to 1867, Emerson delivered some sixty lectures in Ohio. The pattern of public reaction to these lectures is oddly inconsistent. He frequently delivered "the best lecture of the course," and yet no other cultural speaker from the East evoked so much adverse criticism. It is evident that his oratorical powers were limited, particularly in his later years, when his arduous journeys through the West sapped his strength and deprived his performances of some of that vigorous enthusiasm which he had displayed in the fifties.

Despite the limitations of his eloquence and the eccentricities of his manner, Emerson stood apart from most of the cultural lecturers of the day. Bold in his thought and tenacious in his faith in the highest purposes of the public lecture, he was the most individualistic and provocative speaker who visited the West. He was rarely listened to with conventional approbation. He pricked his hearers to admiration, and he stung them to wrath. He demanded the most strenuous attention and mental effort from his listeners, and it is apparent that his meaning was lost on many of them. But the coterie of devoted Ohioans who were willing and able to pursue the intricate and exciting labyrinth of his thoughts were agreed that "To be placed in sympathy for an hour with a mind such as Emerson's, is one of the supremest pleasures of life."[44]

[44] Columbus *Morning Ohio State Journal*, December 31, 1867.

CHAPTER
III

HENRY GILES: *Forgotten Man From Maine*

I

Most of the prominent Eastern orators were celebrated as ministers, journalists, statesmen, or literary writers before they took to the lecture platform. The fame of such men as Emerson, Theodore Parker, Horace Greeley, William Lloyd Garrison, and Bayard Taylor went before them and prepared an audience of curious hearers in the West. But the reputation which Henry Giles brought to Cincinnati in 1851 was that of an eloquent lecturer, and little else. Although he was an ordained Unitarian preacher, he had no regular congregation and had not achieved ministerial fame in the East comparable to that of Henry Ward Beecher, Thomas Starr King, or John Pierpont. As a writer he had pleased a discriminating group of readers with his *Lectures and Essays* (1845) and *Christian Thoughts on Life* (1850), but his contemporary literary renown did not rival that of Emerson, Whipple, or John G. Saxe. When Giles came to Ohio he was not heralded by the newspapers as preacher, poet, or thinker; he stood solely on his growing reputation as "the distinguished lecturer from Maine."

Giles was announced to lecture before the Cincinnati Young Men's Mercantile Library Association on February 11, 1851. However, the lecture was not given until February 18 because Giles, who had been delivering a course before the Mercantile Library Association in St. Louis, was stranded there by an ice blockade in the Mississippi River.

"A crowded and highly intelligent auditory" listened to Giles read his lecture on "Conversation" at College Hall. The high expectations of the audience "were more than realized in the rich intellectual repast served up to them." The lecture, said the *Gazette*, was "truly a magnificent one, and was delivered in a style of impressiveness and oratorical power not often equalled." Its philosophy, brilliance, and beauty "enchained the attention of the large assembly."

After his arrival in Cincinnati, Giles was announced to give a private course of literary lectures entitled "The Actual and Ideal in Life, Illustrated in a Series of Topics from Don Quixote." The schedule of lectures was as follows:

February 20 "The Life and Genius of Cervantes"
February 24 "The Scope and Spirit of the Story"
February 27 "The Censorship in the Library, or Literary Fame"
March 3   "Dulcinea, or Womanhood"
March 6   "Sancho Panza, or the Worldling"
March 10   "Don Quixote, or the Enthusiast"

In reviewing "The Life and Genius of Cervantes," the editor of the *Gazette* (February 24, 1851) informed Cincinnatians that "Mr. Giles, at the urgent solicitation of some of our citizens, has commenced the series here, although he is under pressing Eastern engagements." As for Giles' ability as a lecturer, "He throws around his subject a charm and beauty, which, while they please the fancy, and instruct the judgment refine the tastes, and are grateful to the heart." Here was a speaker who possessed "genius of the loftiest order" and who was "justly entitled to the high encomiums" which he had received from the Eastern press.

In Giles' lecture on "The Scope and Spirit of the Story" he treated the intrinsic literary merits of the book. Once again, said the *Gazette* (March 14, 1851), the audience was completely "enchained" by "the nervous, terse and fresh vigor" of his oratory.

The success of Giles' course was a high tribute to his abilities as an orator. The presentation of a long series of lectures by an individual speaker was not often attempted, because few lecturers could sustain public interest for more than one or two appearances. In this case, the success was especially merited as, throughout the period of his course, Giles was competing for the favor of Cincinnatians with John B. Gough, who was delivering a series of temperance lectures in the city.[1]

Despite Giles' "pressing Eastern engagements," the announcement

---

[1] Gough lectured on February 20, 22, 23, 25, 28 and March 7.

was made on March 7 that he had acceded to "the solicitation of his numerous friends and admirers" to give another series of discourses. The second Cincinnati course, entitled "Illustrations of Civilized Men," was composed of the following lectures:

March 13 "The Hebrew Man, or the Man of Faith"
March 18 "The Greek Man, or the Man of Culture"
March 20 "The Roman Man, or the Man of Law"
March 25 "The Medieval Man, or the Man of Force"
March 27 "The Modern Man, or the Man of Money"

The practical impossibility of being in attendance at all the various lectures, political meetings, and other evening activities in the city prevented Cincinnati's editors from providing reviews for several of Giles' lectures.[2] However, the editor of the *Gazette* (March 18, 1851), who listened to the reading of "The Hebrew Man, or the Man of Faith," wished "that every son of Abraham could have heard this candid and eloquent exposition of the Jewish character, that he might know that there was one Christian at least that could do justice to it." Giles possessed "a great and penetrating insight into the central spirit of a people, and he gave a fine specimen of his power in this effort." By thus going beyond the politics and polemics of the day and "aiming to reach what is essential and eternal, instead of what is phenomenal and ephemeral, he aids every student of History and of Man."

The audience which heard "The Medieval Man, or the Man of Force" appeared "exceedingly gratified with the broad and catholic views advanced by the lecturer, concerning the medieval man, and his place as a man of power in the world's history." The *Gazette* (March 27, 1851) reported that toward the close of the lecture "occurred one of those pieces of impassioned eloquence which are peculiarly Mr. Giles' own." In estimating the writings and character of Dante, "the speaker seemed to catch the glow of sublimity and feeling which animated that most wonderful poet of the middle

[2] Gough was again providing grist for the newspaper mill. After lecturing in Columbus on March 12, 13, 14, 15, and 16, he returned to Cincinnati on March 17 and lectured nightly during the ensuing week.

ages, and rose to a sustained elevation of thought and expression which bore the sympathies of the audience along in breathless enthusiasm to the close." It was rare indeed that a lyceum audience "listened to a peroration at once so beautiful and so stirringly eloquent as this."

At the conclusion of his Cincinnati lectures, Giles postponed his Eastern journey in response to a lecture invitation from the Cleveland Library Association. On April 3 he delivered "The Modern Man, or the Man of Money," and the correspondent of the *Herald* doubted "if a more truly eloquent, instructive and impressive disquisition was ever read in our city." In the midst of this lecture Giles' well-known power to "enchain his audience" was given a severe test. The alarm of fire, the dread of all lecturers, was suddenly sounded outside the hall. But the alarm, "so startling to any audience, did not occasion a stir in the assembly; all kept their seats; the highest compliment that could be paid to the Speaker."[3] Under similar circumstances, other Eastern lecturers, including Bayard Taylor, were to endure the humiliation of seeing their Ohio audiences vanish into the night.

Although the effort of Cleveland lecture-goers to induce Giles to deliver a full course was unsuccessful, there was much satisfaction in the news that the "citizens have prevailed upon Mr. Giles, to tarry with us, and deliver another lecture." In announcing Giles' second discourse, "The Enthusiast," the *Herald* (April 8, 1851) published the following statement:

In many respects Mr. Giles is, in our opinion, superior to Emerson. His instruction is never involved in a cloud of transcendentalisms, but enforced in diction that all can understand. Nor is he a mere imitator. He is altogether an independent and original thinker. His views are sound and practical, and characterized by the golden medium between conservatism and radicalism.

In "The Enthusiast" Giles defined "enthusiasm" as an "exalted ambition" and described the quality as it appears in the ascetic, mystic, thinker, poet, artist, and musician. In reviewing Giles' treatment of the subject, the *Plain Dealer* (April 9, 1851) asserted that

---

[3] Cleveland *Daily True Democrat*, April 5, 1851.

he "excels in the power of generalization," though he did not, like
some lecturers, "profess to put a hay-stack into a thimble." His
phraseology was "entirely choice, expressive, and wonderfully self-
denying, considering the present public demand for exotic words
and sonorous terminations."

2

AMONG Giles' lectures on literary subjects, none was more popular
than "The Comic Powers of Shakespeare," which he presented in
many Western communities during the season of 1854–55. The
skill and dramatic power with which the dwarf-like, deformed Irish
clergyman quoted passages from Shakespeare's plays moved his
hearers with surprise and admiration. At Cincinnati the *Commercial*
(December 14, 1854) reported that "the intensified imagination of
the Lecturer" played upon his theme for two full hours, and yet,
"when he had uttered his last brilliant antithesis, and retired, the
audience seemed then first aware of the lapse of time."

Giles visited Columbus at a time when the lecture course of the
local Atheneum was threatened with financial failure. In announcing
"The Comic Powers of Shakespeare" the press and Atheneum made
a final appeal "to the intelligent and substantial citizens of Columbus."
A small audience would prove that the people were "too poor or
too niggardly to sustain a course of lectures." Thus the public
response to Giles' performance "must settle the question."

Giles "brought down the house." He displayed "a power of
analysis" and "a happy combination of the humorous and the moral"
which the correspondent of the *Capital City Fact* (December 20,
1854) had "seldom seen equalled and never excelled." Never had
a lecturer in the city "commanded more admiration or awakened more
interest." Giles divided Shakespeare's comic characters into three
categories: those we laugh *with*, those we laugh *at*, and those we
laugh both *with* and *at*. His illustrations of these types were re-
peatedly greeted with bursts of applause. And best of all, such
enthusiasm by the large audience provided sufficient proof that
Columbus citizens were "disposed to encourage this species of entertainment and instruction during the long winter evenings."

The Dayton performance of this lecture was described by the *Journal* (December 23, 1854) as "the most brilliant thing of the season" and "fairly bore away the palm from all competitors, who, as lecturers, have sought to win public favor and applause." The *Gazette* (December 23, 1854) described Giles as "very small, and even the little there is of him physically, is deformed," but he was "a man of rare genius and cultivation." Dayton's citizens had "heard no lecturer who equals him."

3

MOST OF Giles' Ohio lectures of 1855–56 were given under the auspices of the Bryant Association, a co-operative lecture agency with member organizations in northern and central Ohio towns.[4] The association arranged a strenuous itinerary which required almost nightly appearances in small communities whose railroad facilities were often undependable. More than one audience waited in vain for Giles while he rode, hours behind schedule, on the cold, drafty "fever and ague" trains. And the press sometimes reported that he appeared worn out from traveling and lecturing. Giles, with his frail body but stalwart spirit, was not a man to be dismayed by hardship, fatigue, or the small fees of the Bryant Association. He belonged to that distinguished group of cultural lecturers who devoted themselves ceaselessly to the highest purposes of the lyceum. He was intent on "doing good."

Giles usually delivered "False and Extravagant Eulogy in Oratory," a lecture designed to show the hypocrisy of contemporary political oratory. Adulation of party drove men to false argument or meaningless eloquence which superseded logic and truth. Liberty required truth and was impaired by the degeneracy of character in the political orator who thrust aside truth for the selfish purposes of party supremacy or personal ambition.

At Sandusky the *Commercial Register* (December 13, 1855) declared that Giles withdrew "the thin veil which guards the motives of men from common sight, and exposed, in earnest declamation,

---

[4] For a discussion of the formation of the Bryant Association, see pp. 189–191 of this study.

the deceit and hollowness—the untruthfulness and baseness which instigate the usual flatteries of demagogues and sycophants." The lecture was "most happily conceived and original"; indeed, "for such words money is poor return."

When Giles appeared in Kenton the editor of the *Hardin County Republican* (December 21, 1855) compared the lecture with Parke Godwin's "The Future Republic," which local citizens had recently heard. While Godwin's discourse revealed more "rhetorical and ornamental finish," Giles' lecture "was more analytical and argumentative and more comprehensive and easier followed by the audience."

Giles' performance before the Whittlesey Academy in Norwalk revealed that he "was considerably exhausted from incessant labor." According to the *Reflector* (January 1, 1856) the lecture was nevertheless highly successful, as Giles "evinced deep, massive thought and clothed it in plain, but beautiful habiliments."

Giles made only occasional visits to Ohio in the next decade. His last lecture in the state, "The Jew in History," was scheduled for delivery in Zanesville on February 5, 1866. A few days before the appointment the lecture association received a letter from the speaker's wife, Louisa L. Giles. Suffering from a long illness, Henry Giles had had to give up his hope "of being able to go West." His wife was thankful for the privilege of reading the lecture for him. "Mr. Giles' long illness has taken from us our only means of support, and it is a pleasure to me to be able to do anything for my family."[5] Mrs. Giles read "with great skill and tact" the discourse which traced the persecutions of the Jews and stressed their retention of "their ideal or national characteristics, their inflexibility of character and adhesion to principle."

Henry Giles was one of the most widely admired cultural lecturers who visited Ohio. Lacking the intellectual depth of Emerson and the polished style of Edwin P. Whipple, he was more eloquent than either of these lecturers. The chief function of the cultural lecture was to instruct, and Giles was "admirably fitted for a public teacher"

---

[5] *Zanesville Daily Courier*, February 2, 1866. The letter is printed in full. Mrs. Giles had previously read her husband's lectures in Boston and Salem, Massachusetts.

with his "energy, originality, and a habit of close, philosophic thinking."[6] "There is matter in what he says," wrote the editor of the
Cleveland *True Democrat* (April 17, 1851), "substantial matter—
and no one can hear him without profit and pleasure." But the
major source of Giles' popularity lay in the fact that he was gifted
with unusual eloquence in an age that loved eloquence unusually
well. He deserved a better fate than the obscurity which has over-
taken his fame.

[6] *Cleveland Daily Plain Dealer*, April 8, 1851.

CHAPTER
IV

EDWIN P. WHIPPLE: *Elegant Essayist*

I

THE OHIO lectures of the critic and essayist Whipple met with considerable success, particularly in those early years when the cultural impulse of the lecture system was still strong. Before 1853 his oratorical talents, which were already famous in the East, were little known in the West. "Mr. Whipple may be justly regarded as the McCauley [*sic*] of America," wrote the editor of the Cleveland *True Democrat* (February 21, 1853). "As a descriptive and analytical reviewer he has few equals; and yet his celebrity in the West is confined mainly to the *reading* circles." But in a single year Whipple earned for himself a reputation as a cultural lecturer which was unmatched in Ohio except, perhaps, by the fame of Emerson and Henry Giles.

The "ripe scholar and accomplished essayist" from Boston delivered his lecture on "The American Mind" before the Cincinnati Young Men's Mercantile Library Association on February 15, 1853. The subject of the discourse "was analyzed and treated as to its different manifestations in Politics, Literature and Commerce." While Whipple's views were "eminently catholic and liberal" and displayed "a generous faith in his countrymen," they also revealed a piercing eye for the "follies and more serious errors" of Americans. The audience was particularly impressed with his analysis of the intellectual characters of Webster, Calhoun, and Clay. Whipple's effort was to show that "Webster pursued the *inductive*, Calhoun the *deductive*, and Clay the *seductive* method of forensic reasoning."[1]

The nice organization of Whipple's lecture materials was evident to his hearers. The divisions of thought, the clear-cut topics, and the simplified analysis of his subject made him entirely comprehensible.

---

[1] *Daily Cincinnati Gazette*, February 16, 1853.

For newspaper correspondents his lecture-essays were as easy to review as Emerson's were difficult.

Whipple's second Cincinnati lecture, "The English Mind," began "with the selfish, pugnacious, sturdy *John Bull*," and ended "with that marvel and darling of nature—Shakespeare." The English mind was firmly rooted in character. While it was not perfect, and exhibited the vices of "servility to the class above and tyranny to the class below," the English mind was yet the strongest in history, and, "in one continent or the other, must ultimate in the most glorious manifestations of Humanity." The *Gazette* (February 18, 1853) reported as the "unanimous expression of the immense audience" the opinion that Whipple's lecture was the best of the season. This was high praise, as the Mercantile Library Association had already presented lectures by Emerson, Park Benjamin, Horace Mann, and Benjamin Silliman, Jr.

From Cincinnati, Whipple went to Cleveland, where he delivered his "masterly analysis of American mind and character." "Seldom, indeed," commented the editor of the *True Democrat* (February 21, 1853), "has a Cleveland audience been favored with a lecture so philosophic, and yet so captivating in style and manner."

Whipple's reading of "Heroism" before the Cleveland Library Association was termed by the *Herald* (February 22, 1853) "the Lecture, and the Lecturer of the season." This writer added, with rhapsodic approval rarely excelled in newspaper appraisals, that a synopsis could hardly do justice to a lecture combining "such depth and profundity of thought, such transcendentally beautiful ideas, such eloquent outbursts of creative fancy, mingled with sublime truths and illustrated by such vast, magnificent and deeply absorbing comparisons."

According to the *Plain Dealer* (February 22, 1853) "Heroism," which was neatly divided into four topics: the Hero Soldier, the Hero Patriot, the Hero Reformer, and the Hero Saint, "evinced such a complete mastery of words, so profound a depth of intellect, that those who heard it were startled into admiration and surprise."

Whipple's lecture on "Eccentric Character," read before the Toledo Young Men's Association, was "very shabbily attended."

"What is the fault?" asked the editor of the *Blade* (December 5,
1853). "Do the lecturers deteriorate as soon as they touch the banks
of the Maumee? or are the people too dull to appreciate wit, and
instruction and classical taste combined?" After complimenting the
lecturer's "keen perception of the ludicrous" and his "very comprehensive knowledge of literature and literary men," this correspondent
described Whipple as "an illustration of what industry and energy
will effect in any pursuit of life." Though from boyhood brought
up "amid the untoward influences of trade and at its severe toil,"
Whipple had at the age of thirty-four risen to be superintendent of
the Boston Merchants' Exchange and had "placed himself in the front
rank of the literary men of the country."

At Columbus the lecture on "Heroism" was "handled with a
severity of analysis and a polished cogency of style, condensed to
a burning point." Here were antithetic brilliancy of style and epigrammatic crispness "clothed in spiritual beauty and cordial appreciation
of true heroism, which indicated at once a generous heart and a
capital intellect."[2] The *Ohio State Journal* (December 9, 1853)
described Whipple as a small, thin person "with full eyes of a
peculiar appearance." As a platform speaker he was "rather slow in
enunciation," gesticulating but little, and never with violence or
rapidity. His voice was not full or powerful, but was distinct and
often musical. "The sentences he utters are perfect, and as they come
from him with his solemn, earnest and impressive manner, they
reach the point of true eloquence by their effect upon the audience."
As a rhetorician Whipple was a model, his every thought being
"beautifully polished and clothed in most apt and appropriate garb."

2

THE RECEPTION of Whipple's later Ohio lectures provides an
illuminating commentary on the cultural taste of the times. The
quiet force and literary grace of his learned essays were sometimes
lost on audiences who came to look with increasing favor upon
those eloquent orators who stirred their passions and did not molest
their minds. At the Cleveland performance of "Young Men in

---

[2] Columbus *Ohio Statesman*, December 8, 1853.

History," the *Herald* (December 15, 1857) complained that Whipple was "a small, mild-looking person, without any of those advantages of size, figure, or feature that at the outset win the favor of the audience." Besides, his voice was "weak and monotonous." And the materials of the lecture, which attempted to show that "most of the great movements and great phases of ancient and modern history, both of good and evil, have been brought about by young men," were "but imperfectly understood or little cared for" by the audience. Such a lecture "would doubtless have been appreciated by the alumni of a college, though certainly 'caviar to the general.' "

During the Civil War Whipple returned to Cleveland with "Grit," an instructive, carefully prepared lecture which discussed the importance of the quality of grit in "society, business, politics and religion." Whipple delighted his very small audience, but most of those citizens who in earlier days would have crowded the lecture-room either stayed at home or were out sleighing in the deep winter snow. "It must be," concluded the editor of the *Plain Dealer* (January 18, 1862), "that the unbounded interest formerly manifested in lectures, no matter by whom delivered, or upon what subject, is dying out."

The main sources of Whipple's success as a cultural lecturer lay in his matter, rather than in his manner. The keenness, originality, and simplicity of his character analyses were enhanced by the striking language in which they were clothed. Like Henry Giles, he was a master in the creation of carefully supported and understandable generalizations. Truth and scholarship—these were the ingredients of the cultural lecture—and Ohioans found them combined in the productions of Whipple. In addition, they found the most pleasing use of the nineteenth-century essayist's stylistic devices—epigram, analogy, antithesis, elegance of diction, and compactness of logic. Even in the years when amusement had usurped the place of instruction on the platform, Whipple was still regarded by discriminating and serious-minded Ohioans as a rare lecturer to be enjoyed on rare occasions.

CHAPTER
V

HERMAN MELVILLE: *Solemn Mariner*

ALTHOUGH by 1858 Melville had written most of his prose romances, he was known principally to the American reading public for his two early narratives of the South Seas, *Typee* (1846) and *Omoo* (1847). His later volumes, including his masterpiece, *Moby Dick* (1851), were indifferently received by his contemporaries. Throughout the 1850's, Melville, living with his family at Arrowhead, a farm homestead near Pittsfield, Massachusetts, attempted to stave off poverty by offering a succession of volumes to an unreceptive public. In an effort to better his finances by emulating the other Eastern writers who had profited from lyceum engagements, Melville read lectures in both the East and West. "If they will pay expenses and give a reasonable fee," Melville once wrote, "I am ready to lecture in Labrador or on the Isle of Desolation off Patagonia." In 1858 his travels brought him to Ohio for lectures in Cleveland, Cincinnati, and Chillicothe.[1]

Melville was the object of much Western curiosity. Home-keeping Ohioans were eager to see the man who had lived as a captive among the cannibals of Polynesia. *Typee* had also related something of his romantic relationship with Fayaway, the island beauty who was accustomed to swimming *au naturel*. However much the decorous women of the West may have been shocked by Melville's unblushing account of his association with Fayaway, at least one Ohio journalist pointed out that "a good proportion of the audience" at Melville's Cincinnati lecture was composed of the city's fashionable ladies. An additional factor which aroused the curiosity of Ohioans to see

---

[1] These lectures are discussed in George Kummer, "Herman Melville and the Ohio Press," *Ohio State Archaeological and Historical Quarterly*, XLV (January, 1936), 34–36. Other Western appearances of Melville are treated in M. R. Davis, "Melville's Midwestern Lecture Tour, 1859," *Philological Quarterly*, XX (January, 1941), 46–57. For the schedule of Melville's lectures between 1857 and 1860 see Raymond M. Weaver, *Herman Melville, Mariner and Mystic* (New York: George H. Doran Company, 1921), pp. 369–370.

Melville was his attack on the missionaries who, so he contended in *Typee* and *Omoo*, professed to teach Christianity among the Polynesians, but had in reality introduced European traders who had spread venereal disease among the natives and had made veritable slaves of them. Such contentions had touched their author with notoriety and had evoked the wrath of many American readers.

In his Ohio lectures Melville did not speak of his experiences in the South Seas.[2] He chose to discuss "Statues in Rome." There was "not a very good house" at his Cleveland appearance on January 11, 1858, "partly from the effect of the forbidding weather, and partly from the competing attractions of the Opera." The *Ohio Farmer* reported that the lecture was very good in point of style but was delivered with a "hazy-lazy air" and a "boozy elocution." It seemed as if Melville "had never forgotten his imprisonment among the Pacific cannibals, and half regretted his extradition from that physical paradise." The discourse was marred by Melville's "affection for heathenism"; indeed, an "under-current of regret, or sorrow, or malice, at the introduction of christianity, seemed to pervade the whole lecture." The *Herald* added that, while Melville had a musical voice and a very correct delivery, "a subdued tone and general want of animation prevents his being a popular lecturer." He was one more illustration of the axiom that "good writers do not make good lecturers."

At Cincinnati, where "Statues in Rome" was read on February 2, Melville was described as

an unremarkable, quiet, self-possessed looking man, seemingly about thirty-five or six years of age, with brown hair, whiskers and mustache, bronzed complexion, above the medium stature, appearing not unlike the captain of an American merchantman.[3]

The lecturer's delivery "was monotonous and often indistinct, but

---

[2] In 1855 Richard T. Greene of Sandusky, who had accompanied Melville on his adventures among the Marquesans, delivered a lecture entitled "Typee" in several northern Ohio communities, including Fremont, Toledo, Tiffin, and Elyria. "Toby," as Melville called him in *Typee*, was well received as a lecturer. Clarence Gohdes, "Melville's Friend 'Toby,'" *Modern Language Notes*, LIX (January, 1944), 52–55.

[3] *Cincinnati Daily Enquirer*, February 3, 1858. Melville was thirty-nine years old.

not devoid of impressiveness, which sometimes approached the
ministerially solemn."

The abundance of newspaper descriptions of Melville's appearance indicates that Ohio journalists were more interested in the man
than in his lecture.

Mr. Melville is rather an attractive person, though not what anybody would describe good looking. He is a well built, muscular gentleman, with a frame capable of great physical exertion and endurance.
His manner is gentle and persuasive, while a certain indefinable sharp-
ness of features, with small twinkling blue eyes under arched brows,
and a rather contracted and rugged forehead, indicates the spirit of
adventure which sent him roving a sailor's sturdy life. His face, three
parts obscured by a heavy brown beard and moustache, still glistens
duskily with the Polynesian polish it received under the tawny influences of a Southern sun, and his voice is as soft and almost as sweet,
barring a slight huskiness proceeding from a cold, as the warbling of
the winds in cocoa groves.[4]

On February 3 Melville delivered "Statues in Rome" before the
Chillicothe Gymnasium and Library Association. The *Scioto Gazette*
declared that Melville made no attempt at eloquence, "but the deep
stillness that pervaded the large audience from the commencement
to the close of the lecture, showed that his brilliant imagination and
charming descriptive powers, could hold hearers as well as readers
entranced." The most adverse criticism of Melville's Ohio lectures
was written by the editor of the *Chillicothe Advertiser*, who complained that Melville did not confine his discussion to "Statues in
Rome" but "telegraphed his audience to Naples and Florence, and
to Amsterdam with little regard to their convenience, and did not
even take the trouble to render the travelling easy." Moreover, the
lecture was "sadly wanting in that polish which gives even to trite
common places a passing interest and endows the germ of originality
with the power of life and beauty."

It would seem from the reviews of the time that Melville's moderate success before Ohio's lyceums was attributable to his somewhat
notorious reputation as an author rather than to his subject matter
or his eloquence. His audiences would doubtless have been better

---

[4] *Cincinnati Daily Commercial*, February 3, 1858.

pleased if he had described his romantic adventures in the South Seas. Melville "was not sufficiently animated for a Western audience," and, as the *Cincinnati Gazette* pointed out, his manner was entirely "too quiet, common-place and unobtrusive for a popular audience,— but he talks as he writes—without the pretension of those who make lecturing a business."

CHAPTER
VI

AMOS BRONSON ALCOTT: *Intoxicated Talker*

I

ON NOVEMBER 3, 1853, when Amos Bronson Alcott set out from Concord on his first journey into the Great West, his enthusiasm for the new adventure was tinged with doubt at the prospects of its success. To be sure, his friend Ralph Waldo Emerson, who had already made two lecturing trips beyond the Alleghenies, spoke "hopefully of the people in those parts." But Emerson and the other intrepid New England lecturers who had visited the Western region agreed that it was a raw, rough country, a vast area of majestic forest land and squat, muddy towns sprawled among rectangular fields of corn and wheat. Many of its citizens were simple, practical folk whose minds stubbornly refused to enter that wonderful realm of transcendental speculation so familiar to Alcott and his philosophical New England friends. And a speaker had to be careful what he said, especially on moral or social themes, lest some irate Westerner rise in his creaky boots and stalk indignantly out of the lecture-room.

Traveling was not a new experience to the former Yankee peddler whose journeys in the East and South had increased his love of human companionship without affecting his natural innocence and impracticality. But the conversation, which Alcott hoped would some day "supply, as a means of culture, the place of popular lectures, discourses, and books," would be a new experience for the West.[1] It was com-

---

[1] Alcott's journals contain numerous passages describing his preference for the conversational method of disseminating culture. See especially Odell Shepard (ed.), *The Journals of Bronson Alcott* (Boston: Little, Brown and Company, 1938), pp. 104–105, 133; F. B. Sanborn and William T. Harris, *A. Bronson Alcott, His Life and Philosophy* (2 vols.; Boston: Roberts Brothers, 1893), II, 508–510. Alcott believed that the public lecture served simply "to lull the soul into vague dreams of knowledge and truth." But the informal conversation, the chosen method of Socrates, Plato, and Jesus, provoked discussion, thus "affording the chance of free intercourse between mind and mind" and giving "life and light to truth."

forting, of course, to have Emerson's encouragement of his venture. One day in August Emerson and Alcott had taken a leisurely walk along the banks of Walden Pond and planned the tour "along the great Canal towns"—Syracuse, Rochester, Buffalo—and on to Cleveland, Medina (where Alcott had relatives), and Cincinnati.[2] Besides giving Alcott the opportunity to instruct his hearers on cultural themes, the project was "to be so managed as to defray its expenses and more." Then in October the detailed arrangements had been made. A prospectus announcing Alcott's willingness to offer a course of conversations on "The Leading Representative Minds of New England" was dispatched to the Western cities. And finally Emerson, who knew and understood Alcott's difficulties in making and keeping money, gave his friend eighteen dollars for his passage to Cincinnati.

In the chill privacy of his room at Cleveland's Franklin House the weary traveler felt the loneliness of a stranger in the unfamiliar West, and perhaps he wondered why Emerson, on his lecture trips, always preferred the solitude of hotel rooms to the pleasant society of private homes. On Friday, November 4, Alcott took the stage to Medina and enjoyed the first of his frequent week-end visits with his relatives. The genial company of his Cousin Hiram Bronson, Aunt Sylvia Alcott, and Uncle Noah Bronson warmed his spirits and revived his enthusiasm.

On November 8 Alcott arrived by train in Cincinnati for his first series of conversations in Ohio. Emerson's friend Ainsworth Rand Spofford,[3] a Cincinnati bookseller and later a librarian of Congress, had made every necessary arrangement for Alcott's appearance; he had engaged the Apollo Rooms, at the corner of 5th and Walnut Streets, had publicized the course of conversations, and had procured and sold tickets to interested citizens. Course tickets admitting "a gentleman and lady" sold for $2.50; single admissions were fifty cents. At the first conversation on November 11, "an audience of near 100 persons" gathered to hear his "sustained" and "pertinent" dis-

---

[2] Shepard, *Journals*, p. 270.

[3] For an account of Emerson's relationship with Spofford, who was responsible for Emerson's invitation to lecture in Cincinnati in 1850, see Louise Hastings, "Emerson in Cincinnati," *New England Quarterly*, XI (September, 1938), 443–469. See also pp. 25, 30, and 33 of this study.

course on "Chaos."[4] When Spofford assured him that the evening
had been a notable success, Alcott was elated and on November 12
wrote to his wife, Abigail May Alcott, and their four daughters:
"You will remember my doubts as to any adaptions of mine to this
wild population, and will share the surprise at the results. Last evening was a decided stroke . . ."[5]

Alcott's subsequent conversations in the Cincinnati series were
well received, although during the discussion of "Paradise" on November 12, his audience, whose thoughts were apparently somewhat
incoherent on that subject, were more timid and reserved than he
would have liked them to be. A "very select and sympathizing company" participated in the discussions of "The Fountain" on November
17 and "The Seminary" on November 21, and Alcott's journals describe these two evenings as "every way delightful." He was especially pleased with the reception given his conversation on "The
Mart," "the flower of the five preceding," by a "large and appreciating company" on November 23.

Alcott concluded his Cincinnati engagement on November 26 with
"The Altar." His first appearances in the West had met with a warm
response, and there was a "good prospect of meetings again in the
coming Autumn and after." Spofford's accounts showed that Cincinnatians had bought sixty-four course tickets, and these, together
with the receipts from single admissions, brought Alcott's total earnings to $209.00.[6] Perhaps, at the age of fifty-four, Alcott had found
an occupation more profitable than peddling in the South or school-
teaching and conversing in New England.

On November 30 Alcott was once again in Cleveland, where he
completed arrangements with H. M. Chapin, a wholesale grocer with
cultural interests, for a course of conversations in that city. Before
opening this engagement, however, Alcott went to Medina for a
five-day visit with his relatives. The Cleveland conversations began

---

[4] Manuscript Journals. The writer is indebted to Mr. Frederick Wolsey
Pratt of Concord, Massachusetts, for his kind permission to use the Alcott
manuscript journals and letters in the Concord Public Library.
[5] Manuscript Letter.
[6] Manuscript Journals. Alcott was not accustomed to such large receipts for
his efforts. The journals reveal that for twenty-eight conversations given
between January and May, 1853, in Boston, Medford, Salem, and Cambridge,
his total earnings were $150.00.

on December 7 with "The Individual," given at the residence of
Chapin. Alcott's journal entries dealing with this and the succeeding
conversations are brief; the audiences were small, "quite select, but
mainly silent."[7] The reluctance of his hearers to enter into discussion somewhat marred the success of the discourses. Alcott's conversational method required a free exchange of views, as the "silent
company" was liable to turn the conversation into a lecture, which,
in Alcott's opinion, applied knowledge from without and did not
endeavor to discover the truth within.

Alcott boarded a train for Buffalo on December 16 after concluding what appeared to be a profitable Western journey. To his Cincinnati earnings was added $50.00 paid by Chapin for the Cleveland
conversations, and, en route to Concord, he received $25.00 for three
evenings spent at Syracuse, bringing his total receipts to $284.00.
Alcott's homecoming is described in the diary of his daughter, Louisa
May Alcott. He roused his family in the middle of a cold winter
night, "and five white figures embraced the half-frozen wanderer
who came in hungry, tired, cold and disappointed, but smiling bravely
and as serene as ever." When his wife and daughters had fed and
warmed him, and "he had told all the pleasant things," little May
voiced the question they were all bursting to ask: "Well, did people
pay you?" Then, a queer expression on his face, Alcott opened his
pocketbook and drew out a single dollar, all that was left of his
earnings. To his brave but disheartened family he summarized his
experience among the "wild population" of the West. "Only that!
My overcoat was stolen, and I had to buy a shawl. Many promises
were not kept, and travelling is costly; but I have opened the way,
and another year shall do better."[8]

---

[7] The Cleveland course included "The Family," December 9; "The Garden,"
December 10; "The School," December 12; "The State," December 13; "The
Church," December 14. "The State" was given at the home of "Mr. Vaughan,"
who was probably John C. Vaughan, listed in the *Cleveland City Directory for
1853* as editor of the Cleveland *True Democrat*. "The Church" was given at
the residence of Daniel R. Tilden, a local lawyer and former member of the
Ohio Senate.

[8] Ednah D. Cheney (ed.), *Louisa May Alcott, Her Life, Letters, and
Journals* (Boston: Roberts Brothers, 1899), pp. 69–70. The unkept promises
may refer to Alcott's expectations of conversing in Medina, Rochester, and
Buffalo. His manuscript letter of November 12, 1853, also notes that he
expected to appear in Dayton "for a conversation or more."

2

ALCOTT did not follow the new way he had opened until the winter of 1857. On December 23 he reached Cleveland, and a week later talked "to a few persons at Chapin's from 8 till 11, and pleasantly, on Intellect and its organs." The next evening he discussed "Hearts, or the Affections" with a slim and apparently unenthusiastic audience. "Hands, or Conduct," announced as the third conversation in the series, was not given, and Alcott, finding that the "season is unpropitious," decided to return to Cleveland on his way East, when he might appear "under better advantages."

On January 5, 1858, Alcott arrived in Cincinnati with good prospects of more financial profit than the eighteen dollars which he received from Chapin in Cleveland. Spofford and Moncure Conway, Unitarian minister, author, and friend of the New England transcendentalists, had already advertised and sold tickets for his course of three conversations on "Human Life, Considered in Its Genesis, Genius and Issues." In introducing Alcott to the city's intellectuals, the correspondent of the *Cincinnati Commercial* (January 11, 1858) commented that "These Conversations are a new style of lecture, in which more freedom and range are secured to the speaker, while his interlocutors are enabled to test a principle or satisfy a doubt as the discourse proceeds."

The opening conversation, "Heads, or Intellect," delivered on January 11, was applauded by "a good company of fifty persons or more, cultivated and attractive." After hearing the next two conversations,[9] admiring Cincinnatians begged Alcott to stay and "give another evening." Alcott agreed, and his final discourse, "Oversights," given on January 15, is exuberantly described in the journals as a "masterly" effort, delivered "with unusual vivacity and magnetism."

Alcott was immensely pleased with his course in Cincinnati, where his audience had been "eager and earnest, well-behaved, and disposed to make the most of these interviews." The *Commercial* (January 15, 1858) disclosed that the "literary coterie" who attended had

---

[9] "Hearts, or the Sentiments," January 12; and "Hands, or Conduct," January 14.

enjoyed "a rich repast." After deducting expenses of $9.70, which
included Alcott's payment of $1.40 for a two-volume "Mystic Book,"
Spofford handed Alcott $60.00 for his services. On January 16, Al-
cott took the train for Cleveland, happy in the thought that his conversations might some day be "as necessary to the winters entertainment as the Lyceum Lectures."

Alcott found Clevelanders more responsive to his second series of
conversations, and three meetings at the home of Daniel Tilden
earned him $40.00.[10] He was obliged to cut short his Western journey
when he received news of the serious illness of his daughter Elizabeth, who died the following March. Alcott had still not come to like
the "slovenly West" with its desolation, its winter mud, and its
dearth of transcendental minds. But there were friends to be made
in that expanding region, and there was a market for his particular
"species of entertainments." He was resolved to return in some future season.

3

In December, 1858, Louisa May Alcott wrote in her diary: "Father
started on his tour West full of hope. Dear man! How happy he
will be if people will only listen to and pay for his wisdom."[11] Alcott undertook this trip in response to an invitation from William T.
Harris to visit the St. Louis philosophers, a zealous group of Hegelian
students. Traveling over the prairies, Alcott found "sparse corn-
fields and log-hovels," a dismal landscape which failed "to awaken the
picturesque and delight the imagination." Even the speech of Western people seemed "flattened, with sudden startings and awkward
leapings into the regions overhead, for fit figures of expression."[12]
On reaching the Mississippi, Alcott was more than ever convinced
that he was "purely Eastern" and had "little . . . in common with the
wild life of the West."

His visit with the St. Louis philosophers was not altogether

[10] The Cleveland course included "The Family," January 18; and "Friendship," January 19. The journals do not reveal the title of the final conversation,
given on January 20.

[11] Cheney, Louisa May Alcott, p. 103.

[12] Shepard, Journals, p. 311.

pleasant. Schooled in the philosophy of Hegel, of which Alcott knew little, they argued vehemently the importance of "the State" and showed no more than a respectful interest in Alcott's glorification of the individual soul. Before accepting a proposition they insisted on examining its logic and its historical relations. When Alcott read them some of his "Orphic Sayings," they recognized that "there might be something to them; but they wanted to question it, turn it this way and that, classify it, rather than merely accept it gratefully as an inspired and prophetic utterance."[13]

On his journey eastward in January, 1859, Alcott stopped in Cincinnati to deliver a course of four conversations on "Life and Its Mysteries" in Conway's Unitarian Church. Course tickets were $1.50, although the journals admit that some of these were sold for $1.00 "to parties who would not pay 1.50."

In his first conversation, "Fate," delivered on January 24, Alcott declared that Fate was a limitation to which all humanity was subject. When men transgressed the moral law, they were bound. "Nature and God were not to be outwitted; they exacted payment for every thing, and when we opposed them Fate held us more securely in its iron embrace." Men were least bound by Fate in their "affectionate moments, when spirit had the ascendancy."[14] The thirty persons who attended "Fascination" on January 26 were somewhat disappointed at Alcott's failure to stimulate their interest. In the journals Alcott confessed that he did not treat his subject satisfactorily, and his company did not "incline or call forth the best things" from him. The *Enquirer* (January 27, 1859) reported that Alcott "believes of conversation, as the orthodox do of divine grace, that it must come of itself—and by some means the Fates were averse on this occasion." After saying some "excellent, subtle, curiously metaphysical things," most of which "were foreign to his theme," Alcott abruptly closed the performance by reading an original poem, "The Saint's Rations."

The audience which heard "Recreation" on January 28 was slim and unresponsive. Alcott lamented that "Spofford is unable to attend

---

[13] Odell Shepard, *Pedlar's Progress: The Life of Bronson Alcott* (Boston: Little, Brown and Company, 1937), p. 476.
[14] *Cincinnati Daily Enquirer*, January 25, 1859.

and help us and Conway is usually a listener only." Nevertheless the conversation was "very entertaining, and often instructive." According to the *Enquirer* (January 29, 1859) Alcott contended that "proper food, rest, exercise and company were what man required for his physical, mental and moral development," and these would do much to render him "in harmony with Nature."

The final conversation, "Worship," was given on January 31. Worship was "the high admiration and esteem we feel for those of superior goodness and purity." For God we feel an "involuntary worship, because we believe him inherently and necessarily all-just, all-merciful and all-perfect. God is every-where, and occupies common territory with every atom of good."[15] At the close of the conversation Alcott's Cincinnati friends gave him a vote of thanks and $25.25 for his course. Late that evening Alcott wrote in his journal: "I have done my work here and shall move on tomorrow for Cleveland, and the East."

Alcott's six Cleveland conversations, given at "D. Atkinson's Rooms," were lively and successful.[16] He was grateful for a gathering of enthusiastic friends who were "free to express their views and defend them with candour and spirit." Among the fifty persons who attended "Recreation" were several spiritualists. Alcott reported that "the Spiritualists seem pleased, and accept most of what I have to say on health and family sensibly." He had intended to conduct only three conversations, but his audience, who enjoyed the proceedings, invited him "to give them three evenings more." Atkinson paid him $50.00 for the series of six conversations.

Back home in Concord, Alcott was thankful for New England's privileges and opportunities, "all the more pleasurable after the privations and discomforts of loafing about that slovenly West." He could perceive that he was "neither a planter of the backwoods, pi-

---

[15] *Ibid.*, February 1, 1859.

[16] The course included "Fascination," February 5; "Recreation," February 7; "Worship," February 9; "Social Life," February 10; "Genesis," February 12; "Marriage and Social Life," February 13. The "D. Atkinson" of Alcott's journals probably means "Doctor Atkinson," as the *Cleveland City Directory for 1859* does not list a "D. Atkinson." William H. Atkinson was a prominent physician and surgeon in the city.

oneer, nor settler there, but an inhabitant of the Mind, and given to friendship and ideas." There were friendship and civility in the West, but the society which most excited his sympathies was "the ancient society, the Old England of the New England, Massachusetts."[17]

4

ALCOTT did not visit Ohio again until 1866. During the tempestuous Civil War years the Western market for cultural discourses was not a promising one. The lyceum, which had previously upheld the superiority of literary and scientific lectures, offered chiefly political discourses. Ohio audiences wished to hear Wendell Phillips, Charles Sumner, and Anna E. Dickinson rather than Emerson, Alcott, or Edwin P. Whipple. But when peace returned and political passions subsided, New England's cultural envoys once more resumed their annual journeys to the Western states.

In February, 1866, Alcott made a month's visit in St. Louis. Here, joining in the stimulating discussions of Harris and his philosophical friends, he gained a new respect for their systematic methods of thought. He became accustomed to their blunt Western manner and found many of their ideas to be surprisingly fresh and original. They greeted his conversation on "Genesis" with warm approval and reconciled some of its theories with their own. "They tell me I am a Hegelian in spirit if not in form, and seem disposed to claim me as of their master's school," Alcott declared in his journal.

On March 6 Alcott reached Cincinnati, and the next evening attended a reading party at the Walnut Hills home of "Mr. Keys."[18] Selections from the works of Dickens and Tennyson furnished the evening's pleasant entertainment. On March 8 Alcott discussed "New England Men and Women" with "an agreeable company at Mr. Kirks, neighbor to the Harrisons."[19] Among the group were "many accomplished women," and Alcott was flattered by their attention.

---

[17] Shepard, *Journals*, p. 313.

[18] Probably S. B. Keys, listed in the *Cincinnati Directory for 1866* as a banker.

[19] Probably John W. Kirk, a Walnut Hills broker. L. B. Harrison, a commission merchant and prominent member of the Walnut Hills circle, was a friend of Emerson.

But the arduous journey to the Mississippi and the fervid discussions with the St. Louis philosophers had wearied him. After the Cincinnati conversation Alcott wrote in his journal: "I am not equal to my theme, and find I must desert from talking and run home . . ." Harrison, after paying him $33.00 for the conversation, persuaded him to lecture on Sunday, March 11, before the Cincinnati Free Congregation Church. For his discourse on "The New Church, Its Faith and Forms" Alcott received $25.00. On Tuesday, March 13, he took the train for the East.

Alcott's journey in 1866 marked the turning point in his attitude toward the West. A major influence in his conversion was his admiration for Lincoln, the assassinated President whose name was already growing into a Western legend. "I reflect that here was the home of the Great American President," wrote Alcott as he was traveling across the prairies. Here in the West were the "skies above, the great river flowing seaward, the wild adventures of the pioneer, the excitements of river and road, to fashion him into the Man he was." The "first real ruler of a Republic," Alcott called him—"a large-hearted, loyal soul, with a plainness and slovenly greatness that the West favors."[20] Alcott had often judged the worth of his native New England by the character of her famous sons; and the West, which produced Lincoln, must be a great and promising country.

Alcott's second visit with the St. Louis philosophers was a pleasant, exciting experience. "If wanting in the courtesies of conversation, these western minds take every freedom of tart debate and drive home the argument at a fearful rate," he wrote in his journal. This "free, frolicsome, slovenly sense of able earnest men has a formidable attraction." Alcott remained four weeks with these aggressive Hegelians, "amazed to find such a company encamped there on the edge of the wilderness and burrowing deeper into the thought of Germany than the academicians of Boston and Cambridge cared to go."[21] Although these Westerners lacked the discretion and refinement of

---

[20] Shepard, *Journals*, p. 378. See also the discussion of Lincoln's influence on Alcott in Shepard, *Pedlar's Progress*, pp. 477–480.

[21] Shepard, *Pedlar's Progress*, p. 482.

the "well-behaved populations" of the East, they were men of original genius. The manners will come, declared Alcott, "and this New England will compete in all things with the land of its ancestry, the school of its culture."

If, in his journey of 1866, Alcott had not become reconciled to the hardships of the West and its lack of picturesque beauty, he had acquired a genuine respect for the questioning, independent spirit of Western people. His enthusiastic acceptance of the Lincoln legend and his admiration for Harris, Henry C. Brockmeyer, and the other St. Louis idealists undoubtedly influenced his attitude toward the entire Western region; numerous passages in the journals provide evidence of Alcott's opinion, which he never altered, "that Western minds and audiences were in many important respects superior to those of New England."[22]

5

IN THE fall of 1869 Alcott set out on a Western tour that lasted four months, took him to fourteen cities, and earned him more than seven hundred dollars.[23] Following the route through Syracuse and Buffalo he arrived on November 23 at Cleveland, where he attended the opening meeting of the National Woman Suffrage Convention. Though the journals report that Alcott was "an interested spectator of the doings," he felt "more in place in drawing rooms, and abler there to promote the deeper end for which the speakers here plead superficially." In those "more private discussions in parlours" he could make "a more lively appeal to the virgin instinct. There is my place ..."

After a week's visit with his Medina relatives, Alcott returned to Cleveland and on December 1 delivered "New England Authors," the first of a series of five conversations.[24] Mrs. Peter Thatcher's

[22] Shepard, *Journals*, p. 377.
[23] *Ibid.*, p. 405.
[24] The course included "Manners and Conversation," December 6, at the portrait studio of C. L. Ransom; "Temperament and Descent," December 8, at the home of Edwin Cowles, editor of the *Cleveland Leader*; "Woman," December 9; "Beauty," December 10, at the residence of C. W. Willey. "New England Authors" is briefly reviewed in the *Cleveland Daily Leader* and the *Cleveland Morning Herald*, December 2, 1869.

drawing rooms were "filled with a curious company," and Alcott talked "at length" on Emerson, Thoreau, Hawthorne, Margaret Fuller, W. E. Channing, Longfellow, Lowell, Holmes, Whittier, and "by request, of the author of 'Little Women.'" According to the journals Alcott was "tempted to dilate so largely on Emerson, that the others get less justice done to their gifts and attainments than were becoming...." As for Louisa, he found that he had a "dramatic story to tell of her childhood and youth, gaining in interest as she comes up into womanhood and literary note." While in Cleveland Alcott was called upon to relate the story of Louisa to the school children, "most of the scholars being familiar with her book and curious to learn what I might tell them about her history. I am introduced as the father of 'Little Women,' and am riding in the Chariot of Glory, wherever I go."

After the conversations in Cleveland, for which he was paid sixty dollars, Alcott traveled to Toledo, where, on Saturday, December 12, he spoke to the Independent Society on "The Coming Church." On Sunday afternoon he addressed the Woman's Suffrage Association at the residence of Israel Hall. Then, to complete an arduous day, he held an evening conversation with the Radical Club, an organization "which meets weekly for discussion of important questions." The conversation ran "broad and deep into Genesis, free will, Personality" and was "enjoyed by all present."

Alcott next went to Elyria, opening a series of five conversations with "New England Authors," given in the parlor of Herman Ely on December 18.[25] The forty ladies and gentlemen present were greatly impressed with Alcott, who was described in the *Independent Democrat* (December 22, 1869) as "a venerable looking man, with white, flowing hair" and possessing "high intellectual culture." In the journals Alcott affirms his pleasure with his audience: "People

---

[25] The other conversations in the series were "Health," December 20, at the home of George Washburn, editor of the *Elyria Independent Democrat*; "Social Life," December 21; "Temperament and Descent," December 27; and "Culture," December 28, at the Beebe House Parlors. Alcott received fifty-four dollars for the five performances. Short reviews of "New England Authors" and "Health" are given in the *Elyria Independent Democrat*, December 22, 1869.

here appear to have a wholesome interest in Eastern Minds and listen with respect to any information concerning these." In his discussion of "Health," Alcott asserted that "the true object of health was to attain that condition which would produce the highest sensibility, and the highest and profoundest thought." This and the succeeding conversations were delivered "to good effect" before enthusiastic audiences.

Alcott's final conversations in 1869 were given in the northern Ohio community of Tiffin. Arriving at the local hotel on December 29, he was visited in the evening by a "miscellaneous company" of villagers. The journals declare that these people were "extremely individual." "Coming from Maryland and Pennsylvania chiefly, they have no New England tradition to speak to, and the conversation runs into difference and debate. The conversation is interesting nevertheless and I am invited to speak again tomorrow evening." Except for the statement that he received thirty dollars for his efforts, Alcott made no comment about "Health and Temperance," December 30, and "Social Life," December 31. On January 1 Alcott took the train for Elyria, intending to travel on to Cleveland for a second series of conversations.

By 1870 Alcott's ambitions to carry his philosophical idealism to the West and to turn the conversation into a profitable venture had been fully realized. Indeed his devotion to the dissemination of culture was in sharp contrast with the fallen ideals of the Western lyceum, which, in the years after the Civil War, "degenerated into a string of entertainments that have no earnest purpose, and minister to no manly and womanly want." He held himself above the level of the popular entertainers, the sensationalists, and the politicians who diluted the tastes of Western audiences and threatened to destroy the market for cultural speakers. Alcott's kindly, genial nature and his rare ability to stimulate his hearers won him the friendship and admiration of hundreds of Ohio people. And he, in turn, outgrew the bounds of his native New England and became, in mind and spirit, an American. His later journeys confirmed his opinion of 1870 that, in some respects, "the West is more hospitable to ideas than the East, less the victim of tradition."²⁶ So, like Emerson, Alcott came to speak "hopefully of the people in those parts." Although the West was raw and rough and ugly, it held great potentialities for America. "Westernize," wrote Alcott in 1871, "is a verb meaning progress."

---

²⁶ Shepard, *Journals*, p. 408. Alcott visited the West in 1872, 1874, 1879, and 1880.

CHAPTER
VII

GEORGE WILLIAM CURTIS: *Critic of the West*

THE THREE brief Ohio visits of Curtis, the New York reformer and world traveler, met with only moderate success. By 1853, the year of Curtis' first Ohio journey, Western people were familiar with his travel books, *Nile Notes of a Howadji* (1851) and *The Howadji in Syria* (1852), and with his letters from abroad to the *New York Tribune*.[1] Although Curtis was not yet well known as a reformer, those discerning readers who had discovered his satirical sketches of New York society, the *Potiphar Papers*, were already acquainted with the keen powers of observation and evaluation which were to make Curtis one of the foremost social critics of his time.

On December 15, 1853, "Young America" was read to "quite a numerous auditory" in Toledo. The editor of the *Blade*, after observing that Curtis habitually "terminates his words in a drawl like that of New England Unitarian clergymen now arrived at middle or mature age," declared that the memorable parts of the lecture were "the successive shots he gave to pretension, and insincerity, and hollowness and ignorance in life and society." Even so, his sarcasm seemed to be "a very little tinged with misanthropy." The lecture was somewhat overburdened with classical and poetical allusions which many of his hearers did not understand. In this respect, his discussion of America, like a Yankee housewife's pumpkin pie, "tasted rather more of every thing else, than the pumpkin."

Curtis repeated this lecture the next evening in Cleveland before "such an audience as any Lecturer might well be proud of." The *Herald* (December 17, 1853) commended him for "an admirable performance" marked by humor, native good sense, youthful imagery, and a clear, distinct delivery. Curtis was a man who had seen the

---

[1] In 1846 Curtis traveled in Europe, Egypt, and Syria. His letters to the *Tribune* were reprinted in many Western newspapers. *Lotus-Eating* (1852) was a collection of letters to the *Tribune*.

civilization of the Old World and had come home "an American in heart, feeling, hope and purpose."

In December, 1854, Curtis read his lecture on "Success" in Cincinnati, Zanesville, Cleveland, and Dayton.[2] The familiar theme that success and happiness are not dependent upon wealth was to reappear in his popular *Prue and I* (1856). The *Cincinnati Commercial* (December 6, 1854) commented that Curtis had "a fine manner, a pleasing voice and a correct elocution, in addition to many of the higher qualifications of an able and interesting lecturer." The *Gazette*'s reviewer added that the purpose of the lecture was to show that "the accumulation of property is not a real success, but only an apparent one; that the only true success is deeper, and is perfectly consistent with what the world calls a failure." Although the lecture was a clever performance, "the lecturer spun out the thread of his verbosity quite as far as the style of his argument would warrant."

Curtis' tendency to relate his theme to the attitudes of polite Eastern society was annoying to some Ohio journalists, who felt that his criticisms were not necessarily applicable to Western society, and that underlying the lecturer's gentle admonitions was a sentimental liking for New York's dandies. There was nothing genteel or sentimental about Western newspaper criticism in the 1850's. The training ground of the critics was the political campaign, where editors learned the uses of strong language and hard blows. And to these journalists the light-fingered tactics of Curtis were unsubstantial and unconvincing.

The *Zanesville Gazette* (December 12, 1854) complimented Curtis' "earnest manner" but accused him of "a too great indulgence for that particular class of fast young men 'who love fierce mustachios and picturesque hats.' " But it was at Cleveland that Curtis was exposed to the uninhibited and inelegant sentiments of an annoyed Western editor. As an intellectual effort, wrote the correspondent of the *Herald* (December 8, 1854), the lecture on "Success" "was

---

[2] Curtis' intentions in making this Western tour were frankly stated in a letter of October 9, 1854, in which he wrote that he would "be away at the West in December, away at the East in February, and home in March. I mean to lecture during two months and make two thousand dollars. I have put my price up to fifty dollars." Edward Cary, *George William Curtis* (Boston and New York: Houghton, Mifflin and Company, 1894), p. 90.

below criticism." It was vague, uncertain, and without any apparent point or application. There was a galling impudence in this Eastern gentleman who seemed to think that the fashionable citizens of Up-town Gotham had discovered the real meaning of success. New York was not all the world. "There is a great tract of land in this country out of New York, and a vast many people who have met with suc-cess in all the avocations of life, have never dreamed that the ac-cumulation of wealth was the only criterion of success." The lecture was, finally, "a waste of time and capital." Curtis' pretty senti-mentality was "a great bore. . . . A lecturer should either *entertain* or *instruct* his audience; and if he cannot do either, he should keep at home."

In 1860 Curtis read his lecture on "The Policy of Honesty" in Toledo and Cleveland. At Toledo "the audience was not large enough to pay the expenses of the Association." The *Blade* (December 3, 1860) reported the lecture to be full of plain truths delivered in "a gentlemanly manner." Curtis tested the practices of "the civil, religious, commercial, and political world by the great standard of honesty" and found that sterling quality to be conspicuously rare among men.

At Cleveland Curtis had a good audience despite the competition of a lecture by the great crowd-gatherer John B. Gough. The *Plain Dealer* (December 4, 1860) praised the discourse, which was "elo-quent in thought, manner and expression." Curtis spoke in a rich and powerful voice, "and its modulation and compass exaggerate but a little the strict line of elocutionary rule." To be sure, the lecture "was that of a reformer" and so "was not palatable to the minds of all who listened to it." But the only serious weakness was that it "was wholly ideal, in conception, thought, imagery and logic." Sit-ting alone in his study, Curtis had pictured forth a society based upon exceptional cases. In the West, at least, the "merchant, clergyman, lawyer and politician, each and all are honest"—or certainly a good deal less despicable than the speaker accused such people of being.

The reception of these Ohio lectures was unfortunately marred by the prejudices of Curtis' hearers, who were quick to take offense at his social criticism. The rough-and-tumble West had not yet outgrown its jealousy and resentment of the more cultured East. Had Curtis displayed some of the bravado and boisterous good-fellowship of Bayard Taylor, he would have been more kindly received, and the real merit of his lectures would have been more fully appreciated. But clad in his fashionably tailored coat and his elegant cravat, he reminded Ohio people of those "parvenu people of the avenues." And from such a man the West disdained criticism, even if that criticism was wise and eloquent.

PARKE GODWIN: *Oracle of Optimism*

AN ASSOCIATE of his father-in-law, William Cullen Bryant, on the *New York Evening Post*, Godwin was an accomplished essayist and "a pleasant speaker, but with no pretensions to oratory." One of the most popular lyceum lectures in America in the middle fifties was Godwin's "Manifest Destiny," or, as it was often called, "The Future Republic." The appeal of "Manifest Destiny" lay partly in its literary excellence, its polished style, but mostly in its subject matter. Godwin pointed out many conspicuous shortcomings in American life, but optimistically concluded that the nation's future was "full of promise and bright hope."

In 1854 and 1855 Godwin read this lecture some fifteen times before Ohio audiences. At Cincinnati the *Gazette* (January 10, 1855) reported that Godwin gave an admirable summary of America's growth, prosperity, and manifest destiny. There was nothing wild or "enthusiastic" about his prediction that America must become "a universal nation, the largest in the world." Of course the precise nature of the country's future "must be wrapped in mystery, for none but bell pullers, table movers, and such like, had ever attempted to solve the mystery." Godwin satirized the selfish motives of politicians and warned against the greedy spirit of "Young America," which was intent on "grasping at every thing within view, from the Arctic regions to the far off South." The lecturer's liking for New England character was demonstrated in his humorous description of the versatile Yankee. "To-day he is a lawyer—to-morrow he is a druggist—next day he is a peddler, and in a few days you find him in the far West, the owner of a thriving village."

The Chillicothe *Scioto Gazette* (January 12, 1855) observed that Godwin's "analysis of American nationality and individuality was keen and subtle." His thrusts at politicians, "for whom he has an unmitigated hatred," and his "strictures upon the love of Americans for the larder" were well deserved. He displayed a sparkling wit in his hits at "Young America" and in his portrayal of Yankee genius.

At Elyria the hall was filled when Godwin gave his "masterly performance." The *Independent Democrat* (December 5, 1855) felt that Godwin's "manly, direct and forcible" style was well adapted to his subject, "now rising into the most animated strains of eloquence, and again attracting more by its simplicity and directness than by any attempt at display." The citizens of Kenton found Godwin's satire and humor to be "highly amusing and instructive." "His hits at 'old fogyism' and 'young America,'" declared the *Hardin County Republican* (December 14, 1855), "were too life-like not to be appreciated even in our own unpretending community."

Godwin's lecture was "one of the best, if not the very best" ever delivered in Springfield. Embodying both "the useful and the beautiful," it was "seasoned with enough of humor to make it very generally acceptable." The *Nonpareil* (December 13, 1855) asserted that "Manifest Destiny" was "illustrated profusely with elegant and beautiful passages, and enlivened with brilliancy, power and unusual eloquence." At Mansfield Godwin drew the largest attendance of the season. Though he was not "what is usually termed a popular orator, yet his powers of thought, and Rhetorical elaboration, are such, as to give him the perfect control of an audience." In this production of Godwin, continued the *Herald* (December 19, 1855), were "a comprehensiveness of view, a beauty of finish, and an appropriateness of combination" which were seldom equaled. His analysis was "sparkling in wit, rich in fancy and profound in thought." Parke Godwin was a man who "will make his mark in history, and will do much to mould the destinies of 'The future Republic.'"

While Ohio citizens were often suspicious of lecturers who criticized American life and institutions, they were unlikely to take offense unless the speaker made remarks derogatory to the West. In "Manifest Destiny" Godwin was on safe ground. The chicanery of politicians, the rash ambitions of youth, the dangers inherent in greed for material things, and the practical genius of the Yankee were subjects which were popular with satirists and could be discussed with impunity. But on December 11, 1855, at Zanesville, Godwin made the mistake of deprecating the social standards of the West in a lecture entitled "American Social Life." The subject was a delicate one, and Zanesville citizens, many of whom did not feel the social necessity of wearing their suspenders inside their coats on lecture night, were incensed at Godwin's encomiums for the polite society of the East and his unflattering opinions of the unsophisticated society of the West.

Godwin, fumed the editor of the *Gazette*, was one of those "imported lecturers from the East" who were so shortsighted or misinformed as to think American society was composed wholly of Eastern socialites, those dandies "who sputter bad French and buy pictures they have no taste to appreciate," and "the border ruffians of the West." But Western people were not all "without decency or intellect—mere brutes of instinct, without dignity or aim." It was time Godwin became acquainted with the great middle class, the industrious people who had built the "material and political greatness" of the West. He had omitted from his analysis any estimate of those citizens who had provided "happy homes, good schools, enlarged benevolent associations and christian churches." By failing to appreciate the labors of substantial Western citizens and by focusing his prejudices on the worst elements in Western society, the lecturer had, "in the general opinion, failed in his subject, both in matter and manner." "Whether he will enlighten us again, in the future," concluded this critic, "is a matter of great doubt. We vote no!"

So Parke Godwin, like George William Curtis, learned that criticism of Western social standards was a topic which Eastern lecturers dared not discuss if they hoped to emerge unscathed.

CHAPTER
IX

WENDELL PHILLIPS: *Irrepressible Agitator*

I

OF THE major lyceum lecturers from the East, Phillips was the most persistent deliverer of political addresses. During his visits to the West, he became the most popular and, at the same time, the most severely criticized of the Eastern political and reform lecturers. He looked upon the platform as a place for partisan oratory and the expression of personal political opinion. Construing the lyceum lecture to be a vehicle by which the people could be informed of the social and political problems of national life, he assumed the responsibility of interpreting those problems in terms of his own convictions and those of his party. While his political adherents praised him as a well of wisdom, his opponents attacked him as a dangerous fanatic. He did not disdain the values of the cultural lecture, but he held that instruction in national affairs would elevate the topics of government and politics to a respected place on the rostrum. But neither his own orations nor those of his followers were capable of fulfilling this ideal; the inevitable prejudices of the political orator were hardly suited to reflect the dignity of the cultural lecturer's more objective search for truth in the problems of literature and life.

All of Phillips' Ohio lectures, with the exception of "The Lost Arts," dealt with combustible topics which frequently aroused the indignation of the partisan press. His announced subjects were deceptive, as they were often mere pegs upon which to hang his antislavery sentiments. In the northern Ohio cities Phillips' reformer's zeal was accepted and praised, except for occasional mild protests from the *Cleveland Plain Dealer* and other Democratic newspapers. But in the Ohio River communities, where sympathy with slavery was prevalent, he stirred up an antagonism which in 1862 was to break forth in open rioting at Cincinnati.

Phillips' bitterest assailant among Ohio's newspapers was the *Cin-*

cinnati Enquirer, and in December, 1856, he provoked an enmity
with the editors of that journal which was to endure for many years
after the Civil War. The antipathy of the *Enquirer* for Phillips'
political opinions had long been smoldering. This was a period of
strenuous partisanship, and the *Enquirer*, like many other Democratic newspapers, frequently printed excerpts from Phillips' speeches
for the express purpose of attacking the political views contained in
them.

On December 2, 1856, Phillips read "The Philosophy of Reform"
before the Young Men's Mercantile Library Association. Smith and
Nixon's Hall was "filled with a fashionable and highly intelligent
audience" despite the rain and sloppy streets. The opening paragraphs
of the lecture were without offense. Phillips approached his subject
by a few remarks on the growing importance and influence of the
lyceum in America. Men most appreciated "the palpable which
could be seen, rather than the thought, silent and imperceptible in
its workings." Especially in America, "where the New York *Tribune*
and *Herald* were more really the government than Franklin Pierce
and Caleb Cushing," the public lecture "must exert much influence
as a public instructor and educator."

In the remaining portion of his lecture, however, Phillips gave what
the *Commercial* described as "an able and highly polished, though
slightly indirect defense of popular agitation as a means for abolish-
ing Slavery." The *Gazette* found the discourse to be "terse and
Emersonian in style, abounding in epigrams and apt quotations and
illustrations." Though "brilliant and sparkling" it was nevertheless
"partial in its analysis rather than comprehensive." The editor of the
Enquirer, who was in no such temporizing mood, attacked not only
Phillips, but also the organization which sponsored him. Under the
pretext of lecturing on "The Philosophy of Reform," Phillips had delivered "an Abolition harangue" before the Mercantile Library Association. If the members of the association were all abolitionists, "who
are determined to force down the throats of this community the most
offensive disunion and disorganizing doctrines, it would be far more
open and manly to proclaim their true character and to change their
name." It was apparent that the lecture system was being overrun

with men who belonged to "the Black-Republican Disunion party, and have acquired distinction as 'shriekers' in that cause." Many of the leading lyceum speakers were "downright disunionists, whose very names offend the patriotism and good sense of the country." The "Greeleys, Beechers, Hales, Phillipses, Garrisons, Quinceys, Sumners, Burlingames, and others of that ilk" were coming to monopolize the lyceum. If organizations like the Mercantile Library Association continued to foster such partisanship, it would "inevitably result in the downfall of the whole system."[1]

The president of the Young Men's Mercantile Library Association answered the *Enquirer*'s accusations in a letter to the *Gazette* (January 5, 1857). The charge of partisanship was declared to be unjust, malicious, and libelous. The association was not to be blamed because the East was "richer in the lecture element" than other parts of the country. Indeed the lecture committee had found it impossible to get speakers from the South. The association had no political views to advance, but was rather "the representative of great conservative interests, the maintenance of which should be the duty of every good member."

Beneath the personal and partisan prejudices of the *Enquirer*'s strictures and its apprehensions for the future of lyceum culture lay a vein of prophetic truth. By the mid-fifties the political issues of a tempestuous era in American history were already being caught up by the platform orators. Phillips and his fellows were the precursors of the reform lecturers who were to dominate the lecture system in the sixties.

2

DURING the Civil War public lecturers were well aware of the advisability of treating political subjects with prudence and caution. In

---

[1] December 3, 1856. Beecher, Josiah Quincy, Jr., and George Sumner appeared before Cincinnati audiences in 1855–56. Sumner's "Spain and Her Revolutions," delivered before the Cincinnati Young Men's Mercantile Library Association on November 25, 1856, was branded by the *Enquirer* "a singular compound of historical errors, false logic, feeble rhetoric, traitorous sentiment, narrow-minded sectional prejudice and passions, and bad pronunciation." (November 28, 1856.)

the communities of northern Ohio, eloquent appeals to patriotism and
for the support of the Union cause were publicly acclaimed by lecture-
goers, and the deprecation of the Confederate slaveholders was a
common means employed by lecturers to rouse audience enthusiasm.
But as the lecturer traveled southward toward the Ohio River he
was likely to discover small groups of listeners who sat silently
through his attacks on Southern institutions, and if his eloquence degenerated into wordy abuse, he ran the risk of being interrupted by
the hisses and catcalls of stern-faced citizens. Perhaps their friends
or relatives were fighting with the Confederate army or their patriotic regret over the rupture of the Union was tinged with mis-
giving at the spectacle of a traveling orator who used the tragic circumstances of the war to incite hatred and to fill his own pockets
with money.

The chief danger spot for political lecturers was Cincinnati, which
was a stronghold of the Democratic party in the North. Many par-
tisans of that city took the view that the antislavery lecturers were
a fanatical lot whose orations in support of the "Black Republican
Disunion Party" had weakened the social and political fabric of the
Union and had hastened the country into a needless war. The most
outspoken of the abolitionists and the lecturer most certain of inciting
violence in the city was Wendell Phillips. On March 22, 1862, Cincinnati's newspapers announced that Phillips had arrived.

It seemed at first as though the visit of Phillips would be innocuous.
He was advertised to speak in Conway's Unitarian Church on Sunday,
March 23. According to the *Commercial* his discourse on "The Democracy of Christianity" was "characteristic" and "Phillipian." Phillips
took as his text a passage from Matthew, "observing that Christ looked
to the masses of men especially, having no partiality for the lawyers
and members of church, that is Scribes and Pharisees."

On Monday the *Gazette* announced that "at the request of the
citizens of Cincinnati" Phillips would lecture at Pike's Opera House
on "Slavery and the War." The speaker's profits would be given to
the Sanitary Commission "for the relief of sick and wounded soldiers."
The news that Phillips would lecture on slavery provoked much comment and speculation among Cincinnatians. "Threats of disturbance

were common, and the prediction that he would not be permitted to address his audience, was in the mouth of every body."[2] The opposition forces quickly made plans for Phillips' reception. A fund of $125.00 was subscribed by the lecturer's enemies, and 500 tickets were distributed to a gang of ruffians, many of whom were from Kentucky, engaged to promote a riot.

On the evening of March 24 Pike's Opera House "was filled at an early hour" with Cincinnati citizens "of all shades of politics." At eight o'clock Phillips appeared upon the stage and was introduced by Judge J. B. Stallo to the audience, who greeted the lecturer "with mingled hisses and cheers." Stallo, who had defended Kossuth against the censure of Orestes Brownson ten years before, introduced Phillips by comparing him "to a piece of artillery, the report of which had disturbed the quiet of the Potomac."

Phillips began his lecture by saying that "the future of nineteen millions of nineteen states" would be determined "by the policy which the representatives shall force upon the Cabinet." The war itself was not the fault of any one section of the country or any political party. It was a conflict with complex causes and might endure for a generation. Turning directly to the subject of slavery, Phillips proudly announced that "he had been an Abolitionist for sixteen years." His remark was greeted "with hisses and a few cheers."

A moment after this mild outburst Phillips declared that "The North represents a democracy, founded on industry, brains and money; the South an aristocracy, founded on slave labor—an aristocracy whose right hand is negro slavery, and whose left is the ignorant white man."[3] This remark was the signal for the first serious demonstration of the evening. There was a roar of derision from the upper tier of the Opera House; among the printable epithets hurled at the speaker were "Down with the traitor!" "Egg the nigger Phillips!" "Lynch the traitor!" "Tar and feather the Abolitionist!" Amidst the confusion "two or three rotten eggs were thrown from the second tier, one of which struck the speaker on his right side and covered his coat and pants with the filth." Seemingly unconcerned,

[2] *Cincinnati Daily Enquirer*, March 25, 1862.
[3] *Ibid.*, March 25, 1862.

Phillips continued talking, when suddenly "a paving stone, thrown with great violence, struck near his feet." Phillips still tried to go on lecturing though frequently interrupted by hisses and catcalls, "and at every remark distasteful to the rowdies who were present, rotten eggs were showered upon the stage."

The second uprising occurred after "a reference to the employment of the poor, ignorant whites of the South as tools of the despotism that was warring upon the liberties of the Nation."[4] The rioters, "apparently three or four hundred strong," began to move ominously toward the stairs, while several fights broke out in the upper tier. There were no policemen in the building at the time, and the few persons in the gallery who attempted to put down the disturbance were soon overpowered. The confusion was increased by "ladies screaming, crying, jumping on chairs, and falling in all directions." The lecture was completely interrupted for ten or fifteen minutes when one of the mob "took his stand at the head of the stairs leading from the dress circle to the gallery, and called for cheers and groans alternately."

A number of ladies, frightened by the growing violence, rose and moved toward the door. In doing so, they were obliged either to elbow their way past the jostling rioters, who were swarming down the stairs from the upper tier, or clamber unceremoniously over the rows of seats. As the mob pushed into the middle aisle, the cries "To the stage!" and "Hurrah for Jeff Davis!" were shouted by the leaders of the gang. The owner of the Opera House, aided by many gentlemen who hurled their chairs and canes into the crowd, tried unsuccessfully to stop the advancing rioters. In the meantime, Phillips, who had given up all hope of finishing his lecture, disappeared from the platform and, unknown to the mob, reached safety through the back entrance of the building.

The two main exits of the Opera House "were beset by gangs determined to lynch the obnoxious speaker." As the members of the audience made their way into the street they were shocked by the violent threats made on the life of Phillips and by the sight of revolvers gleaming under the open coats of the rowdies. When a

---

[4] *Cincinnati Daily Commercial,* March 25, 1862.

bottle of deadly vitriol was discovered in the vestibule, there was general agreement that Phillips had been fortunate to escape without injury.

On the day after the lecture Cincinnati's newspapers featured irate editorials about this "lasting disgrace to Cincinnati" and the city's Democratic administration, which had failed to provide the customary police protection at the Opera House. The *Gazette* accused the mayor and the chief of police of complicity in the riot and declared that "the City Government, to which our citizens have entrusted their protection from violence, is in the hands and under the influence of the most dangerous element in the community." This writer concluded with the assertion that the city government "would to-day set up the flag of Jeff. Davis in this city if it was threatened by an approaching Confederate army."

The *Commercial*, after heaping opprobrium upon the heads of the city authorities, agreed that the instigators of the outrage "would be open traitors to their country if they dared." The "whisky-faced blatant wretches" who roared in the galleries and threw eggs and stones upon the stage were the serfs of traitorous conspirators and "were as faithfully doing the bidding of their masters, as if they had received special orders from Jeff. Davis, or any of his villainous aristocracy." The *Enquirer* refrained from criticizing the city's Democratic administration but took the view that the riot was disgraceful because it violated the right of freedom of speech. The rioters had "inflicted a stain upon the reputation of our city for adhesion to law, order and general decorum." Though Phillips' views were flagrantly in error, "he had a right to be heard by those who chose to attend his lecture."

On March 28 the mayor and chief of police published cards in the *Gazette* in which they lamely defended themselves against the accusation of negligence. They both contended that since Phillips' lecture at the Unitarian Church had aroused no disturbance, they did not anticipate trouble at the Opera House. Their declaration that the manager of the Opera House did not desire any special police protection was publicly refuted by the treasurer of the Opera House. Members of the audience recognized several of the the leaders among the rioters, but when the latter gentry piously denied any knowledge of the affair, no charges were brought against them. Phillips himself reported in Garrison's *Liberator* (April 11, 1862) that the mob did him no harm except smear his clothing with eggs. "Its stone and vitriol department did not reach me," he wrote. Phillips was convinced that the riot had not occurred because of any particular remarks in his lecture; "it was no sentiment of mine they mobbed, but me."

3

The lectures which Phillips delivered in Ohio in 1867 and 1868 were usually of a political nature, although he occasionally read "The Lost Arts," a cultural discourse which had been a lyceum favorite since its first presentation in the East in 1838. On April 17, 1867, when "The Lost Arts" was delivered in Toledo to "as many people as White's Hall would conveniently hold," the *Blade* termed it "the most instructive lecture we have been favored with this season, and one of the most entertaining." But Phillips' Toledo hearers desired something more than a review of the cultural attainments of ancient civilization. "At the request of many citizens," Phillips, after concluding his lecture, remained in the hall "to make a few political remarks." He affirmed his belief "in thorough reconstruction; in the complete and entire destruction of the Southern idea, and the carrying of Northern principles to the Gulf." He also revealed that he had "no faith whatever in Gen. Grant" and deprecated the idea of making him a candidate for the Presidency.

The next evening Phillips made his first appearance in Cincinnati since the egg-throwing episode of 1862. His subject was "The Times," and, "owing to the great expense attending this Lecture," the usual fifty-cent admission fee was advanced to seventy-five cents. The announcement that Anna E. Dickinson would be present at the performance was calculated to attract a large number of sight-seeing lecture-goers.

In his prefatory remarks Phillips spoke of his previous speech in the city, "when two thousand citizens of Cincinnati" gave him a kind welcome, but "some two or three hundred lawless men" broke up the lecture and thus proved "the irrepressible antagonism between free speech and the institution which they defended." Phillips then made the following comment about the nation's lyceums:

This platform has done more than any one other instrumentality to prepare the American people for the great strife through which they have passed. Oh! remember how vast the stride which the nation has made in ten years—how many prejudices it has flung away. Here it was, from this platform, that you first forgot your prejudices, and learned as a nation to thrill beneath the eloquence of that matchless among American orators—negro though he be—Frederick Douglass. It was in the lyceum, too, that men first learned how they could bend beneath the power of eloquence on the lips of Anna Dickinson. I claim both of these triumphs for the lyceum.[5]

The editor of the *Enquirer* carried on his long quarrel with Phillips, the "paid attorney of the New England bond holders," by attacking his "liquorish descriptions" of New England's wealth and influence over "Southern poverty and despair." The performance was "a grand fanatical love-feast." Anna E. Dickinson "was exhibited in one of the private boxes," where, "with that freedom of spirit for which she is noted, she gave the signal for each round of applause by clapping her hands and murmuring in a suppressed voice, Halla-lujah! as each traitorous declaration dropped from the lips of the speaker." When Phillips eulogized Frederick Douglass he "very ungallantly brought in Miss Dickinson as the colored gentleman's co-partner in the work of enlightening, with the weight of their forensic talent, the semi-civilized people of the mighty West."

Phillips concluded his Ohio lectures for 1867 with the reading of "The Perils of the Hour" at Cleveland on April 19. This lecture, which "was able and eloquent in the highest degree," was cordially received. According to the *Herald*, the chief point of his argument was "in favor of the introduction of an element south of Mason and Dixon's line that would gradually absorb all rebel feeling," or, in practical terms, "he favored sending capital, enterprise, spelling books, &c., to aid the South in regaining her former wealthy position, provided she accepted the institutions of the nineteenth century as promulgated through those agencies."

In February, 1868, Phillips returned to Ohio and undertook an

---

[5] *Cincinnati Daily Gazette*, April 19, 1867.

extended series of lecture engagements. At Cleveland, where "The Times" was read on February 18, the city's journalists objected to the lecturer's rough treatment of Ulysses S. Grant, whom Phillips considered too "reticent" and "irresponsible" to be a fit candidate for the Presidency, and complained of the "impracticability" of the discourse. The *Herald* declared that Phillips recognized no obstacle in the way of Reconstruction "that cannot be disposed of by a glittering generality or an amusing hit." The public would always lend a delighted ear to Phillips' roseate views of how things ought to be done "but would long hesitate to trust anything but the fine oratory to his hands."

On February 20 "Two veteran allies in the cause of anti-slavery, Wendell Phillips and Oberlin, met . . . at the First Church." Oberlin's citizens set a high value on knowledge and instruction, but the cultural taste of the day was clearly indicated when "The subject of the lecture was submitted to the choice of the audience, and instead of 'Lost Arts,' 'The Times' was selected." The *Lorain County News* reported that the lecture fully displayed Phillips' "genius in argument, and his strong enunciation of the principles of liberty and justice, and his denunciation of half-way measures and uncertain and non-committal men." Though the speaker's ability and masterly eloquence were much admired, "a large portion of the audience would hesitate to accept all Mr. Phillips' conclusions, or to endorse all his opinions of public men."

On February 20 the *Delaware Herald* announced that Phillips, that "Disunionist of a third of a century," would read "The Times" on the twenty-sixth. Of course, "the loyal heroes who sat on the street corners whitling [*sic*], and thirsted for the blood of Democrats during the war, will go in a body to hear him." Such hale fellows "should always kiss through a black cloth when they meet." The *Gazette* (February 28, 1868) wrote that Phillips, "a fine-looking old gentleman, and without doubt a great orator," complained of "Grant's refusal to make known his political sentiments" and gave President Andrew Johnson "his portion in due season, and rejoiced that there was now a prospect of his being brought to justice." The *Herald* (March 5, 1868) felt that Phillips' large audience was "drawn out mostly through curiosity and not from any love for the man." Phillips was "a tall, square-faced man, nearly sixty years of age, with a keen eye, bright intellect, and wields a powerful influence over his audience." If he were engaged in a useful cause, such as "defending the Union of our Fathers," he would be a useful member of society, "but disunionist as he has been for the best part of his life, his great talents are of but little account."

On February 27 Phillips lectured in Columbus on the life of Daniel O'Connell, the Irish patriot and orator who, during the second quarter of the nineteenth century, agitated for the admission of Catholics to the British Parliament and for the separation of the English and Irish Parliaments. Phillips selected O'Connell as his subject "because he was a man who had accomplished much for his race by agitation." The lecture gave a "vivid and impressive picture of the condition of Ireland" and a description of O'Connell's "wonderful and magic control of the fiery Celts, and of the great works he accomplished." The *Ohio Statesman*, a Democratic journal, objected to the lecture, as much of it "was in reality an appeal for negro suffrage." If Phillips' sponsor, the Young Men's Christian Association, desired the support of all citizens, they "would find it to their advantage to engage lecturers who will let the political prejudices of their audiences alone, and who will keep in view the object of these lectures, the information and instruction of the people."

When Phillips read "The Lost Arts" in Cincinnati on February 28, "the most noticeable fact in connection with his lecture" was that "Phillips has lectured twice in Cincinnati within as many years, without being egged." The waning popularity of the cultural lecture, particularly with those plain citizens who in the fifties were the main support of the lyceum, was illustrated by the *Commercial*'s observation that the "lower part of Mozart Hall was filled by a very intelligent audience," but the "gallery, the cheap part of the house, did not contain a single occupant." The lecture was given "in an easy, conversational style of delivery peculiar to the class of New England scholars, of which Mr. Phillips is a type."

The audacity of Wendell Phillips on the lecture platform was demonstrated in Cincinnati on March 2, 1868, when he read a discourse on the combustible subject of "Impeachment." The Republican Congress at the time was instituting procedures to impeach President Andrew Johnson, ostensibly because of his efforts to remove Secretary of War Stanton from office, but actually because of his insistence that the administration of the Reconstruction program was an executive problem and not a legislative one.

Many Democrats in the nation were indignant at the impeachment agitation and its supporters. On the day that Phillips was to lecture, his old enemy, the editor of the *Enquirer*, announced that, "at fifty cents a head, the people of Cincinnati are invited to attend and hear the falsehoods set afloat to justify one of the most flagrant invasions of right and the Constitution that has been attempted." Since the day the plan of getting rid of the President had first been suggested this "political incendiary and mischief-maker" had "never ceased to howl for impeachment."

Phillips began his address by offering his views of the purposes and progress of the lecture system:

Ladies and Gentlemen:—When I had the honor to speak to you two or three nights ago, I spoke of the change which had taken place within the last fifteen years in the range of lyceum topics, in the subjects treated of upon this popular platform. It has been remarkable within the last seventeen years, within the last fifteen years especially it has been absorbed into the great maelstrom of political agitation. It has done great service there. I value it especially on that account, considering it not a transient provision, but a permanent addition, and an indispensable element in the educational machinery of the Republic. I do not think our children will ever dispense with it. Having once planted it firmly among the habits of the American people, my belief is that it will deepen its roots and broaden its hold on the active mind of the community, till it becomes one of the recognized channels, one of the great levers by which public thought and parties are lifted to that level where parties, technically speaking, can afford to enter.[6]

The next forty-five minutes of the discourse were devoted to discussing the Reconstruction program, or, as the *Enquirer* put it, "to demonstrating how much untruth, half-knowledge and total ignorance could be crowded into an entertainment to which the people were invited under a promise of instruction."

---

[6] *Cincinnati Daily Commercial*, March 3, 1868.

Phillips was a long time approaching his announced topic. In fact it was nine o'clock before he said, "And this brings me around to impeachment." He then proceeded to discuss "the faults which he claimed make the President unfit for his office." The audience made "but few expressions of feeling on the subject proper of the evening." The main point of Phillips' argument was that official misconduct was sufficient cause for impeachment. He maintained that, while President Johnson had not violated a statute, he had failed "to come up to Congressional notions of the spirit of the age" and had not united with Congress in the enforcement of the Reconstruction program.

After his brief treatment of the impeachment problem, Phillips concluded with his customary description of the inadequacies of General Grant. These remarks "were received in quite a guarded manner." According to the *Enquirer*, "Phillips placed in a strong light the folly of the Republican party in choosing, in these critical times, a candidate without opinions." This critic was quite amused when Phillips "ridiculed to considerable effect the attempts that had been made to superinduce ideas upon that piece of impracticable humanity." Taken as a whole, this "inferior, rambling and inconsistent" lecture was saved from "falling dead" only by "rhetoric, elocution, cant phrases, clap-traps, and expressions more impudent than elegant." As an essay, "no magazine editor in the United States would have accepted it as a contribution to his pages."

The most notable trait of Phillips as a lecturer was his outspokenness. He prided himself in his independence and often, in his lectures, asserted the superiority of the lyceum over the press because of the latter's hesitancy to put forth ideas which might be unpopular. Although his own political views aroused antagonism among a minority of his hearers, they really conformed with the preconceptions and prejudices of the majority. And Phillips, despite his faith in the independence of the lyceum, was, like most lecturers, fully aware that conformity bore a close relationship to future engagements. His political lectures were popular because they voiced the partisan opinions of his audience. His individualism consisted in his willingness to desert the cultural ideals of the early lyceum and introduce, as the principal function of the platform, the indoctrination of political opinions. The lyceum was established as a place for cultural instruction; Wendell Phillips did more than any other man to make it a place for agitation.

CHAPTER
X

BAYARD TAYLOR: *Voice of Young America*

I

In 1854, the year of his first visit to the West, Taylor was one of the most admired and talked-about young men in America.[1] His fame had been established in the forties, when he began his career as a world traveler, newspaper correspondent, and author. After touring Europe in 1844 and 1845 he published his popular *Views Afoot* (1846), which ran to twenty editions in nine years. In 1848, while manager of the miscellaneous and literary department of Horace Greeley's *New York Tribune*, he followed the gold rush to California and, before returning to New York, journeyed through Mexico. His experience was recounted in *Eldorado* (1850). In August, 1851, Taylor's restless spirit again took him abroad, and for more than two years he lived among the strange people of Egypt, Palestine, Syria, Turkey, India, and China. At Shanghai he joined Commodore Perry's squadron and spent the summer of 1853 as a master's mate, studying the habits of the Japanese.

The American public followed Taylor's adventures through his letters to the *Tribune*, which were reprinted in hundreds of news-papers. These fascinating accounts of foreign lands and mysterious people were greatly enjoyed and lavishly praised by a generation of Americans whose practical, mercantile pursuits kept them at home. Throughout the fifties and sixties there was a thriving market for Taylor's undistinguished poems and entertaining travel books. The announcement that Taylor would lecture in Ohio in 1854 was accom-panied by an unprecedented clamor to see and hear "the most traveled man in America." To the women of the West he was an

---

[1] For an account of Taylor as a lecturer and of the subject matter of his speeches see Richard Croom Beatty, *Bayard Taylor: Laureate of the Gilded Age* (Norman: University of Oklahoma Press, 1936), pp. 146–169; Robert Warnock, "Unpublished Lectures of Bayard Taylor," *American Literature*, V (May, 1933), 123–132.

adventurous hero, a romantic Marco Polo who had glimpsed the guarded secrets of the Orient; to the men of Ohio he was an embodiment of the industry and culture which were idealized in the contemporary conception of "Young America."

Taylor was most successful in those lectures which were factual, descriptive, and enlivened with personal anecdote. He was apparently wise enough to recognize his limitations and to refrain from over-burdening his travel lectures with any depth of thought or "philosophy." He was primarily a dealer in facts; he satisfied the curiosity of his hearers and sent them home with the feeling that they had been instructed, that they had imbibed valuable information about the strange countries of the earth. Thomas Wentworth Higginson has accurately said that "Bayard Taylor represents the indefatigable travellers, and his reports of his latest trip are always well received by that large class who (as Goethe says in his analysis of playgoers) do not care to think, but only to see that something is going on."[2]

Taylor's first Ohio appearance was made at Toledo, where he read "The Arabs" on March 20. The *Blade* described the lecture as "a flattering and poetic view of the tastes, mental characteristics, habits, and religion of the roving Arabs of the present day." As a literary performance the lecture showed "great power for nice discrimination and a highly cultivated mind."

Though their local Atheneum had no lecture course in 1853–54 the citizens of Sandusky had long wished for a visit from Taylor. The editor of the *Commercial Register* (January 23, 1854) insisted that Taylor could be induced to come if there were "any taste in this town for any thing except fiddling, dancing and silly parties." When C. L. Derby, a Sandusky citizen, secured a lecture appointment from Taylor, the *Commercial Register* proclaimed that the lecturer would be welcomed with particular pleasure, "for as a man of genius and a gentleman, he has no superior among the young men of America, and we want him to stand before our young men to show them what labor and a noble ambition can do in developing character."

As the day of his arrival, March 21, was "breezy and chill, but

---

[2] "The American Lecture System," *Macmillan's Magazine*, XVIII (May, 1868), 55.

too tempting for a stay upon the land," Sandusky citizens took Taylor
sailing on Lake Erie. In the evening "Japan and the Japanese," or,
as it was sometimes called, "Japan and Loo Choo," was read at
Euterpean Hall. The audience included a "large party" from Fremont, and a special train was run for the accommodation of Mansfield people. The intense expectations of the audience were more
than gratified, for in Taylor "they beheld a perfect impersonation
of a 'splendid' man, with a head on his shoulders which might
serve as a model for Canova." Tall and erect, he had the chest and
limbs of an athlete, while his expressive features were "set off with
a handsome beard and moustache." His style of speaking was "not
marked with action," but "his voice is richly attuned, and his words
fall so full and sonorous from his lips as to fasten the slightest
syllable on the hearer's attention."[3]

Enthusiastic Sanduskians sought a promise from Taylor to return
for a second lecture on March 27. Taylor agreed, but not until the
superintendent of the Sandusky, Mansfield and Newark Railroad
had arranged to have a special train ready to leave Sandusky immediately after the lecture, thus enabling the speaker to meet an
appointment in Pittsburgh. "The Arabs" was just as successful as
the first Sandusky lecture. Taylor's journey aboard the special train
to Pittsburgh was perhaps the kind of exhibition that was expected
from a bold adventurer, but his conduct was strikingly different from
the usually sober demeanor of the Eastern lecturers. Taylor, "always
up for adventure, . . . signified his willingness to jump astride the
iron horse." But as Sanduskians could not find a saddle big enough
to fit over the boiler, he had to content himself with riding in the
cab with the engineer. The trainman found Taylor to be "one of *the*
men," with "a heart as big and full of energy as a locomotive."

At Cleveland "The Arabs" was delivered to "an overflowing
house." Taylor, "tall, athletic, and erect," spoke "in a slow measured
manner, employing little or no gesticulation, and never changing
his position on the platform." His second Cleveland lecture, "Japan
and the Japanese," was heard by twelve hundred people. The *Plain
Dealer* (March 24, 1854) reported that this travel lecture "was

---

[3] *Sandusky Daily Commercial Register*, March 22, 1854.

worth a hundred metaphysical essays." It could not have been written by a scholar in his study, but only by a man who had known "toil, privation and fearless adventure." Taylor himself was "a shining triumph of American energy and go-aheadativeness."

Taylor's delivery of "Japan and the Japanese" at Mt. Vernon was somewhat marred by the circumstances of the evening. One of "the largest and most intelligent audiences ever convened in Mt. Vernon" was assembled in Woodward Hall when, a few minutes before the lecture was to begin, the fire alarm sounded, and the cry went up that the town's woolen mill was burning. The citizens' curiosity about Japan was lost in the excitement; Taylor soon stood alone in a deserted hall. It was "near nine o'clock" when the townspeople despaired of extinguishing the fire, and Taylor's audience, or what was left of it, returned to the hall. Many people, supposing that the lecture would be called off, went home after the fire. Nevertheless, the *Ohio State Times* (March 27, 1854) reported that the lecture was "well attended."

At Newark Taylor's lecture on the Japanese delighted "a large and respectable audience." "There is a charm in that gentleman's manner and voice, as a speaker, that is irresistible," declared the *Advocate* (March 29, 1854). His manner was "dignified, simple, and unaffected." As a reader, Taylor was a model, and "the young ladies and gentlemen of the town, who are now being educated, would have listened to him with pleasure as well as profit."

Taylor's other appearances in Ohio during April and early May met with almost unqualified praise.[4] "Affable, witty, and wide awake, he is just the man to be popular, anywhere," wrote the editor of the Columbus *Ohio State Journal* (April 10, 1854). "He draws better

---

[4] Taylor's triumphal tour was not without its hardships. Writing to his mother from Newark on April 30, 1854, Taylor declared: "I am quite fagged out, not with speaking, but with traveling, and with being shown up, introduced, questioned, visited and made to visit, handshaken, autographed, honorary membershiped, complimented, censured, quizzed, talked about before my face by people who don't know me, written about in the papers, displayed on hand-bills, sold on tickets, applied to for charitable purposes, and the Lord knows what else." Marie Hansen-Taylor and Horace E. Scudder (editors), *Life and Letters of Bayard Taylor* (2 vols.; Boston: Houghton, Mifflin and Company, 1884), I, 275.

houses than any man in America." At Chillicothe, where Taylor was announced to tell his hearers "something new about that selfish and unsociable empire of Japan," the *Scioto Gazette* described the lecturer as "highly intellectual, a poet from the impulse of native genius, the world's great traveller, the acute observer, the man of action and energy, earnest and hopeful, with an intellectual argosy of wealth from Oriental lands." Taylor was starting out, at the age of twenty-nine, "with better capital and better prospects than any American who has ever trod the path-way of honorable ambition. God speed this true embodiment of 'Young America.' "[5]

Two thousand people gathered in the village of Oberlin to hear "The Arabs." The audience was entertained, both before and after the lecture, with music, and "the words sung were Taylor's own production." The music for the occasion was composed by G. N. Allen of Oberlin. The first song, beginning with the line "From the bosom of ocean I seek thee," was written by Taylor for Mary Agnew, whom he married a few months before her death in December, 1850. The closing number was Taylor's "The Storm Song." The poet was "tenderly affected" by these unexpected performances.[6]

These lectures established Taylor's popularity, which was unchallenged among travel lecturers until the emergence of George Kennan of Norwalk in the 1860's. Taylor came near to fulfilling the ideal of the Western lecture public in the 1850's; he instructed with his colorful materials about far-off people and places, and he entertained with his exciting anecdotes and reminiscences of personal experiences. He attained no depth of thought in these productions; indeed, beside the rich, intellectual strength of Emerson's essays, Taylor's lectures, as well as his published writings, were decidedly superficial. Nor was there "anything wonderful, or strangely peculiar in the manner or style; but to have before you the actual live Yankee

---

[5] April 8, 1854. At Chillicothe Taylor was escorted by a party of citizens to Bellevue Height, where he saw "the Ancient Capitol and adjacent country.— He pronounces it one of the finest views he ever saw. This coming from a man who has seen more of the world than any other living man, is no small compliment." *Daily Scioto Gazette*, April 4, 1854.

[6] Letter from "H. J.," *Sandusky Daily Commercial Register*, May 8, 1854.

who has strolled all over creation, awakens an interest and gives a zest to the subject matter which is not experienced in reading."[7]

2

BEGINNING January 4, 1855, with the delivery of "India" before the Steubenville Atheneum, Taylor gave some twenty lectures before Ohio audiences during the months of late winter and early spring. These discourses were received with consistent approbation, although some of the exuberance and idolatry which greeted his first tour of the state is missing from the newspaper reviews. There is rather a succession of "large and intelligent" audiences listening through the conventional hour and a half with "fixed attention" to "The Arabs," "Japan and the Japanese," or one of his three new lectures, "India," "The Philosophy of Travel," and "The Animal Man."

From the lecture reviews of the time can be gleaned some of the qualities which made Taylor's popularity with Ohio audiences endure for a decade and a half. "Mr. Taylor's elocution is good, and he speaks 'right on' like a man of sense, without making any pretensions to display."[8] "His descriptive powers are of the highest order," observed the editor of the Chillicothe *Scioto Gazette* (January 19, 1855). It was this skill in description which enabled Taylor to discuss the geography, people, and customs of foreign lands so that "his listeners can see clearly in their mind's eye the things of which he speaks." Taylor's informality, his ability to treat his subject "in an extemporaneous and off hand manner," was especially pleasing to the unsophisticated audiences of the Western towns. His appeal was conscious and calculated; he had no share in the ideal of spreading culture. Lecturing was to Taylor a means of gaining financial independence and leisure for the pursuit of his literary career.

During the fifties Taylor provoked less adverse comment from Ohio's newspapers than any other major Eastern lecturer, with the possible exception of Henry Giles. Occasionally there was a mild dissent. The Canton *Stark County Democrat* (February 7, 1855) protested that "The Arabs" "was destitute of that fund of information

---

[7] Akron *Summit Beacon*, May 10, 1854.
[8] *Daily Toledo Blade*, January 15, 1855.

which a lecture—a fifty dollar lecture—should impart." And the
Zanesville Gazette (January 30, 1855) declared that "The Philosophy
of Travel" was not extraordinarily fine. "Though listened to atten-
tively, it was but faintly applauded or praised by ladies and gentlemen capable of judging and criticising correctly."

The high regard for Taylor was shared by cultured and unsophisticated lecture-goers alike. This flattering lecture invitation was
written to Taylor by Horace Mann, president of Antioch College at
Yellow Springs, and Ohio's most eminent educator in the fifties.

JULY 1ST, 1854
B. TAYLOR ESQ.

DEAR SIR,

There is at this place a small village, perhaps containing one thousand people. In our Institution, there are three or four hundred students
whose average age is more than 20 years. Our villagers wish to hear
the great man of whom they have heard so much, & I am most anxious
that our students should see high specimens of the combined effect of
talent and culture—the young men that they may have notable examples
to aspire to & emulate, & the young women that they may see the difference between men & butterflies.

I invite you, therefore, to give us a Lecture during the ensuing "Lecture season." Our means, of course, are limited, but I will ensure you
$30, can probably give you $40, & rather than our young people should
not hear, I will be personally responsible for $50.

Saturday evening will be acceptable to us, & will probably steer clear
of the preference of all others.

If you come,—as I earnestly hope you will,—Mrs. Mann & myself
will be most happy to entertain you as our guest, as long as you may
find it agreeable to remain.

Yours very truly,
HORACE MANN

P. S. Our place may be reached on the same day from Cincinnati, Columbus, Cleveland, Sandusky or Toledo.[9]

Taylor did not disappoint his correspondent. On the night of
January 21, 1855, a young student at Antioch College recorded in
her diary that "Bayard Taylor spoke of different religious customs
of Asia Europe & Africa."[10] And two days later Taylor wrote to his

---

[9] A photostat of this letter is in the Antioch College Library. The letter is
quoted here with the permission of the library.

[10] Manuscript Diary of Maria L. Moore (Antioch College Library).

mother that at Antioch he was asked to "preach in the chapel on Sunday afternoon, on the 'Religions of the World.' I spoke for more than an hour extemporaneously, a new thing to me. I was a little scared, but got through with credit."[11]

3

FROM 1856 to 1858 Taylor traveled in Europe, mostly in the northern countries of the Continent. His experiences were narrated in his letters to the *New York Tribune* and in his travel volumes *Northern Travel* (1858), *Travels in Greece and Rome* (1859), and *At Home and Abroad* (1860). In January and February, 1859, Taylor journeyed through Ohio lecturing on "Moscow" and "Life in the North." The materials of these lectures were already familiar to his readers. Nevertheless, the opportunity of seeing the famous world traveler in the flesh was sufficient inducement to attract throngs of curious Ohioans to his performances.

At the reading of "Life in the North" before the Cleveland Library Association, the Melodeon was so jammed that Taylor had difficulty "finding a passage through the densely crowded stage to the lecture-desk." According to the *Plain Dealer* (January 26, 1859) the audience was highly pleased with Taylor's discourse, which "was made up of observations made by him of the country and people, during a year's travel in the lands of the Swede and Fin." After the lecture Taylor attended a Cleveland celebration of the centenary of the birth of Robert Burns. Called to the platform, Taylor recounted the story of his attendance at a Scottish festival honoring Burns' three sons.

Twenty-five hundred people were present at Taylor's reading of "Life in the North" in Cincinnati on February 3. The *Gazette* reported that the lecture was "an admirable condensation of the letters which he wrote from 'high latitudes,' many of which have been copied into almost every paper in the country." Though most of his listeners had "some notion of what his lecture would be," his selections of material were made "with a taste and judgment that

---

[11] Hansen-Taylor and Scudder, *Life*, I, 297–298.

were very creditable and gave great pleasure to those who had read his epistles."

Since Taylor's lecture schedule was too crowded to enable him to give a regular evening performance before the Delaware Young Men's Lecture Association, he delivered "Life in the North" to "a large and appreciative audience" of Delaware citizens at one-thirty in the afternoon on February 4. In the evening he read the same lecture in Columbus. The editor of the *Ohio State Journal*, who was not greatly impressed, declared that Taylor gave "a rambling, desultory sketch of his travel, in a style not polished nor particularly attractive." Speaking without manuscript, he employed a tone that was "conversational" and a manner that was "self-possessed" and "undramatic." This critic concluded that the lecture was successful chiefly because the people were permitted to see the celebrated man who had experienced an adventurous journey into the Northland. "It is not every day that cats may look at kings, though adage cheerfully accords them the privilege."

After reading "Moscow" to an audience of four hundred in the Antioch College chapel at Yellow Springs on February 5, Taylor returned to Cincinnati. That his romantic appeal to Western women had not faded since his early Ohio visits is evident from the fact that an unusually large number of ladies attended the delivery of "Moscow" on February 7. As the stage itself was crowded with women, "the lecturer had the honor of speaking in the midst of a bevy of grace and beauty not easy to surpass." The *Enquirer* found the lecture to be "colloquial in style, and not approaching nor pretending to any literary excellence." Taylor's manner was "easy and gentlemanly, and his voice clear and distinct. Without aspiring to or attempting the oratorical, he is much more pleasing than many men who do."

Taylor's Ohio tour of 1859 was concluded with lectures at Cleveland and Toledo. The Cleveland *Ohio Farmer* (February 19, 1859) commended Taylor the man but showed little admiration for his performance as a lecturer. To begin with, the discourse was concerned not so much with "Moscow" as with "Bayard Taylor himself." As a lecturer Taylor was "prosy and heavy" and incessantly waved his hands and arms about, "without any force or meaning in his gestures." He attracted a large crowd because "everybody wants to see the man that has seen everybody and everything." But those people "who had read Mr. T.'s letters in the Tribune, heard nothing new about Moscow."

Taylor opened his 1860 series of Ohio lectures on January 5 at Cincinnati with a discourse on the life of Baron Alexander Von Humboldt, the German naturalist and traveler.[12] The lecture was "a sketch of a great man drawn by one who had the rare fortune of being numbered among his intimate friends." The *Enquirer* declared that Taylor's laudatory account of "the mighty intellect, extraordinary attainments, and nobility of character of his departed friend" was "pleasant in its conversational character" and "interspersed with anecdote." The audience was "pleased, amused, and instructed."

When Taylor gave this lecture in Cleveland on April 2 he drew a large audience despite the "excitements of election night." The *Leader* reported that "the story of Humboldt's life and character" was told "in the eloquence of hearty admiration and faith." While in Cleveland, Taylor employed his traveler's wisdom to add a few dollars to the proceeds of his lecture tour. In a column adjacent to the *Leader*'s review of his lecture was printed his testimonial of the virtues of one "Wm. Raebel's Bath," which was happily "arranged after the best Russian model." This "cure of colds" and "mitigator of rheumatisms" had so impressed Taylor that he assured Clevelanders it would be "a fortunate thing if the Russian Bath should be permanently naturalized in the United States."

Taylor reappeared in Cincinnati on November 20 with a new lecture entitled "Man and Climate," which was read at Smith and Nixon's Hall before "one of the largest audiences ever assembled within the walls of that building." This discourse was delivered on November 22 before the Cleveland Library Association. The *Leader* stated that Taylor's aim was to show that "each of the great divisions of the human race is assigned its proper location on the earth, the

---

[12] Humboldt traveled extensively in Europe and South America, making investigations in natural science. His *Cosmos* (1845–48), a study of physical laws and their effects, had a great influence on the study of physical geography. During his European travels Taylor had become acquainted with Humboldt, who died in 1859.

climate best adapted for the development of one race being destructive to another division of the human family." The *Plain Dealer* added that the lecture "was of the highest order of interest and of solid practical utility, often sparkling with the finest hits of dry wit."

After a brief trip into Pennsylvania Taylor returned to Ohio on November 26. "The City Hall was filled with the fashion and talent of Springfield" to hear "Life in the Arctic Regions." In describing the pleasure with which the audience received the lecture, the *News* pointed out that "Everybody likes Bayard Taylor because he is a man of and from the people and puts on no airs."

Taylor's final appearance in 1860 was made on December 8, when he read "Man and Climate" before the Irving Lecture Association in Oberlin. The audience of one thousand contained many people from Elyria, Wellington, and other nearby towns. Taylor was introduced by the president of the association as "one whose feet have gone all over the earth, and whose fame has gone farther than his feet." The correspondent of the *Lorain County News* was "somewhat disappointed in Mr. Taylor's appearance." The lecturer was "very large, being considerably more than six feet high and heavy in proportion. . . . His countenance is not so much indicative of refinement as it is of strength, and his general appearance not so much that of the poet as of the traveler."

Oberlin College's student editors estimated the ability of Taylor and the worth of his lecture with more discriminating accuracy than was usually displayed by more experienced critics. These reviewers felt that "some of the points made by the lecturer admit of successful refutation, and in such a way as to sadly interfere with his conclusions." His best points were those "fortified by arguments drawn from his own extended observation as a traveler." Though Taylor had had much experience in foreign countries, the lecture brought to mind "the repeated remark of Humboldt" that Taylor "has seen the most and knows the least of any living man." The lecturer did not appear to be "a man of great breadth of mind or elevation of purpose."[13]

[13] *Oberlin Students' Monthly*, III (January, 1861), 92. The uncomplimentary remark attributed to Humboldt was invented by Park Benjamin, "who confessed the fact shortly before his death." Hansen-Taylor and Scudder, *Life*, II, 523.

4

TAYLOR was the only major Eastern lecturer who visited Ohio during every one of the war years. Because of the curtailment of the state's lecture system he was obliged to forego his customary appearances in the small communities, except in northern Ohio, and to confine his lecture activities to the large cities. ". . . what is the state of our business this winter? I get precious few invitations, and from widely scattered places," Taylor wrote to George William Curtis in 1861. "As for the 'business,'" replied Curtis, "it is certainly depressed. I have had, I think, not more than half of the usual invitations."[14] It is evident from the reviews of the time that this restriction of the lecture market was disadvantageous to Taylor. He had no new materials for travel lectures, and the city lyceums had listened to his entire stock of essays on the countries of northern Europe.

In 1861 Taylor partially evaded the problem by appearing in several communities where his old lectures were not very familiar. Among these were Ashtabula, Wooster, and Conneaut. On February 26, when Taylor appeared in a benefit performance for the Cincinnati Union Bethel, he rehashed the materials of old lectures by reading a production entitled "Moscow and the Russians." In pondering the ability of Taylor to attract an audience to hear such a stale theme, the *Gazette* commented that, next to Henry Ward Beecher, Taylor was probably the most popular lecturer in America. There were others, "such as Phillips, Emerson, Curtis, head and shoulders above him as thinkers, writers and speakers, but they do not draw such houses as he." The explanation was that Taylor "has *seen* more of the world than any other man, and has a happy way of communicating to others his impressions, and placing before them a picture of strange countries, people and customs."

The *Enquirer* objected to Taylor's use of old materials. His discourse "lacked the very letter and spirit of a lecture—something new." The repetition of his observations on Moscow "was certainly a poor compliment to the intelligence of our citizens." From a man of Taylor's reputation "the audience present certainly had a right

---

[14] Hansen-Taylor and Scudder, *Life*, I, 382.

to expect an original lecture that had never before been delivered in this city."

In 1862 Taylor laid aside his travel lectures and turned to social and political themes. He was not well fitted to join the growing corps of lecturers who treated such topics, as his observations of life were broad rather than deep. His travel lectures, which exhibited considerable skill in description, owed little of their popularity to his powers of analysis. But the fame of Taylor in the West was such that the people of Ohio would eagerly turn out to hear him speak on any subject.

On January 7 Taylor delivered "The American People, Socially and Politically"[15] in Zanesville. The *Courier* reported that the "keen observation of the great traveler has given him the ability to deal justly, though somewhat sarcastically with the follies and foibles of Americans." Taylor attempted to point out the "glaring" and "wicked" practices in American social and political life.

Advertised as "American Civilization," this lecture was given in Columbus on the following evening. The city's journalists did not review the discourse in any detail, but the editor of the *Capital City Fact* did "not think the subject which he selected, very happily suited to his peculiar style of thinking and writing."

At Cleveland, where Taylor read "The American People, Socially and Politically" on January 9, the *Leader* declared that "his object was to show the arbitrary and despotic character of our social system as compared with that of Europe, which he claimed to be liberal and democratic." The political materials of the address were "intended to demonstrate that there is a great amount of corruption in politics, the root of which is with the people."

Taylor concluded his four-day visit in Ohio by lecturing in Cincinnati. The *Gazette* (January 11, 1862) found "The American People, Socially and Politically" to be a decidedly thin and un-original discourse. Since Taylor was a very popular lecturer it was "a requirement of fashionable life to give ear unto him whenever he

---

[15] Although Ohio journalists invariably used this title, the lecture is usually known as "The American People." In his correspondence Taylor calls the discourse "The American People in Their Social and Political Aspects."

comes along." But he said "a great many things not brilliant in themselves" as well as "a great many things that others have said before him." His digressive lecture conveyed only "a poor idea of the subject." In many places, too, it was "evident that the facts ran out, and the lecturer was obliged to supply their place by a draft upon his imagination."

After his unenthusiastic reception as a social critic, Taylor resorted, in most of his subsequent wartime lectures in Ohio, to his much-used discourses on Russia. The *Cleveland Plain Dealer* (December 4, 1863) stated that his lecture upon "Russia and Her People" combined "amusement and instruction, embodying a masterly sketch of the great Muscovite realm, the peculiarities of its inhabitants, its system of government, &c."

A crowded audience assembled at White's Hall in Toledo to hear Taylor read this lecture before the Young Men's Association. It was evident to the editor of the *Blade* (February 25, 1864) that Taylor "had seen the best side of Russia." The speaker tried "to explain the circumstances which had heretofore made despotism the only principle of government there, and to show that the advance in this respect was as rapid as the case would admit."

On January 17, 1865, Taylor read "Ourselves and Our Relations" at Cincinnati's Mozart Hall. The lecture "consisted of a comparison of some of our social and political forms with those of the more prominent European nations." The *Gazette* complained that, although the lecture "was listened to with a certain degree of apparent pleasure," Taylor took his seat, "having entertained every one of his hearers without having taught any one of them any thing."

At Taylor's reading of "Russia and the Russians" in Cincinnati, the *Enquirer* (November 10, 1865) observed sympathetically that "if he a little overestimated the character of Russian sovereigns and their Government, it is perhaps no more than a fair offset to the pretty wholesale and elaborate detraction to which they are now and then exposed." But the editor of the *Gazette*, who found the lecture to be commonplace, objected vigorously to Taylor's analysis of Russian character. Since Taylor had held a diplomatic position in the court at St. Petersburg, the audience anticipated "much valuable information and pleasant gossip respecting Russia." The lecture was "not only devoid of these features," but "it contained little that could not be found in any book of travels or Encyclopaedia." Taylor's high regard for the Russians was irritating. "From the Czar to the lately emancipated serfs, no class of people in the Muscovite Empire failed to receive affectionate praise." His "indiscriminate laudation of Russian institutions" revealed Taylor's "almost entire blindness to the evils inherent in the greatest military despotism of the globe." A serious defect in many writers and public speakers was that "they are boundless either in their praises or their censures." Taylor was "a remarkable example of the former class."

5

TAYLOR's final Ohio journey occurred in 1869, when he undertook a series of some forty lectures in the Western states. He usually spoke to full houses, as he had acquired, during his many lecture trips, a large following of admirers who were eager to have one more look at the great traveler before his retirement from the lyceum platform. His first Ohio appearance was made at Cincinnati, where he read "Views of American Society" on November 2. The lecture advertisements stated that the discourse had never before been delivered. Taylor told his audience that when he first began lecturing, sixteen years before, "he did so in response to a call from the public, with his travels as his theme." Now that his travels were over "he could afford to choose his own topics, and speak upon things nearer home." He had therefore turned to his discussions of American society. He was pleased at the recollection that always, on his Cincinnati visits, he had "received the same hearty and generous welcome." He had lectured in America nine hundred times and could honestly say there were three cities where he felt "especially at home," where he was sure of a "generous, intelligent and sympathetic hearing." Those cities were Cincinnati, Baltimore, and Boston.[16]

On December 11 Taylor came to Ohio from Detroit and delivered "Life in Europe and America" at Toledo. According to the *Blade* his ideas "were of a philosophic nature, and embodied the mature

[16] *Cincinnati Daily Commercial*, November 3, 1869.

reflections upon the experience of the lecturer in his extensive travels and observations." In comparing American and European society Taylor pointed out the abuses and follies in American life that called for reform. He emphasized particularly the need for "tolerance of different views" and a "less exhausting pursuit of wealth for the sake of its outward splendors."

In Cleveland his "Views of American Society" was "much better attended than such entertainments usually are." The *Leader* (December 14, 1869) reported that after Taylor's absence of four years "the public hailed his return with pleasure, and greeted his appearance in the hall with prolonged applause." The lecture, which was "replete with advanced moral ideas, boldly and clearly expressed," touched on "many abuses of society for which philosophy has not yet discovered a remedy."

After entertaining a "well filled house" at Massillon "with graphic descriptions of 'Life in Europe and America,'" Taylor read the same lecture at Springfield on December 15. His plea for "a higher, broader, more pervading intellectual and social culture" was enthusiastically received by an audience which "should have been thrice as numerous as it was." Those personal qualities that had made Taylor a favorite with Ohioans for fifteen years were summarized by the *Republic*. Taylor had the "polish of a perfect gentleman" and a mind furnished with "the resources of the ripest scholarship and the inexhaustible data afforded by travels." Though he was not a man to stir or "enthuse" the popular heart, he touched it none the less. He was a model speaker, "almost too well-bred to raise his voice above a certain range of modulation, and he never strikes the desk with his fist." Massive and stately in form, "graceful in gesture, delicate in speech," Taylor was "a gentleman in every fibre, but not a swell."

At Columbus, where Taylor delivered "Life in Europe and America" on December 16, the editor of the *Ohio State Journal* wrote a flattering tribute to the lecturer as a thinker. Taylor spoke "less as a traveler and an observer" than formerly, and "more as a thinker, and more as a poet." Most lecturers "were prepared to meet the demand of the people," but in this address Taylor had "a *strong pur-*

pose as the moving principle." He demonstrated "the depth of careful study given by the Thinker to social and political problems, the symmetry that is the guiding star of the Author, the practical common sense that comes as the result of observation and the beautiful figures incident to the story-telling and arguments of the poet."

Taylor's last Ohio lecture was given at Chillicothe on December 18, 1869. "Life in Europe and America" was reported by the *Scioto Gazette* to be "a good lecture, full of homely truths, well considered, and spoken in excellent spirit." The audience "recognized the truthfulness of his thrusts at American faults" and agreed that "it was full time to reform them altogether."

Throughout the period of his Western lectures Taylor was pictured in the minds of Ohioans as an ideal American gentleman. He was held to be the embodiment of culture and ambition; he represented what the men of Ohio would have liked to be and what they desired their sons to be. He combined the adventurous spirit of their pioneer forefathers with the cultivation and learning of the nineteenth-century world. This contemporary estimate of Taylor was an exaggerated one, and his fame has receded with the passing years. To the people of Ohio he was one of the great figures on the lyceum platform, and his limitations, including the absence of a serious cultural purpose in most of his discourses, were seldom censured. He was thought to be one of the people, and his modesty, his democratic spirit, and his patriotism were consistently praised in newspaper estimates in which sentimentality sometimes usurped the place of reason.

CHAPTER
XI

ORESTES A. BROWNSON: *Enemy of Insurrection*

IN FEBRUARY, 1852, the members of the Cincinnati Young Men's Mercantile Library Association, learning that Orestes Brownson was "accidentally in the city," prevailed upon him to deliver a lecture. The association was nearing the end of a successful lecture program featuring, for the most part, local orators. The presentation of the celebrated Brownson not only would bring before the Cincinnati public one of New England's most gifted minds, but also would add a considerable sum to the association's lecture profits. While Brownson was probably not so well known in the West as Theodore Parker or Henry Ward Beecher, his outspoken articles in the *Democratic Review*, the *Boston Quarterly Review*, and *Brownson's Quarterly Review* were familiar to some Ohio readers; and his interest in the Workingmen's party and in the transcendentalists' experiment at Brook Farm was known to a much larger public. Brownson's conversion from Unitarianism to Catholicism, and his writings describing the experience, had aroused a great deal of comment in the churches and in the journals of the West. The Catholic population was particularly eager to see and hear him.

At the time of Brownson's visit in Cincinnati the city was entertaining Louis Kossuth, the Hungarian patriot. For several years the people of the West had been reading about this famous revolutionist and lover of freedom. As a member of the Hungarian Parliament he had incited his countrymen to throw off Austrian domination, and, had Russia not intervened, he might have been successful in leading his country to independence in the Revolution of 1848. Kossuth had fled Hungary in 1849 and, after two years' imprisonment by the Turks, had been liberated through the influence of England.

Throughout the year 1852 the newspapers of America were filled with news about Kossuth. Since his arrival in the country in December, 1851, he had been celebrated as a hero and martyr to the cause of freedom. Receiving countless invitations to speak, he appeared in the assembly halls of legislatures, in Boston's Faneuil Hall, and in the remote crossroads communities of the West. On February 6, 1852, he addressed the Ohio legislature. As he journeyed by railroad across the land he was greeted at every station by enthusiastic crowds. People drove for miles over the rutted, muddy roads of winter to hear him plead for the support of Hungarian freedom. He received many generous contributions of money to be used in his country's struggle for independence. The acclaim of the people surpassed even the ovations which had greeted Jenny Lind's triumphal American tour in 1851.

Orestes Brownson shared none of this enthusiasm for Kossuth. In January, 1850, Brownson had braved the hisses of his audience by attacking the Hungarian revolutionary in a public address in New York.[1] When President Millard Fillmore welcomed Kossuth to America in an address to the Congress, Brownson took Fillmore to task for his misunderstanding of Kossuth's character and motives. Brownson denounced both Kossuth and Joseph Mazzini, the Italian refugee, as leading conspirators in a grand European plot to overthrow by violence "every monarchical, and indeed every legally constituted government in the civilized world." Kossuth was a dangerous character, a traitor who abused liberty to stir up hate and insurrection. Brownson mistrusted him and warned against his cleverness and persuasive eloquence.

At Cincinnati, Kossuth received a "hearty Western welcome." He was banqueted and entertained by the mayor and other leading citizens. Lavishly praising his free spirit, the newspapers carefully preserved his every public utterance. A large purse was subscribed and presented to him by the people of Cincinnati.

On February 17, in the midst of these exciting events, Brownson lectured on the subject of "Non-Intervention." Because it was his first public appearance in Cincinnati, the new Concert Hall was filled

---

[1] Brownson's antagonism toward Kossuth is discussed in Henry F. Brownson, *Orestes A. Brownson's Middle Life: From 1845 to 1855* (Detroit: H. F. Brownson, 1899), pp. 418–424. For Kossuth's enthusiastic reception in Ohio see Andor M. Leffler, "Kossuth Comes to Cleveland," *Ohio State Archaeological and Historical Quarterly*, LVI (October, 1947), 242–257.

with eager listeners. As Brownson discussed the wisdom of America's minding her own affairs and staying clear of foreign entanglements, he did not mention Kossuth, but there was a growing tenseness, a perceptible uneasiness in the faces of his audience. And then suddenly Brownson shouted: "We have no traitors in this country—but we import traitors from Europe and make heroes of them!" For a moment there was silence and surprise; then from every part of the hall came shouts of anger, and Brownson's voice was indistinguishable in a storm of hisses. Had the audience been an ordinary one it is doubtful that the speaker would have been allowed to continue, "but Mr. Brownson's religious friends (constituting the largest portion of the audience) came to his rescue with every imaginable species of applause, and finally drowned out the voices of the dissenters."[2]

The rest of Brownson's address was listened to in sullen silence by many of his hearers. He elaborated the view that Hungary was an integral part of the Austrian empire and that there was no justification for the country's ambition to become an independent nation. He denied the right of revolution, declaring that the people of a country had no right to oppose a legal government. He concluded that the Hungarian cause was unjust and undeserving of the sympathy which it had received.

The people of Cincinnati were so incensed that J. B. Stallo, one of the city's prominent judges and most eloquent orators, was given the responsibility of refuting Brownson's opinions. At Smith and Nixon's Hall on February 20 an enthusiastic crowd listened to his reiteration of the virtues of Kossuth and the Hungarian cause.[3] With a lawyer's careful logic he attacked Brownson's autocratic principles, particularly the denial of the right of revolution. The address was received with complete approbation by his applauding listeners, the grandfathers of many of whom had fought in the American Revolution.

Brownson's rough treatment of Kossuth was especially embarrassing to the Young Men's Mercantile Library Association. The organization's lecture committee, which had always exercised painstaking care to prevent the discussion of political topics in its lecture program,

[2] *Daily Cincinnati Gazette*, February 18, 1852.
[3] Stallo repeated his address at Smith and Nixon's Hall on February 26.

had had no foreknowledge of Brownson's inflammatory remarks. At the lecture on February 24 by O. M. Mitchel, the noted astronomer of the Cincinnati Observatory, the president of the association, after apologizing for Brownson's speech, asserted that the lecturer had "abused the confidence of the Association by travelling outside the proprieties of the lecture hall, to indulge in an indecorous and wanton personal attack."[4]

A public comment on Brownson's lecture was made by Kossuth himself. In his farewell speech at Cincinnati's railroad depot on February 25 he said to his large audience:

Remember that you are Republicans, and still here in the very metropolis of Ohio, a man was found to lecture for Russo-Austrian despotism, and to lecture with the astonishing boldness of an immense ignorance.

But that good man, I can dismiss with silence, the more because it is with high appreciation and warm gratitude that I saw an honorable gentleman, animated with the most generous sentiments of justice and right, take immediately upon himself the task of refutation.[5]

Cincinnati was well pleased with Kossuth's answer to Brownson. But America's ardor toward Kossuth cooled considerably in the months that followed, and the Hungarian patriot left the country in June, 1852, amid what Brownson described as "the perfect indifference of the American people." Cincinnati's denunciation of Brownson was soon forgotten by its citizens and by the press. In 1861 he was again asked to lecture before the Mercantile Library Association, but he did not accept the invitation. In 1858, however, he returned to Cincinnati to deliver two religious lectures before the Young Men's Catholic Literary Institute on "Popular Objections to the Church" and "Charity and Philanthropy."

[4] *Daily Cincinnati Gazette*, February 25, 1852.
[5] *Ibid.*, February 26, 1852.

CHAPTER
XII

HENRY WARD BEECHER: *Eloquent Profiteer*

IN THE columns of Ohio's newspapers of 1855 lies the dramatic account of Henry Ward Beecher's rejection as a lecturer by the indignant citizens of the West, a story which has not been revealed by the biographers of the great Eastern divine. Not that Beecher was the first celebrity to be humiliated by Ohio's lecture public in the boisterous 1850's. Ralph Waldo Emerson, during his Ohio journeys of 1850 and 1852, had been reminded often enough that he was a pantheistic dreamer whose disjointed, unintelligible philosophizing had little to do with the practical affairs of life.[1] In 1854 the New York reformer George William Curtis had visited the state with a "namby-pamby, up-townish" lecture on "Success." His listeners, men who had experienced the struggle of the West to escape the economic bondage of the Eastern bankers and who loved their mercantile account books next to their homes and families, resented his implication that wealth had nothing to do with success in life.[2] And the Western press, in reminding Curtis that he would do well to remain at home, could not suppress a sneer at the fashionable cut of his coat "or the particular shade of *yellow* gloves." Parke Godwin of the *New York Evening Post* suffered when he took the liberty with Ohioans in 1855 of contrasting the social standards of the East and West in a discourse entitled "American Social Life."[3] His hearers objected vehemently to his disparagement of the West's great middle class, "the substantial architects of our greatness," and dismissed both Godwin and his lecture as "a miserable and disgraceful failure."

But these orators antagonized Ohioans merely by their opinions. They offered nothing worse than annoying philosophical speculation; Beecher, however, was associated with something much more offensive —a financial speculation. In 1855 the eloquent minister of Brooklyn's

---

[1] See pp. 24–61 of this study.

[2] See pp. 92–95, above.

[3] See pp. 96–98, above.

Plymouth Church hired himself out to a shrewd lecture agent, a speculator, and set out for the West, his right hand raised in ardent praise of religion and truth, while, according to contemporary accounts, his left hand sought to unfasten the purse strings of the public. Western citizens were not usually averse to financial speculation; indeed they throve on it. During the early decades of the century their economic lives sometimes depended on it. In 1855, the very year of Beecher's journey, Ohioans flocked by the thousands to hear Phineas T. Barnum, the greatest speculator in America, the "Prince of Humbug," deliver his lecture on "The Philosophy of Humbug." They cheered and applauded a discourse which was admittedly a collection of "stale newspaper scraps and stump anecdotes, which have been bawled in all the school houses of the country during the campaigns of the last twenty years." Barnum appealed to their own sense of humbuggery. Besides, he was an eminently successful speculator, and many of his listeners secretly hoped they would learn something that could be turned to advantage in their relations with their fellow citizens.

In the minds of Western people, however, Barnum and Beecher were as unlike as two Americans well could be. Barnum appealed to the gullibility of the people; Beecher appealed to the highest motives of human conduct. Beecher was the idol of American Protestants and one of the most sought-after lecturers in the East. Western citizens were familiar with his oratorical fame; they read his published works and the excerpts from his sermons which were scissored from Eastern journals and reprinted by the Western press. Each year Beecher was besieged with a great volume of invitations to appear before Ohio's lyceums.[4]

The source of Beecher's difficulty lay partly in his attempt to lecture under conditions running contrary to customs developed by Ohio's lecture system during the early fifties. The standard admission price for lyceum lectures was twenty-five cents; higher prices were not countenanced by lecture-goers except on special occasions when

---

[4] In addition to the lectures treated in this study, Beecher's Ohio engagements included appearances at Painesville, July 4, 1854; at Cincinnati, November 16, 1856; and at Cleveland, July 2, 1854; October 20, 1857; October 21, 1857; February 26, 1862.

the proceeds were for charitable purposes. Appointments for lectures were normally arranged by lyceum secretaries through direct correspondence with prospective lecturers. Lecture agents were not numerous, and large agencies for scheduling speakers' itineraries were not successfully established until after the Civil War. Lyceum secretaries annually wrote many invitations to speakers, and no orator was likely to attempt the discourtesy of lecturing privately in a community whose lyceum invitation he had refused.

In 1854 and 1855 the Cincinnati Young Men's Mercantile Library Association had applied for Beecher's services but had not secured an appointment. It came as a considerable surprise to the Cincinnati lecture public, therefore, when the announcement was made in the local newspapers that Beecher would speak in the city under the auspices of a Chicago lecture agent on October 22, 1855.

The press was quick to exploit this discourtesy to "the first of lecture associations." The details of Beecher's lecturing arrangements were available in the Chicago papers, as the orator had begun his Western tour in that city. Soon all Cincinnati knew that Beecher, ignoring the invitations of lecture associations in Cincinnati, Columbus, and Cleveland, had arranged with E. S. Wells, a Chicago agent, to appear in these Ohio cities. Beecher had agreed to deliver twelve lectures in the West for a sum of $1500.00, or $125.00 per lecture. The *Cincinnati Daily Gazette* reminded its readers that the great popular idol had hired himself out to a speculator, had offended the Young Men's Mercantile Library Association, and, to pad the pockets of Wells, was charging the exorbitant admission price of fifty cents.

Beecher lectured on October 22, as announced. On the following day the *Gazette* noted with satisfaction that only three hundred people had attended the lecture. It was apparent that Wells had made a bad speculation and that Beecher had "not added to his reputation by accepting the contract." Had Beecher visited the city under the auspices of the Mercantile Library Association, "to whom an unfulfilled promise to lecture has been out for two years," he would have "filled the largest church in the city every night for two consecutive weeks." But he had come as the property of a speculator, and the Cincinnati public, by staying at home, "expressed in a manner as decided as it is severe, their opinion of the course the gentleman has pursued."

Beecher defended himself in a letter published in the *Gazette* on November 15, 1855:

In regard to the charge of the Cincinnati *Gazette*, that I had broken an engagement of two seasons in that city, I pronounce the charge unfounded and untrue. And no gentleman having official connection, or having had such connection, with the Young Men's Association, will choose to assert any such thing over his own proper name.

In answer to the accusation that Wells was a mere speculator, Beecher declared that his agent was "an upright Christian gentleman, a member of the Presbyterian Church, active and useful." As for the fifty-cent admission charge, Beecher asserted that "the price is not an unusual one, nor is it unusual for the avails of a lecture or a course of lectures to go to the lecturer and not to local associations."

On the evening of October 23, Beecher lectured at Neil's New Hall in Columbus. The editor of the *Daily Capital City Fact* (October 18, 1855) had prepared the city's lecture public for Beecher's appearance with an editorial entitled "The Lecture Monopoly." This correspondent protested that it had become the practice of some of the country's most distinguished and talented lecturers "to hire themselves out to some *Barnum* for the lecture season at a gross sum to be carried around the country." As the sole object of the speculator was to make money, he would not hesitate to demand an exorbitant admission fee for his "show." Thus Beecher "was made to play cat's paw to put money in the pocket of a heartless speculator," and the people of Columbus would serve the public interest if they would "decline the honor of contributing to Mr. W's *missionary* box."

This newspaper's review of Beecher's discourse provides ample evidence that Columbus citizens quite agreed with the editor's opinions of the lecture monopoly:

Last evening this gentleman read, very indistinctly, to forty persons, all told, a lecture on "Beauty." He had advertised to read his lecture on "Patriotism," but after discovering the want of patriotism in our citizens, in the gross receipts of *fourteen dollars and fifty cents,* he concluded to treat them to a desertation on the love of the beautiful, not inaptly supposing, that "money" was an article possessing peculiar charms in this locality.

Beecher did not read very well, "and who could—to a beggarly account of empty boxes?" At the very outset he "called up the mourners" to draw close around the stand so that he could see them. Then, "very incoherently at times," he delivered his lecture to his "woefully slim auditory." No doubt Beecher's mission as a lecturer was a noble one, but the name of a "traveling showman" had been attached to him, and, "until the name of Barnum has become obsolete, his highest and most worthy endeavor to ... ameliorate the condition of man, will in a measure prove futile, proportionately as the public has resolved to be humbugged no longer."

In his Cincinnati letter, Beecher commented briefly on his visit to Columbus:

Of Columbus, O., I have nothing to say. I spent a pleasant day at the Neil House with a circle of much-loved friends; and if, the next day, any of its citizens were found with heretical notions they certainly were not infected by coming to hear my lecture. The Secretary of the Association there, who wrote me a letter, will one day be an older man and I trust a wiser one.

At Cleveland, where he lectured on October 24, Beecher met the full wrath of the press. The editor of the *Herald* (October 22, 1855), maintaining that Beecher broke an engagement with the Cleveland Library Association to deliver this lecture, exhorted the public "to effectually put a damper upon all such *gouging* designs of showmen, by staying away, and thus leaving this clerical imitator of the example set by traveling curiosities to discourse to bare walls, and the exhibitor, Mr. Wells, to pay expenses out of his own pocket."

On the day of the lecture, Wells and several of Beecher's Cleveland friends posted handbills which announced that the lecturer would vindicate himself from the slanders of the Western press. The *Herald* called this action "A Trick Worthy of Barnum," adding that "for this privilege of setting Mr. Beecher right before the public, this Mr. Wells *charges that public only fifty cents per head*. Viva la humbug!!"

The announcements of Beecher's lecture were an undignified mixture of robust Western humor and sharp editorial temper:

GRAND LITERARY CIRCUS

Mr. Wells, of Chicago . . . . Manager
Unparalleled Attraction, for One Night Only
The Manager announces that, at an expense of $125 per
night, he has effected an engagement with that distinguished
individual, the

REV. HENRY WARD BEECHER,

Who will make his *only appearance* in Cleveland, on Wednesday evening, Oct. 24th. The public are requested to contribute fifty cents each towards paying the celebrated performer more money for an hour's talking than an intelligent
mechanic can make by *nine hundred hour's labor*, in three
months.[5]

Mr. Wells, the Chicago showman, will let his fifty-cent lion
roar at Concert Hall, to-night. The smooth walls of that Hall
are excellent for the reverberations of the lion's voice, and
we hope there will be few woolen coats and silk dresses to
deaden it.[6]

The newspaper editors had their way. According to the *Herald*,
only a hundred and four persons attended Beecher's lecture on
"Patriotism," and there were not more than sixty paid admissions.
Beecher's humiliation was complete. He attempted to salvage
something of his reputation in a letter printed by the *Cleveland Plain
Dealer* on October 25. He denied that he had broken an agreement
to lecture before the Cleveland Library Association.[7] He upheld the
character of Wells, whom he described as a merchant and president
of Chicago's Metropolitan Library Union. Commenting on the
fifty-cent admission price, Beecher wrote:

[5] *Daily Clevelander*, reprinted in *Sandusky Daily Commercial Register*,
October 24, 1855.
[6] *Cleveland Morning Leader*, October 24, 1855.
[7] The correspondence of the Cleveland Library Association is reviewed in
the *Cleveland Herald*, October 27, 1855. Most of the letters are communica-
tions between the secretaries of the Cleveland and the Chicago Library Associations. The Chicago secretary talked with Beecher in the East and attempted
to make arrangements for lectures in both Cleveland and Chicago. He reached
no satisfactory agreement and wrote that Beecher's treatment of him was
"rather shabby." It is clear that Beecher broke no promises to lecture associations
in the West. He simply did not reply to their invitations.

I think not only that fifty cents (except for lectures devoted to some charitable end in the community, and where the fee may be regarded as a contribution to some public end) is too much, but that it would be better to charge less than twenty-five cents. It would answer the ends of *popular education* better were lectures to be afforded for a shilling, and this could be done with profit to the managers if Halls were large enough.

On this occasion Beecher declared that, because of his agreement with Wells, he had no control over the admission price for the lecture. Later, in his Cincinnati letter, he defended the fifty-cent admission as a just one.[8]

On October 25, the day of the lecturer's departure, the *Cleveland Herald* pointed out that in the largest cities in Ohio—Cincinnati, Columbus, and Cleveland—Beecher had "had the pleasure of addressing 449 men, women, and children." But if he had come to the state as his respect for himself should have demanded, he would have had audiences in these cities "of many hundreds, night after night." As for Wells, he had perhaps learned that "clergymen are poor showing stock," and that "the people of Ohio are not quite so green as he took them to be."

In November, 1856, Beecher returned to Cincinnati and delivered two lectures before the First Congregational Church Society. His success was almost without precedent in the city's lecture annals. The debacle of the previous year was completely forgotten by the lecture public. Describing the crowd that assembled to hear "The Ministry of the Beautiful," the editor of the *Commercial* (November 17, 1856) asserted that he had "not observed such a multitude, excited and swarming about any place of public meeting in this town since the Buchanan Convention, when the same ground presented a similar scene."

Beecher, "dressed in black, his coat buttoned tightly up, displaying to advantage his portly proportions in a style rather military than clerical," completely captivated his audience with the beauty and power of his eloquence.

---

[8] The Cincinnati letter, written about three weeks after the Ohio lectures, was much less apologetic than the Cleveland letter. In the former, Beecher declared that the attitude of Ohio's lecture associations was "arrogant avarice."

Twenty-three hundred people jammed Smith and Nixon's Hall to hear the lecture on "Patriotism." The audience, eager to see and hear the great pulpit orator, sprawled over the stage and stood in the aisles and doorways. Hundreds more, unable to gain admission, were sent away disappointed. Henry Ward Beecher had returned to the West in triumph.

CHAPTER
XIII

THEODORE PARKER: *Scholarly Divine*

I

THE ELOQUENT pastor of Boston's Twenty-Eighth Congregational Society was one of the first of New England's fiery divines to follow the lyceum circuit beyond the Alleghenies.[1] In 1852, the year of his first appearance in Ohio, Parker's reputation as a courageous, outspoken thinker was well known to the Western public. His pronouncements as a minister had often been reprinted in Ohio's newspapers; his opinions on the mediation of Christ, his disbelief in miraculous revelation, and his sermons on temperance, slavery, and woman's rights had made him, to some Western minds, one of the most notorious of New England's freethinking clergymen.

As the forces for and against slavery slowly gathered themselves during the decade preceding the Civil War, the propriety of antislavery discussion in the pulpit was a topic which aroused nationwide comment. The question was debated in every lyceum in the land, and antislavery sermons delivered by Parker or Henry Ward Beecher were frequently followed by accusations of treason and disunion in the Democratic press. Westerners who knew Parker chiefly through the newspaper accounts of his sermons and his passionate orations in Faneuil Hall against Webster's Seventh of March Speech or the Fugitive Slave Law, and who expected him to repeat his incisive opinions on the platform, were often surprised by the calm, intellectual quality of his lectures.

In announcing "The Progress of Mankind" and "The False and True Idea of a Gentleman," the *Cincinnati Gazette* (November 3, 1852) predicted that Parker's lectures not only would "excite a good deal of interest among the literary portion of our citizens" but also

---

[1] For a general discussion of Parker as a lecturer, see Henry Steele Commager, *Theodore Parker* (Boston: Little, Brown and Company, 1936), pp. 144–150.

would offer sentiments to which "there would be a very general dissent." But as Parker was "undoubtedly a man of great ability," his opinions, however offensive, would be "worthy of consideration."

"The Progress of Mankind" contained no inflammatory statements, Parker choosing to avoid any controversy over his "peculiar views." A correspondent of the *Cleveland Herald* (November 9, 1852) wrote from Cincinnati that Parker's audience, accustomed to hearing lectures read from manuscript, was delighted when he strode to the front of the platform and delivered his discourse "with all the freshness and added interest of extemporaneous speaking." He impressed "a crowded audience of the best intelligence of Cincinnati" as a "man of great directness, remarkable affluence of thought," and "learning of universal variety." In appearance, Parker was "intellectual and scholarly, and his elocution reminds you, in some particulars, of Emerson."

On Sunday, November 7, Parker delivered two sermons to "very crowded audiences" at Moncure Conway's Unitarian Church. The *Gazette* testily branded these discourses "a vigorous attack on the prevailing opinions in regard to the Godhead, to Christ, and upon most other received views on religious topics." Indeed this correspondent had supposed that, because of Parker's objectionable religious opinions, "Sunday would not have found a Christian church open to him, or professing Christians amongst his hearers." But the "immense audience that thronged the inside and outside of the Unitarian Church" proved that "these are progressive days."

"The False and True Idea of a Gentleman" apparently evoked no comments from Cincinnati's journalists, but when this lecture was delivered before the Cleveland Mercantile Library Association the *Herald* observed that Parker's large audience generously applauded the discourse, "abounding as it did with lofty and noble ideas, interspersed with flashes of humor and satire on the principal follies of the age."[2] The editor of the *True Democrat* (November 11, 1852)

---

[2] November 10, 1852. The title of this lecture was usually reported by the press as "The True and False Idea of a Gentleman." In his manuscript Lyceum Diary, Parker calls the lecture "The False and True Idea of a Gentleman." Parker's manuscript Lyceum Diary is used with the kind permission of the Massachusetts Historical Society.

withheld his usual political antagonism toward abolitionists when he declared that "this eloquent, finished, truthful Lecture" could never be forgotten by those who heard it. Parker ranked among the great thinkers of the age, and his lecture possessed "a chaste, easy and flowing style, a lurking, pungent, but apparently unsought sarcasm and wit."

Parker occupied Cleveland's Melodeon again on January 12, 1854, when he delivered "The Progress of Mankind" to a "crowded house." The *Herald* reported that "He is about as graceful a speaker as Horace Greeley, and yet his peculiarities secured the earnest attention of his audience through a very long lecture."[3] This editor made a further, and more ill-tempered, comment on Parker's lecture on January 25. After hearing William Henry Channing's "Great Men and the Elements of Greatness," given before the Cleveland Library Association on January 24, the reviewer pointed out that "Mr. Channing is not an orator, yet he is eloquent. His lecture was in strong contrast with the rigmarole, disjointed, visionary '*talk*' of the man who is so deeply in love with himself, Theodore Parker."

In October, 1854, the Ohio Mechanics' Institute, in Cincinnati, presented a course of weekly lectures on "American Slavery." The project was a money-making scheme, as the offering of political topics by lecture associations was considered to be in poor taste and detrimental to the true cultural purpose of the lecture system. The speakers announced included Parker, William Lloyd Garrison, Frederick Douglass, and Wendell Phillips, all of whom were calculated to attract large crowds and rich profits to the Mechanics' Institute.

Parker delivered the introductory lecture of the course on October 19. His subject, "The Condition and Prospects of Slavery in America," drew a large and "oddly assorted" audience, "a considerable number of negroes being present, and also a delegation of gentlemen from Covington." According to the *Commercial* (October 20, 1854) the lecture was "principally made up of statistics, by which it

---

[3] January 13, 1854. Although Greeley was notoriously poor as a speaker, his editorial fame and bold opinions made him a favorite with Ohio's lecture public. In the fall of 1853 he had campaigned strenuously in Cleveland and Cuyahoga County for General Winfield Scott, the Whig presidential nominee who was defeated by the Locofoco candidate, Franklin Pierce.

was attempted to be shown that the South is the master of the North." Parker dwelt upon the effects of slavery on society, morality, and industry. As a remedy for slavery he proposed that the slaves be "purchased by the general government."

Parker's Ohio journey in 1854 took him also to Toledo, Dayton, and Yellow Springs, where he visited Horace Mann, president of Antioch College, and lectured before the students on "The Condition, Character and Prospects of America."[4] Parker's generosity and his esteem for Mann were illustrated by his returning his forty-dollar lecture fee as a gift to the college.[5]

During these early lecture trips Parker developed small liking for the West. He observed "a certain largeness to everything"—plains, trees, pumpkins, apples, swine, and men. In Ohio he marveled at a huge hog weighing 2,150 pounds. But in addition to largeness there was "a certain *coarseness of fibre* also noticeable in all things." Here were ugliness and squalor in sharp contrast with the neatness, beauty, and refinement of New England. The climate was raw and unhealthful and seemed to sap the energy of the inhabitants. "The men look sickly, yellow, and flabby," Parker wrote in 1854. "The women are tall and bony, their hair lank, their faces thin and flabby-cheeked." His conclusion was that "the West deteriorates Americans."[6]

2

UNLIKE many of the orators who spoke before Western lyceums in the 1850's, Parker was more concerned with popular education than with financial profits for himself. "The business of lecturing," he once wrote, "is an original American contrivance for educating the people. The world has nothing like it. In it are combined the best things of

[4] Manuscript Lyceum Diary. Manuscript Diary of Maria L. Moore (Antioch College Library).
[5] According to the manuscript Lyceum Diary, Parker's fees for individual lectures ranged from $30.00 at Toledo and Dayton to $50.00 at Cleveland and Cincinnati. After deducting expenses and gifts, he had net earnings of $310.15 for twelve lectures in the West in 1854. In addition to his Ohio lectures, Parker appeared in Pittsburgh, Indianapolis, and Adrian, Michigan.
[6] Commager, p. 147. John Weiss, *Life and Correspondence of Theodore Parker* (2. vols.; New York: Appleton and Company, 1864), I, 327.

the Church, and of the College, with some of the fun of the theatre."[7]
The pleasant excitement of lecturing before curious audiences in the
West and the assurance that he was spreading truth and knowledge
more than compensated for the hardships of his winter journeys and
his reluctance to leave his Boston congregation.

In the season of 1855–56, during one of Parker's most ambitious
Western trips, he delivered nine lectures and two sermons in twelve
days among the communities of northern Ohio.[8] This tiring schedule
illustrates Parker's devotion to the lyceum's aim of "doing good," as
none of the lecture fees was more than $25.00. His first performance
was on November 7, 1855, at Hudson, where he spoke to the students of Western Reserve College.[9] The next evening he gave "The
Progress of Mankind" in Ravenna. The *Portage Sentinel* (November 10, 1855) commended Parker as "a model lecturer." "There is
no attempt at display, no flourish, no declamation. He is plain, frank
and candid."

A "large audience" heard this lecture in Salem. The editor of the
Columbiana County Republican (November 14, 1855) was pleased
because Parker's oratory was "not boisterous." He depended for
effect upon "the merits of his subject" and an "argumentative manner" and did not display "any of the spasmodic efforts and exertions
of the body, so common among speakers who are compelled, for
want of ability, to attract attention by noise."

At Wooster, Parker's declaration that "the progress of mankind"
had been hindered by slavery, that "monument of misdirected industry," aroused the ire of the antiabolitionist editor of the *Wayne
County Democrat* (November 15, 1855). This critic wished to "warn
democrats and Union men, that it looks like a Massachusetts Abolition Disunion trick to get their abominable and fanatical ideas before

---

[7] Commager, p. 144. Weiss, I, 304.

[8] Two additional lectures, scheduled at Cleveland, November 6, 1855, and
at Sandusky, November 16, 1855, were not given. Manuscript Lyceum Diary.
At Cleveland his lecture negotiations apparently were not completed; at Sandusky he disappointed an audience of four hundred when he failed to arrive
in time to lecture.

[9] Manuscript "Minutes of the Phi Delta Literary Society" (Western Reserve
University Library).

the people, under the plea of Moral Lectures." The people should "not be humbugged by any abolition tricks" or "party fanaticism" aimed at "sowing the seeds of disunion broadcast in the land."

The "very crowded" Akron audience which attended "The False and True Idea of a Gentleman" expected to hear a fiery orator. "Instead of such an one," reported the *Summit County Beacon* (November 21, 1855), "was a plain and quiet man, plainly clad and not extremely prepossessing; concealing a small keen eye behind a pair of spectacles; making little more use of his hands than was consistent with profound repose of manner, and barely raising his voice above the conversational pitch." His attempt "to gibbet 'cod fish aristocracy'" and "satirise proud ignorance" was entirely successful.

For two hours Parker "enchained his audience" at Toledo "with illustrations of the wonderful strides that mankind had taken in civilization." Parker's power as a lecturer resulted from "the easy composure of his manner, the thoroughness with which his ideas are matured in his own mind, his mastery over forms of expression." Though "pretending to none of the graces of oratory nor mere elegancies of diction," he was "one of the most powerful and instructive speakers" the people of Toledo had ever heard.[10]

Parker's success upon Ohio's lyceum platforms was greatly enhanced by the sincerity and earnestness of his delivery, his manner of talking "like an apostle who has a great mission to fulfil." Here was a man with "a boldness about his speech," a determination to say what he thought "without any unnecessary circumlocution or whipping the devil round a stump." Indeed, except where political issues were involved, Parker and the other "eccentric but brilliant" orators from the East were likely to meet with less adverse criticism in the West than they were accustomed to receive in New England. The pioneers' long struggle against the hardships of the frontier had given to the Western mind an independent spirit and a curiosity to hear all sides of a question. To Westerners, the distinction between moral right

---

[10] *Daily Toledo Blade*, November 19, 1855. On Sunday, November 18, Parker delivered two sermons in Toledo: "False Rules of Action and False Guides of Conduct" and "Overruling Providence." Both were attended by large audiences.

and wrong was not so clearly marked as it was to New Englanders.[11]
There were doubtless many Ohio people who were prepared to find
offense in Parker's opinions, but the newspaper reviews of the day
suggest that among his hearers was a goodly number of independent
Western citizens who were inclined to agree that "Mr. Parker speaks,
as he believes, the whole truth, caring little where it hits. His fear-
lessness is grand. He stands up before earth and heaven a true man."[12]

---

[11] This "moral instability" of the Western mind was disturbing to many
Eastern people, and especially to the New England supporters of the Society
for the Promotion of Collegiate and Theological Education at the West. ". . . we
want principles of stability," declared a speaker before the society in 1846; "we
want a system of permanent forces; we want deep, strong, and constant influences, that shall take from the changefulness and excitability of the western
mind, by giving it the tranquility of depth, and shall protect it from delusive
and fitful impulses, by enduing it with a calm, profound, and pure reason."
Albert Barnes, "Plea in Behalf of the Western Colleges," *Third Annual Report
of the Society for the Promotion of Collegiate and Theological Education at
the West* (New York: J. F. Trow, 1847), pp. 12–13.

[12] *Daily Toledo Blade*, January 16, 1854.

CHAPTER
XIV

OLIVER WENDELL HOLMES: *Literary Jester*

HOLMES WAS not, like Emerson or Giles, a lecturer who startled his audiences with "profound truths."[1] "I am forced to study effects," he once said to Emerson. "You and others may be able to combine popular effect with the exhibition of truths. I cannot. I am compelled to study effects."[2] Holmes viewed the lyceum lecture as a means of spreading knowledge among the plain citizens of America. "A thoroughly popular lecture," declared the Autocrat of the Breakfast Table, "ought to have nothing in it which five hundred people cannot all take in a flash, just as it is uttered." And, he added, "I tell you the *average* intellect of five hundred persons, taken as they come, is not very high."

The opening of Smith and Nixon's new music and lecture hall was the occasion of Holmes's only lecture visit to Ohio. In September, 1855, the management, in conjunction with the Cincinnati Young Men's Mercantile Library Association, arranged an elaborate program presenting "James E. Murdock,[3] Esq., the celebrated Tragedian, and Professor Oliver Wendell Holmes, the distinguished Poet and Lecturer." Murdoch, from Warren County, Ohio, was the most famous tragedian of his day, and for more than twenty years his dramatic readings were much in demand by Western lyceums.

The program of events was advertised as follows:

September 4 Murdoch—Dramatic and Miscellaneous Readings and Recitations, consisting of Selections from Shakespeare, in Tragedy and Comedy, Byron, Scott, and other Poets, and humorous selections from Dickens.

---

[1] For a discussion of Holmes as a lecturer see Eleanor M. Tilton, *Amiable Autocrat, A Biography of Dr. Oliver Wendell Holmes* (New York: Henry Schuman, 1947), pp. 203–218.

[2] *Journals of Ralph Waldo Emerson*, VIII, 424.

[3] Newspaper writers frequently spelled Murdoch's name with a "k."

September 5 Holmes—"Lectures and Lecturing."
September 6 Holmes—"Physical Life in New Eng-
           land."
September 7 Holmes—"The Poetry of Keats."[4]

The newspaper reports of Holmes's Cincinnati lectures reveal surprisingly little enthusiasm. He was appreciated for his learning and his literary reputation; he was complimented for his wit and genial spirit. But his appearance in the West was not attended by the rush of lecture-goers who greeted Park Benjamin and John G. Saxe. Holmes came to Ohio on short notice, and his lecture subjects offered little promise of any display of his famous wit. "Lectures and Lecturing," the only humorous discourse in the series, was marred by inclement weather and a slim audience. "Physical Life in New England" "touched on the border of science," while "The Poetry of Keats" was "purely literary." Holmes's drawing power in Cincinnati proved to be much less impressive than that of Murdoch.

On the evening of September 4 the new hall was packed by two thousand Cincinnatians who had come to hear the stirring recitations of James E. Murdoch and to admire the costly decorations of the lecture auditorium. Promptly at eight o'clock Murdoch was introduced to the audience, who, filled with the genial spirit of the occasion, greeted him with hearty applause. The tragedian responded by announcing that he had chosen as his first selection "The American Flag" by Joseph Rodman Drake. The events that followed were of a surprising character.

Murdoch recited a few verses and then suddenly stopped, put his hand to his head, and declared, "There are times when my nervous irritability overcomes my memory. Accustomed as I have been to facing audiences in fictitious characters, yet this scene comes too near home to me; and although I would not venture to say I am frightened, yet I feel exceedingly nervous."

He then tried a reading from Shakespeare, "Hotspur's Account of the Fop." But once again, after a few lines, his memory left him

---

[4] *Cincinnati Daily Gazette*, September 1, 1855. Single tickets sold for 50 cents; course tickets admitting one person, $1.50; course tickets admitting a gentleman and lady, $2.50.

completely. Murdoch stood for a moment as though dazed, and finally said, "Ladies and gentlemen, I am compelled to suspend this reading by a nervous irritability which affects my memory."

The audience was stunned by these strange proceedings. As Murdoch remained standing on the platform a gentleman in the audience "rose and suggested that they suspend for half an hour to enable him to recover." But Murdoch replied, "I would not like to keep this audience waiting. The sensation is an unaccountable one which struck me on first entering the Hall. I feel my mind wandering."[5]

It was ten minutes past eight when Murdoch was led off the stage. A physician was called for, and it was soon announced that the tragedian, though not seriously ill, would be unable to continue his recitations. As the audience milled about, comparing diagnoses of the attack and conjecturing on the prospects of further entertainment, the announcement came that Dr. Holmes had arrived in the city and had been sent for. At half past eight Holmes appeared, the soot of railroad travel still upon him, and was promptly hurried to the stage.

Holmes began by expressing his regret at the circumstances which had brought him before his audience. He felt that he could only inadequately fill the place of Murdoch. As he had expected to make only three appearances in Cincinnati, he had brought only three finished lectures with him. However, he had the draft of a lecture on "Byron and Moore," which he would read. This discourse "was imperfect and full of pencil marks," since he had not had time to alter or revise it. If his audience observed any defects "his apology was, that he had also discovered them, and made a pencil mark at the very place, designing when he had time to make it a great deal better."

Holmes sketched for his hearers the early life and loves of Byron. Turning his attention to Byron's poetry and its reception he declared that "Childe Harold" "came ringing down from the placid firmament like the shield of Paris cast into the city of Ilium." Exactly at that moment, fifteen minutes before nine o'clock, "a glass shade over a burner in the ceiling, just in front of the stage, having been broken

---

[5] *Ibid.*, September 5, 1855.

by the heat, fell, a large piece of it striking Mr. Wm. Green on the head." This incident caused considerable excitement until the audience was assured that Mr. Green's head was neither burned nor otherwise damaged. Holmes then completed his first Ohio lecture by supporting the view that Byron, despite his immoral qualities, was the foremost English poet of the nineteenth century and by reviewing the early works of Moore, whom he described as the greatest master of lyrics in his time.

On the next evening a severe storm held the audience at "Lectures and Lecturing," one of Holmes's most amusing and popular lectures, to fewer than three hundred persons. In his introduction Holmes commented on Cincinnati's fine buildings and his pleasure at seeing the river and the landing. He was delighted by the greenness of Ohio's vegetation, which surpassed that of New England, and by the musical song of its locusts. The strength and enterprising character of Western mosquitoes had also "touched and struck in upon him."

Holmes said of the lyceum lecture that its true purpose was to enlighten men, that it held many advantages over book-reading, and that it should not consume more than an hour in delivery. It was mankind's fondness for menageries that brought many people to see the "lions" of the lecturing profession. Factual lectures were the easiest to write, and those which discussed principles were the most difficult. Audiences in the East and West were pretty much alike, as "their silences and applause came always in the same places." The *Enquirer* reported that the lecture "was happily arranged, embracing sufficient variety to keep the audience interested and in a very good humor." As a lyceum speaker Holmes was "good natured, piquant, truthful, and in no respect dull or prosy."

The hall was not full when Holmes delivered "Physical Life in New England," although the audience was larger than it had been on the preceding night. The lecture contrasted physical life in New England and Old England. Holmes's medical knowledge colored his description of the physical attributes of dwellers in the two regions and the effect of climate on human health. At his final lecture, "The Poetry of Keats," Holmes thanked his Cincinnati audience for "their

kind attention to him." He had much enjoyed his visit to the West.
He regretted that it had been "hard to form a programme" for his
three lectures, but he "had no course comprising just that number,
and his invitation here, was too short to prepare one." His treatment of Keats's life and poetry was well received by an audience
which "nearly filled" the lecture hall.

CHAPTER
XV

PARK BENJAMIN: *Platform Poet*

I

AMONG the Eastern lecturers who endeavored both to entertain and instruct their audiences was the New York humorous poet and recalcitrant editor of *New World*, who enjoyed a remarkable vogue in the West in 1852.[1] Benjamin owed much of this vogue to his mediocrity. He was "popular" in a sense that the cultural lecturers could never be. He repeated the commonplace moral sentiments that the people never tire of hearing and made them the more palatable by presenting them in undistinguished rhyming couplets garnished with satire and wit. He was a high-grade entertainer whose place on the platform was equidistant between Emerson and the Swiss Bell Ringers.

In January, 1852, Benjamin was introduced to the citizens of Cleveland as a "distinguished literary man, poet and highly popular lecturer" and "the author of many enviable additions to American Literature." He had come from Detroit, where he had "taken the City of the Straits by storm," to deliver a course before Cleveland's Forest City Lyceum.

There was a full audience at Empire Hall to hear Benjamin's poem entitled "Fashion," a "keen and cutting satire upon the follies and foibles of fashionable life." As a literary work it had little merit, declared the *Herald* (January 5, 1852), "but as a satire its hits are piquant, and truthful, and when aided by the masterly delivery of the author, must convulse the listeners." Benjamin spoke "with great clearness and rapidity, and unquestionably makes a finer thing of his own poetry, by repeating it himself, than any one could do for him."

---

[1] For a general discussion of Benjamin as a lecturer see Merle M. Hoover, *Park Benjamin: Poet and Editor* (New York: Columbia University Press, 1948), pp. 164–183.

Benjamin's ability to "convulse the listeners" was the mark of his popularity. In announcing "Intellectual and Popular Amusements" the *Herald* was content to term Benjamin a "distinguished *caterer* to the laughing community." After hearing the lecture this critic concluded that Benjamin "possesses rare tact in popularizing every topic he discusses." The discourse "gratified a large audience and shortened up all the long faces assembled." The *True Democrat* (January 10, 1852) added that if Benjamin did nothing for the rest of his life but deliver this lecture, which aimed to show that "American people have too few Holidays and amusements," he "would do great service."

"Fashion" was read before the Franklin Lyceum in Columbus on January 5, 1852. The *Ohio State Journal* reported that "the strokes of wit, sarcasm and humor were pert, irresistible and full of real wisdom," and "everybody seemed delighted."

The success of his first Ohio visit encouraged Benjamin to return in the autumn. Again entering the state from the west, he appeared in Toledo and Cleveland before traveling south to Cincinnati and Dayton. His lecture on "Matrimony," read before the Toledo Young Men's Association on November 20, was intended to show the responsibilities of marriage. Benjamin was complimented by the *Blade* because "in all his jokes, witticisms, and humorous observations, the lecturer never once forgot the importance, the dignity, and the delicacy of the marriage relation."

"Matrimony" evoked a strong protest from a female correspondent who signed herself "Tabitha Lutestring." This lady declared that Benjamin, and, for that matter, the editor of the *Blade*, took a naïve view of matrimony. She contended that the lecturer underestimated the importance of a maid's knowing thoroughly the character of her prospective husband. The marriages of Benjamin's lectures were made too easily. Tabitha understood the character of men. She had personally refused six offers of marriage, and she got much pleasure from the knowledge that, of her six spurned suitors, four had become drunkards, one a wealthy tyrant, and one a bankrupt. She therefore advised young women to be wary and, in preference to unhappy marriage with the wrong man, to "live as I have done, and intend to do, until the right man comes, a cheerful, contented, happy old maid."

The height of Benjamin's success in Ohio was reached at Cincinnati. On November 30 he delivered "the first of the course of lectures before the first of Literary institutions—the Young Men's Mercantile Library Association." When the *Gazette*'s reporters reached Smith and Nixon's Hall, it was jammed "with the largest audience we ever saw assembled within doors in this city." More than five hundred people went away because they were unable to find even standing room. Benjamin was described as "a fine looking man, considerably under the ordinary height, stoutly built" and having "a tolerably well shaped head, and a pleasant and rather intellectual countenance." Though neither brilliant nor profound, his lecture was "well written" and "well received."[2]

"Fashion," Benjamin's second Cincinnati lecture, was heard by nineteen hundred people. "The Poem, as a literary effort, was good," declared the *Gazette* (December 3, 1852), "but we prize its moral effect still higher." The "weaknesses and excrescences of fashionable life" were boldly attacked with pointed satire.

Benjamin read his poem "Money: a Love" at the reopening of Cincinnati's Melodeon, which had been newly decorated. The Melodeon was a "magnificent Hall, with its new and gorgeous adornments, its glittering and costly chandelier, its rich frescoes and beautiful paintings, illuminated by more than one hundred gas-burners." The announced program for the evening was a pretentious one and was symptomatic of the kind of entertainment that eventually threatened to crowd the cultural lecturers from the platform. In addition to Benjamin, "the most accomplished and exquisite Lecturer of the day," a ballad singer and "two charming young ladies and exquisite musical performers" entertained the audience. Despite this array of talent the Melodeon was only "about three-fourths full." Benjamin's lecture, according to the *Gazette* (December 7, 1852), "was the best

---

[2] December 1, 1852. Benjamin again delivered "Intellectual and Popular Amusements," a discussion of various forms of amusement such as books, foreign travel, and costume parties.

he has delivered in Cincinnati, and drew down frequent and hearty applause."

When Benjamin visited Dayton, the *Journal* (December 6, 1852) was delighted "to see Clegg's beautiful Hall affording a higher grade of entertainments than those furnished by Bell Ringers and Ballet Troupes." "Fashion" was "one of the notable things of the season," while "Money: a Love" was marked by an attractive style and "the charm of originality."

2

BENJAMIN returned to Ohio in 1855 with a new stock of wit and an old collection of moral platitudes that too often passed for wisdom. He did not undertake the rigorous life of the traveling lecturer because he was moved by a desire to spread culture and knowledge. Lecturing was to Benjamin a purely commercial venture; he had learned during his lecture tours of 1852 that the way to acquire the Western dollar was to make its owner laugh. He also knew the power of advertising. In the fall of 1854 he had run the following notice in the Cincinnati newspapers:

> THE LECTURE SEASON. — Managers of Lyceums, Institutes and Associations, desirous of securing the services of the subscriber, are requested to address him by letter, during the months of October and November.
>
> Park Benjamin
> *Guilford, Connecticut*

When he arrived in Cincinnati early in November, 1855, Benjamin lost no time in promulgating that he would "make Cincinnati his headquarters till the first of December, and be willing to make engagements to lecture in Ohio and the neighboring States." He had brought with him two new lectures, "Americanisms," a satire of the country's social follies, and "True Independence," a long patriotic poem. "Americanisms" was enthusiastically received by Ohio audiences; capacity audiences were the rule. In Columbus, said the *Ohio State Journal* (November 29, 1855), Benjamin was met by "the largest and most intelligent audience we have ever seen assembled on such an occasion." The lecture "abounded in happy hits at the vices and follies of the times, and discriminated properly between the good and bad traits of our Americanisms." The *Springfield Non-pareil* (December 1, 1855) called the lecture "a masterly production" and Benjamin a man of "noble appearance" with "a fine, intellectual head and a pleasing countenance." The correspondent of the *Cleveland Plain Dealer* (December 4, 1855) declared that "the wit and sarcasm of the speaker had full scope in the subject chosen, and the good hits at the weak points in our national character produced a constant succession of explosions of laughter."

The presentation of "True Independence" came near being Benjamin's undoing. First read at Cincinnati, the poem was attacked by the *Commercial* (November 17, 1855) as being nothing more than "pointless twaddle." And in the comments of the critic was a spirit of dissent against the reception of Eastern lecturers, an incipient dissatisfaction that was an omen of things to come. The people of Cincinnati were "accustomed to set a pretty high value upon whatever, in the literary line, comes from the East." But it was time to exercise a severer judgment on the "Yankee lecturers." Though they usually produced something "showy or solid," a distinction ought to be made between mere display and genuine worth. As a lecture, Benjamin's effort was empty and futile.

At Dayton, where Benjamin tried "True Independence" once more, the *Gazette* (November 29, 1855) bluntly called the poem a mere collection of rhymed exercises, and "not very good exercises at that." But the greatest defect of the poem was its "lack of anything valuable or original in its reflections and observations." It "imparted no instruction"; most of it "was occupied in enforcing morals, some of which were false, and the rest extremely common place."

Ohio audiences heard no more of "True Independence." The poem illustrated well enough that Benjamin's province was that of the entertainer. His attempts to make his audience think were certain to result in failure. He was not one of those lecturers who "go about saying sage and thoughtful truths, in a sober and positive manner." Benjamin's true mission, declared the *Sandusky Commercial Register* (December 8, 1855), was "to follow in the wake to arouse the people into a smile again, and so his work is not a bad one if it is not wonderfully wise."

3

WHEN BENJAMIN returned to Ohio in 1857 he brought his satirical, humorous materials with him and left his thoughtful productions at home. Even so, this final journey ended in a bitter quarrel with the Cincinnati Young Men's Mercantile Library Association and Benjamin's ultimate humiliation and defeat in the Ohio law courts. In arranging a lecture program for the winter of 1857–58 the Mercantile Library Association offered two separate courses; the first lecture series was given in November and December, 1857, and the second series was announced to begin on January 19, 1858, with a lecture by Park Benjamin. The invitation to the New York lecturer was made in September, 1857, "at the request of a friend of Mr. Benjamin." An appointment was readily secured, Benjamin agreeing to speak, for a fee of a hundred dollars, before the association in Cincinnati on January 19.

On November 26, 1857, Benjamin appeared unexpectedly in Cincinnati and announced that he would deliver "on his own account" a satirical poem at Smith and Nixon's Hall. An audience of twelve hundred listened to "Hard Times," a "pointed satire upon the financial and fashionable social customs of the day." The *Gazette* (November 27, 1857) pointed out that the size of the audience "was a little remarkable on the eve of Thanksgiving," especially for "an independent lecture delivered under the auspices of no association." No other lecture of the season had "drawn any thing like the audience" which greeted Benjamin.

The subject matter of "Hard Times" was conspicuously appropriate, as the country was suffering at the time from the economic stress of the Panic of 1857. The poem was "full of withering sarcasm, vinegary jibes, and racy puns, which hit right and left without mercy, —chiefly at those honorable members of commercial and banking circles, who take advantage of Hard Times to fail with their property secured to their wives."[3]

---

[3] *Cincinnati Daily Commercial*, November 27, 1857.

On November 28 Benjamin repeated his lecture on "Hard Times" at Smith and Nixon's Hall. His audience numbered about six hundred. Then on November 30 he read his poem on "Fashion" in a benefit program sponsored by the Cincinnati Home of the Friendless. The audience dwindled to four hundred for this performance.

The Mercantile Library Association was somewhat bewildered by this succession of appearances by Benjamin, who was under contract to lecture under its sponsorship. Some members and friends of the association supposed that the lecture committee had altered its arrangements with Benjamin and had sponsored the recitations on November 26 and 28. When the lecture committee denied any such action, the association's perplexity turned to sudden anger. In giving his three Cincinnati lectures, Benjamin had succeeded in "making himself decidedly a stale article in the lecture market," and had deprived his scheduled January performance before the association of any attraction of novelty. Since the association had agreed to pay Benjamin a hundred dollars for his January lecture, a small audience would jeopardize the organization's financial profits, while Benjamin would be secure from loss.

The association quickly made public its resentment. On December 1, at the lecture of B. P. Shillaber, the Boston author of the popular *Life and Sayings of Mrs. Partington* (1854), the president of the association told the audience that the impression that Benjamin had been lecturing under the auspices of the association was erroneous. The association "had had nothing to do with Benjamin's lecturing," and, what was more, the New York poet "would not lecture in the next course of the Association." This last statement was warmly applauded by the audience.[4]

Before leaving Cincinnati, Benjamin was informed by the association that his lecture scheduled for January 19 had been canceled. Benjamin was neither humble nor apologetic. His attorney immediately notified the association that on January 19 Benjamin would be on hand prepared to lecture and that if he was "not given the opportunity" he would "seek redress in a court of justice."

The *Cincinnati Commercial* gave a vehement editorial defense of

---

[4] *Ibid.*, December 2, 1857.

the association's action. Commenting on Benjamin's reading of
"Fashion" before the Home of the Friendless, this journal declared
that Benjamin had "the kindness, in consideration of the fact that he
repeated an old lecture and had already retailed out his reputation
until he had not the power to draw a full house, to read his dog-eared
MS. for the sum of $55." When the ladies in charge of the organiza-
tion had paid all expenses, they realized, "as the net profit of Mr.
Benjamin's effort, the sum of *eighty-seven and a half cents*, more or
less."[5]

In discussing Benjamin's threat to "seek redress in a court of
justice," this writer observed that he had long "had apprehensions
that a gentleman who was vehemently nervous in the fear that
reporters for the press would catch a few of his jingling words and
print them, would turn out a first class humbug."

On December 7 the irascible Benjamin, then lecturing in St. Louis,
wrote his ultimatum to the Mercantile Library Association. He
accused the association of instigating the insertion of "a grossly
libelous paragraph" concerning him in the *Commercial* and resolved
that the authors of that "tissue of lies" should suffer, "if there
be any law punishing libel in Ohio." He assured the association
"with perfect sincerity" that he "never dreamed" that its members
would object to his Cincinnati lectures. As he had more lecture invitations than he could possibly accept, he would gladly have relinquished
his engagement of January 19 if he had been, "with decent courtesy,
requested to do so." "But," wrote Benjamin, "I do not choose to be
treated in the style, which the brainless youths, who are unhappily
in the direction of your affairs at this moment, seem to think gentlemanly and business-like." The "first principle of commercial ethics"
was that, "as it takes two to make, so does it take two to unmake a
bargain." Since the lecture contract was "without conditions," it
could not legally be broken without his consent. And that consent he
refused to give. "As to my lecturing on the 19th of January, as
agreed, we will see about that," continued Benjamin. "You shall pay

[5] December 2, 1857. The editor was in error here. The Home of the
Friendless made a profit of about sixty dollars, according to the "managers of that
Institution." *Cincinnati Daily Gazette*, December 12, 1857.

the $100 either for having or not having my lecture, as you please, if there be any law enforcing the obligation of contracts in the State of Ohio." He had been "informed by eminent counsel" that the association was guilty of breach of contract. However, if the president and members of the association had such weight and authority "as to establish an entirely new precedent," he hoped the judges of the Ohio courts would hasten to promulgate the decision. Knowledge of such an interpretation of the law would be useful to nonresidents "in any future contracts which they may have occasion to make with such *merchants* or *merchants' clerks* as yourself and your compeers, who seem to be ignorant of the heretofore universally admitted arithmetical fact, that one and one make two."[6]

Benjamin's letter was answered by the editor of the *Commercial* (December 11, 1857) and by the president of the association. The journalist wrote that if Benjamin sought the authors of what he was pleased to call a "grossly libelous paragraph," he need not "look beyond this establishment." The editor had written it and had "not yet the grace to be sorry for it." Benjamin, who was both a humbug and a charlatan, was indebted to the journal "for telling the truth and thereby putting an end to rumors still more injurious." And if Benjamin insisted on bringing a libel suit into court, the editor wished to assure him that even if he did not "keep retained so extensive an array of legal talent" as seemed necessary for the transaction of Benjamin's "business," he expected to be "good on execution" for all the lecturer was likely to recover.

In a newspaper statement to the organization's members, W. I. Whiteman, president of the Mercantile Library Association, declared that while it was not usual in making lecture contracts to stipulate that the speaker should not give other lectures in the same city prior to the date of the appointment, such a condition was "always implied." It was an unwritten agreement "established by usage, and observed by gentlemen from instinctive delicacy." Benjamin's lectures were calculated "to surfeit and oppress the public," thus diminishing the receipts of the association. The association considered itself "ill-

---

[6] Benjamin's very long, angry letter was printed by the *Cincinnati Daily Commercial*, December 10, 1857.

treated" by Benjamin and was determined to have no further negotiations with him. It was apparent that a lecturer "whose audiences dwindled so largely upon each successive evening, had already appeared before our public quite as often as was desirable."[7]

After reading Whiteman's statement the editor of the *Commercial* (December 12, 1857) gleefully commented that "It places that waspish pedlar of draggle-tailed rhymes in a position not at all enviable."

On the evening of January 19, 1858, the second course of the Mercantile Library Association was brilliantly opened with a lecture by Charles Mackay of the *Illustrated London News*. His subject was "Poetry and Song," and Smith and Nixon's Hall was crowded to capacity by an audience that contributed gross receipts of four hundred dollars.

While this highly successful performance was being given, Park Benjamin sat sulking in his room at Cincinnati's Burnet House. During the day he had "addressed a note to the Young Men's Mercantile Library Association, informing them that he was here, ready to deliver a lecture, as he had agreed to do. The Association paid no attention to the note."[8]

A short time later, Benjamin, in "a deliberate exhibition of meanness and malice" which could "neither be forgotten nor forgiven," sued the Mercantile Library Association for breach of contract. The case was heard on June 21 in the Superior Court of Cincinnati. The defendants alleged that a usage existed "by which it is customary for lecturers not to deliver any lectures previous to the one contracted for." Benjamin denied the existence of any such usage, asserting that, since his contract was in writing, the association was bound by its terms.

Benjamin's chances of success were considerably impaired by the legal arguments of Thomas Corwin, United States senator and former governor of Ohio, who, with several other prominent Cincinnati lawyers, volunteered to defend the association without charge. The sources of Corwin's wide reputation as a wit were evident in

[7] *Cincinnati Daily Gazette*, December 12, 1857.
[8] *Ibid.*, January 20, 1858.

his speech to the jury, a plea which was dramatically rendered with frequent leers at Benjamin and his lawyers and meaningful winks at the jury.

Park Benjamin, began Corwin, was but another instance of "the difference with which all mankind in general and lyric poetry in particular, are in the habit of estimating their own merits, and the estimate which the world places upon them." Each time Benjamin lectured in Cincinnati he lost one-third of his drawing power, "so that in the end there was nothing left." He was one of those "grand gentlemen, who come out to the West to instruct us poor ignorant fellows in the woods," and his attraction lay solely in the fact that he was a stranger. If some "poor, unlettered back woodsman should lecture with the wisdom of fifty Solomons," nobody would want to hear him. Were people attracted by the greatness of Benjamin's poetry? His name was "in the book that contains all the American poets gathered up in a heap." But all Benjamin had to offer was novelty. If a poet lived on one of Cincinnati's hills, "he might pour out all the waters of Hybla, and nobody would call his poetry sweet." Benjamin had lectured on "Hard Times," "and about one thousand gentlemen who wanted to find out some way of paying their debts, went to hear him." But they discovered that it was all in poetry, "and who ever thought of paying debts in poetry?" About six hundred people went to hear Benjamin lecture for charity, and all of them "had to be pulled there." The married men "were carried there by their wives," the young men "were persuaded to go by their sweethearts," and all free, unmarried men "staid away." Finally, Benjamin had, with a minimum of effort, got up a lecture which he hoped to deliver "in every town of 300 inhabitants east of the Rocky mountains." For "this amount of mental preparation" the jury was being called upon "to appropriate the funds which the Association have been accumulating for its laudable purpose of furnishing instruction to the young men of this city." "Won't you do it, gentlemen of the jury?" Corwin mockingly concluded.[9]

Corwin's stinging, half-serious arguments were convincing, as the jury, after retiring for five minutes, returned a verdict for the de-

[9] *Cincinnati Daily Commercial*, June 22, 1858.

fendant. Benjamin's motion for a new trial was overruled and judgment entered in behalf of the association. The legal decision, which
established an important precedent in defining the responsibilities
of lecturers, was published as part of the association's annual report
for 1859:

The decision establishes that the lecturer shall deliver no other lecture at the same place prior to the time appointed by his engagement
with a literary society, without the consent of the other party; and 1st,
That the custom being general, public lecturers are presumed to have
knowledge of its existence, and to make their engagements with reference to the observance of it, and will be held to such observance,
unless the contract otherwise provide, either in express terms or by
words of necessary implication. And 2nd, That such a usage is reasonable and lawful as conducing to the just protection of such associations,
it adds to the mutual benefit of the parties, and as not imposing an
unjust restraint on a lawful occupation, either to the prejudice of the
party or of the public at large.

Ohio lecture-goers never again heard the "draggle-tailed rhymes"
of Park Benjamin. He was announced to lecture in Cleveland on
December 22, 1862, but the performance was canceled because of
Benjamin's illness. The most tempestuous of the Eastern lecturers
died a little more than a year later. By 1864 the memory of his
Cincinnati dispute was doubtless overshadowed in the minds of Ohio
people by the more pleasant recollections of the happy occasions on
which he had "convulsed the listeners."

CHAPTER
XVI

JOHN G. SAXE: *Green Mountain Wit*

I

IN THE mid-nineteenth century, Saxe, lawyer, wit, and editor of the *Burlington* (Vermont) *Sentinel*, was thought by many Americans to be a brilliant satirical poet. His *Progress: A Satirical Poem* (1846) and *Humorous and Satirical Poems* (1850) were widely read and often quoted. Although this critical estimate has not endured, his contemporaries considered him a rival of Oliver Wendell Holmes and Thomas Hood.

Ohio's lecture public received much pleasure from Saxe's wit; indeed, his popularity led to exaggerated estimates of the quality of his verse and of his wisdom. The "Green Mountain Boy" was apparently an impressive figure, and his geniality made him many Ohio friends. Mingled with his satirical shafts were the household truths reverenced by New Englanders in the West. But his success, like that of Benjamin, was a "popular" success, a triumph of mediocrity.

At Saxe's first Ohio appearance, made before the Cincinnati Young Men's Mercantile Library Association on February 22, 1853, he "was presented to a very crowded house, as a poet, scholar, wit and ('by your leave sir') a live Yankee." The *Gazette* reported that Saxe's poem, "New England," was "a pleasant and truthful description of this mother of States, in her natural features and general habits." Special tribute was paid to New England's great men, Generals Knox and Stark, Ethan Allen, John Hancock and the Adamses, with special mention of

Him whom friendship's license christens Swarthy Dan.[1]

---

[1] The subject of this poem is usually given as "Yankee Land." The reference to Daniel Webster was apparently one of the "sharp points" of the poem, as newspaper reviews often refer to it.

The New Englander's "curiosity, fondness for bargaining, and other traits of character, were by no means spared while his domestic worth, his sacred regard for liberty, his skill and enterprise, were painted with a liberal hand." Saxe was described as "a fine looking 'Green Mountain Boy,' standing six feet and more in his stocking feet, and wears quite as much the look of a bold Captain of Dragoons as of the studious Poet." The *Commercial* commented that Saxe "painted in the most amusing manner the genuine Yankee, his virtues and his faults." His courage, patriotism, hospitality, Boston-pride, and inquisitiveness "were all touched off with the most admirable tact— and he made the audience roar in his description of him:

> Whose very nose is vocal with the twang
> That spoiled the psalms when Cromwell's army sang.

When Saxe, en route to Cincinnati, passed through Columbus on February 21, he was invited to return and read "Yankee Land." Saxe accepted the invitation and was greeted on the evening of February 23 by a Columbus audience "flattering to the author in point of numbers." The *Ohio State Journal* described Saxe as "tall, not bad looking, but not graceful in his form." Socially, this "genial, clever fellow" was "one of the people." His humorous description of Yankee character abounded in "passages of rare wit and brilliancy." The *Ohio Statesman* added that Saxe impressed Columbus people most agreeably, "and he will always be hailed here with a right hearty Western welcome."

At the reading of "Yankee Land" before the Cleveland Library Association the *Herald* (February 25, 1853) observed that the poem was received with "pleasure and delight." The Yankees were "about the only people who can bear to hear the whole truth told about them." Saxe's description of New Englanders "was very exact, and our Boston Buckeyes enjoyed the pictures much."

The next evening Saxe delivered "Yankee Land," a "chaste, beautiful production," in Toledo.[2] From Toledo, Saxe went to

---

[2] The following correspondence, published by the *Cleveland Herald* February 25, 1853, occurred before Saxe left Cleveland:

ROOMS LIBRARY ASSOCIATION
CLEVELAND Feb. 25th, '53

DEAR SIR:—Many of our citizens having expressed a great desire to hear you recite your well-known poem, entitled "Progress," and being desirous not

Detroit to lecture. "Owing to delay at Detroit" he did not return
to Cleveland until March 2, when he read "Progress," which was
advertised by the *Herald* as "the best satirical poem ever written
by an American," and a short poem, "The Proud Miss McBride."
The *True Democrat* (March 4, 1853) thought Saxe's second lecture
"better than the first one." Dwelling with "much emphasis and wit
on moral, political, and social progress," Saxe struck out at "a species
of 'crawfish progress' peculiar to 'fashionable society.'" "The Proud
Miss McBride" "effectively ridiculed that class of fashionables who
always walk on the 'proper side of the street,' boast of their ancestors,
and who, if their parents' strong box suddenly becomes empty, become
unprofitable members of society."

On March 3 Saxe read "Yankee Land" at the reopening of
Sandusky's Euterpean Hall. Donald G. Mitchell was expected to
lecture at this rededication, but, "called away by a long engagement
South, he unwillingly had to disappoint his many friends hereabouts."
"Yankee Land" was said by the *Commercial Register* to be "full of
humor, wit and sense, and pleases Yankees particularly well." Saxe's
recitation, however, did not add to the occasion, "since the Poet's
manner and delivery is neither polished or pleasant, and somewhat

---

only to meet their wishes, but also to partake of the same pleasure ourselves,
we would respectfully and earnestly request you, should it coincide with your
other arrangements, to gratify us, by delivering it upon Tuesday next, March
1st. Hoping that you will comply with our request, I have the honor to be
                    Respectfully yours,
                        CHAS. HERRICK
                            In behalf Lec. Com.

                                    CLEVELAND, Friday A.M.
                                    February 25th, '53
Charles Herrick, Esq., Sec'y Library Association,
    DEAR SIR:—Your polite note, requesting me to again address a Cleveland
audience, has been received. It was my intention to recite the poem on New
England, only, during my visit to the West, and I feel somewhat reluctant to
repeat that which has been so long a time before the public. But as I shall have
a spare day or two on my return, I think I can accept your invitation, and will
deliver the poem on "Progress," as you desire, on Tuesday evening next.
                    I am Sir,
                        Yours very truly,
                            JOHN G. SAXE

dissipates the charm which a reading of the poem had spelled for it."

On January 18, 1854, the Akron *Summit Beacon* announced that Saxe, "the inimitable satirist, of Burlington, Vt.," would probably lecture in Akron on February 6, as he was engaged to speak in Cleveland about that time. The committee of the Young Men's Lyceum were "corresponding with other distinguished Lecturers, who are engaged by the Cleveland Association." This method of obtaining lecturers was a common one. The corps of Eastern lecturers appearing in the smaller communities of northern Ohio was usually determined by the selections of the Cleveland Library Association. In central Ohio the less populous towns relied on the lecturers appearing in Columbus; in the communities of southern Ohio the choice of speakers was made by the Cincinnati Young Men's Mercantile Library Association. In some cases lyceums did not negotiate appointments directly with lecturers, but called upon these large associations to serve as lecture agencies in securing speakers.[3]

Saxe's poem was received in Akron "with the most flattering marks of gratification, throughout." On the following evening "Yankee Land" was delivered in Zanesville, where the poem was termed "a perfect triumph" by the *Courier*.[4] "The tribute to Webster was a graceful and exquisitely conceived little gem; and the apostrophe

---

[3] The manuscript "Minutes of the Dayton Library Association" carry the following entry under date of November 11, 1856: "The Secretary was directed to correspond immediately with the Secretary of the Cincinnati Library Association and to procure if possible the services of Geo. Sumner, Wendell Phillips and D. G. Mitchell also of S. S. Cox of Columbus before the Holidays."

[4] Saxe's acceptance of an invitation from the Zanesville Popular Lecture Association had been in the hands of the chairman of the lecture committee for about a month. The poet's letter was published by the *Daily Zanesville Courier*, January 18, 1854:

BURLINGTON, (Vt.), Jan. 2, 1854

ADAM PETERS, ESQ.   DEAR SIR:—I have received your favor of the 24th ult., and have to say in reply that you may announce me for Feb. 7th (Tuesday), and rely on my punctuality. Subject, "New England—a Poem."—(or, if you prefer the title, "Yankee Land—a Poem") the same delivered in Boston, New York, Philadelphia, Cleveland and elsewhere.

I am, dear sir, yours truly,
JOHN G. SAXE

to our country not inferior to Longfellow's beautiful and widely celebrated 'Ship of State.'" In describing the lecturer the *Gazette* (February 14, 1854) pointed out that his head was "a fine one, just such as a sculptor would delight to put on a poet's shoulders." Saxe's forehead was expansive "and sufficiently protuberant just where phrenologists locate ideality." His eyes were "strongly marked with that humor which is the prevailing trait in his poetry."

Saxe read "Yankee Land" at Whittlesey Academy in Norwalk on February 10, but in his other Ohio appearances in 1854 he delivered a prose lecture, "Poets and Poetry." The Columbus *Ohio Statesman* (February 9, 1854) found the "analysis of poetry, and his remarks on poets, both witty and wise; but it seems tame beside the flashing eye and jolly humor of his verse." The *Capital City Fact* thought the lecture "was filled with many poetic gems, but lacked the 'substantials,' found in the essays of Greely [*sic*], King, etc."[5]

At Cleveland, Saxe's remark that "Pegasus does not ride well under a side-saddle" evoked the anger of "A Lady" who wrote a letter to the *Forest City Democrat* (February 11, 1854) in which she accused the poet of being "an insolent imitation of Tom Hood." Nevertheless, Saxe "riveted the attention" of the "largest audience of the season."

Before leaving Ohio to deliver lectures in Detroit and Chicago, Saxe read his "Poets and Poetry" at Sandusky. "It was a beautiful production," declared the *Commercial Register* (February 13, 1854), "full of telling hits and startling thought, and has left an impression on the minds of his hearers as will always treasure the lecturer in memory."

2

During the years 1855 and 1856 Saxe made three brief journeys into Ohio. His popularity had not diminished since his first appearance in 1853. He could always depend upon a following of transplanted Yankees to praise his wit and his "sharp hits" at New England's foibles. He gave variety and humor to the lyceum pro-

---

[5] February 9, 1854. Horace Greeley delivered his "Reform and Reformers" in Columbus on February 7, 1854. Thomas Starr King read "Substance and Show, or Facts and Forces" before the Columbus Atheneum on February 1.

grams, which usually were dominated by serious lecturers. But Ohio audiences did not regard Saxe as a mere "funny man." Beneath the witty exterior of his poetry they detected a vein of wisdom, a fund of moral truth which gave his lectures a worthy purpose.

The general pattern of newspaper reaction to Saxe's poetic lectures emphasized two points, an extravagant opinion of the poetic worth of his productions and recognition of the weaknesses of his oratory. In criticizing "The Money-King," the *Sandusky Commercial Register* (February 13, 1855) reported that "the Satire, as a whole, is one of the best in our literature, and confirms the judgment of critics and the discerning many that John G. Saxe is the truest Wit now before an American public." The same reviewer added that "the Wit was in admirable voice, which is not saying too much, as Saxe is not celebrated for the mellifluousness of tone and moving oratory which render speech impressive."

Ohioans did not allow Saxe's deficiencies in eloquence to mar seriously their appreciation of his wit and robust good nature. Adverse criticisms were usually delivered in a kindly tone. The editor of the Chillicothe *Scioto Gazette*, after hearing "Yankee Land," labeled it "a very good and witty poem," but added, with a careless good nature that marked his spelling as well as his criticism, that

a poem recited, and reading a poem from the printed page, are two different things for its proper appreciation. And such a recitation! You have listened to the fileing of a saw in some country saw-mill, when the echoes brought back a sort of terrible music, that caused a shuddering tremor through your frame as if a dentist were fileing your tooth, now and then touching the nerve as delicately as possible,—if you have heard and felt this, you can realize how John G. Saxe delivers himself of his Parnassian gatherings.—Having never heard a New England frog, we couldn't say that he had tuned his voice to the melody of its music; but we can say that the silvery tones of the poet, would find a living rival in the king-frog of a Muskingum swamp. But Saxe is a genius of no ordinary mould, a pleasant conversationalist and a good fellow. Long may he live to provoke the merry laugh and sattirize the follies of men. American literature could "better spare a better man."

In Ohio, as in his native New England, Saxe held a considerable reputation as an occasional poet. He was invited to deliver a poem on October 11, 1855, at the dedication of the Sturgess Library at Ohio Wesleyan University. Arriving in Delaware too late for the dedication ceremony, he read his poem of newspaper life, "The Press," before the townspeople.[6] At the dedication of the Mansfield Female College two weeks later, Saxe made his first appearance before a Mansfield audience. According to the *Herald* (October 31, 1855) "Yankee Land" was enthusiastically received, as the audience "testified their approbation by frequent and hearty applause."

Saxe returned to Ohio in early 1856 to deliver lectures at Dayton and Cincinnati. His experience at Cincinnati illustrates one of the hazards run by lecturers who traveled by railroad through the Western states in the fifties. On February 5 Smith and Nixon's Hall was filled at an early hour with a fashionable audience awaiting the delivery of "The Money-King," a poetic satire "aimed at modern follies and cupidity." Though the lecture was announced to begin at seven-thirty in the evening, it was discovered that Saxe's train would not reach the city until eight. Arrangements were therefore made to entertain the audience until he arrived, and "Menter's band accepted an invitation to beguile the time, which they did by playing several popular airs in their own excellent style. But no concord of sweet sounds would bring Mr. Saxe." The next day's *Gazette* explained that Saxe "was on his way from Chicago, and missed the connection at Michigan City, and telegraphed that he would be here at 12 o'clock yesterday, but he missed the connection at Lafayette, and telegraphed again that he would be here at 8 last evening, but he missed the connection again at Indianapolis, and telegraphed that he could not reach here last night. He had every motive to come but the loco-motive." Saxe lectured on February 7, breaking an appointment at Circleville to do so. The Vermont poet intended to make another visit to Ohio in 1856, but the reason for the postponement of the journey is made clear in a letter to the chairman of the executive committee of the Xenia Lyceum:

SYRACUSE, N. Y., Feb. 29

W. B. Fairchild
DEAR SIR:
    I came here from the west a fortnight ago, sick and broken down, and leaving behind me some twenty appointments west of Chicago. I

---

[6] Delaware *Olentangy Gazette*, October 19, 1855.

had intended to return again soon enough to meet my engagement in Xenia—but, on venturing out again, I find myself too feeble to go further, and must return home. I am very, *very* sorry to disappoint you, and wish I could give you a longer notice.

Yours in haste,
JOHN G. SAXE[7]

3

SAXE MADE only a few appearances in Ohio during the late 1850's, and these occasions did not add much to his reputation. It is evident from the reviews of his lectures that the Vermont poet reached the peak of his popularity with "Yankee Land" and that his later long poems suffered by comparison. He was still persistently criticized for his lack of eloquence, but in his new poems his "matter" as well as his "manner" was sometimes received with weak enthusiasm.

On March 17, 1857, Saxe read his poem on "The Press" at Cleveland's Melodeon. The poet had come from Baltimore, "where he said he had received a very warm reception and a very bad cold." The *Ohio Farmer* explained that since Saxe was himself an editor, he was "well qualified to put into rhythm the merits of the press." Nevertheless, in treating his interesting subject, Saxe "did not seem to rise to the grandeur of his theme," though he "called on the muse several times to help him." The poem not only lacked a coherent plan, but many of its puns were bad. Although Saxe had a knack of "happily disguising his quotations," there was evident in his work "a felicitous borrowing from other persons." The poet was usually "a superior punster, and unrivalled epigrammatist" but could not sustain interest in a long poem. Finally, his reading was wretched. "It would be bad enough, if it were natural; but his conceit makes it almost insufferable. If he can't keep from advising the audience of the good things coming, he would better set somebody to read his productions for him, and let us find out their good points for ourselves."

In February, 1859, Saxe appeared in Cincinnati with a new poem entitled "Love," which "treated of the one grand subject Love,

---

[7] *Xenia Torch-Light*, March 5, 1856. Saxe's Xenia lecture was scheduled for March 7.

under several divisions" including maternal love, love of country, love of race, and divine love. The reading at Smith and Nixon's Hall on February 17 drew only two hundred and fifty people. The *Enquirer* commented that while the poem contained "a few sparkling couplets, and an occasional happy allusion or hit provocative of mirth," it was "not worthy of Mr. Saxe's reputation, whom we have always considered the American Tom Hood." Moreover, Saxe's delivery was "less agreeable and his lisping more perceptible than when Cincinnatians last heard him."

Because of the small audience at its first recitation, "Love" was repeated on February 19. The performance was attended by a "larger audience than on its first reading, though by no means a full one." The *Gazette* declared that Saxe's style of oratory was "not particularly pleasing, and from a peculiar nasal twang, mars the effect of many pretty *puns*." The poem would have been much more effective "if delivered in a popular style."

Saxe's appeal to those people who reverenced conservative, old-fashioned, Yankee notions was touched upon by the *Enquirer*:

Mr. Saxe seems somewhat tinctured with old-fogyishness, being an ardent admirer of fat babies, stocking-darning wives and other such incumbrances, and sharing the popular prejudice against social transcendentalism and progressive humanity—all of which is well enough for those believing with him, who, we are free to confess, form a large majority of the community.

Saxe delivered "Love" in Cleveland on February 20, 1860. He was scheduled to lecture before the Young Men's Christian Association on the following evening, but when George William Curtis failed to arrive for his discourse on "Education and Democracy" on February 20, Saxe substituted for him. The poem, which was well received, was described by the *Plain Dealer* as "a sparkling and splendid affair, abounding in happy and palpable hits, sterling sense and sarcasm."

On February 21 Saxe filled his original engagement by reading his always-popular "Yankee Land." Saxe, wrote the *Leader*, "is a true Yankee and hits off New England character to the life." His picture of Yankee Land was "glowing and truthful" and was well appreciated by the Cleveland audience, "nine-tenths of whom were New Englanders or their descendants."

During the late sixties Saxe gave occasional lectures in Ohio. His "Yankee Land" continued to be his most popular production, especially with New Englanders in the West. The attractiveness of this lecture to Ohioans seems to have been little impaired by the mediocrity of its verse. It provided agreeable entertainment; its mixture of jokes, puns, and pleasant satire was held worthy of the lyceum platform because, as was emphasized by the Oberlin *Lorain County News* (January 23, 1861), "beneath the sharpest point and broadest humor could be seen an earnest purpose and a genuine moral."

APPENDIX A

A History of Ohio's Lecture System

1. 1850–1854 *The Years of Cultural Growth*

BY 1850 lecturing was an established profession in the major cities of Ohio. A few Western professionals were in the field, and the route of the Eastern lecturers was gradually extending westward. From Pittsburgh, fast packet boats steamed down the Ohio on regular schedules during the navigation season; and from Buffalo, the steamship lines carried passengers to Sandusky, Cleveland, and Toledo. For several years the Cincinnati Young Men's Mercantile Library Association[1] had been giving variety to its annual lecture course by occasionally presenting such celebrated platform speakers as Henry Giles of Maine and John P. Hale of New Hampshire.[2] The Cleveland Library Association, founded in 1848, was sometimes fortunate enough to acquire the services of an intrepid Eastern lecturer traveling the Lake route from Buffalo to Detroit. The citizens of Columbus, Toledo, and other cities had listened to the rousing oratory of the great temperance lecturer John B. Gough, whose vivid tales of his escape from alcoholism moved strong men to weep and take the pledge, while Ohio's women busied themselves with the formation of temperance societies. Next to Gough in popularity were Benjamin Silliman, America's most eminent scientist in the first half of the

---

[1] Organized in 1835, this institution was the earliest important sponsor of professional lecturers in Ohio. Until its lecture program was suspended in 1863, the association consistently paid the highest lecture fees in the state.

[2] Giles, educated as a Roman Catholic in his native Ireland, became a prominent Unitarian minister. After his immigration to America in 1840, he devoted most of his energies to lecturing and writing. His *Lectures and Essays* (Boston, 1845) was familiar to the Western reading public. See pages 62–69 of this study.

Hale was an insurgent Democrat who in 1847 became one of the first antislavery men to be elected to the United States Senate. Good-humored, eloquent, and witty, he was a favorite lecturer with Western audiences. In 1852 Hale was an unsuccessful candidate for President on the Free Soil ticket.

nineteenth century, and Frederick Douglass, the eloquent son of an unknown white man and a Negro slave woman.[3]

In addition to being inaccessible by railroad, most of the smaller towns and villages could not afford the luxury of professional lecturers, but in those communities possessed of a few public-spirited citizens, weekly free lectures were delivered by local clergymen and other prominent residents. Occasionally a distinguished visitor was persuaded to lecture, or the local congressman used his invitation to edify the people by slyly fortifying himself for some future election.

The lecture system in Ohio had not yet become tainted with commercialism. Lyceums and lecture associations were supported by earnest citizens desirous of improving their minds and morals. The lecturer's aim was to "do good" by educating the public, by counteracting the evil influence of frivolous amusements, and by encouraging young men to avoid saloons and billiard halls. The lecture was sometimes employed as a means of fostering charity organizations or of supplying small funds for local libraries. In almost every case the public lecture retained the qualities given to it by the New England lyceums: it combined instruction and sober amusement.

In later years the lecture system was to receive its chief support from the members of fashionable society, but in 1850 the enthusiasm for lecture-education reached nearly every social level. At a time when firemen's riots were the commonest of civil disturbances, the people of Cincinnati could feel a just pride in the weekly scientific lectures delivered before the city's Northern Fire Company. Such a lecture program, wrote one civic-minded journalist, "bespeaks a strong difference between our boys and the firemen in any other city in the

---

[3] Silliman, who founded *The American Journal of Science and Arts* in 1818, was professor of chemistry and natural history at Yale from 1802 until 1853. His scientific lectures before the Lowell Institute in Boston, and in other cities, met with remarkable success. To Western audiences he was the embodiment of an ideal: the unselfish lecturer who used his energies not for personal gain but for the love of spreading knowledge.

Douglass was an ex-slave who escaped from his master at Baltimore in 1838. After a series of flights to Canada and England, he succeeded in buying his freedom. Self-educated and naturally eloquent, he lectured tirelessly in America for Negro emancipation, and after the Civil War his speeches in behalf of social and economic equality for his race were among the most popular on the lyceum platform.

Union. In fact, in almost every other city the firemen put their heads together for the purpose of breaking them."[4]

During the early fifties the number of lyceums and lecture associations in Ohio steadily increased. Often the lyceum was established as a debating society with weekly meetings at which the members argued the moot topics of the day. Lectures by the society's more eloquent young men were sometimes substituted for or alternated with the weekly debates. When the society was surfeited with the oratory of its members, the community's ministers, lawyers, the local judge, or the newspaper editors were called upon to lecture. If a lyceum was prosperous, it invited paid lecturers from abroad or used its funds to establish a reading room where current periodicals and newspapers, and books donated by the townspeople, were made available. Often such reading rooms developed into community libraries.

The lyceum came to be looked upon as a panacea for all the dissolute tendencies of the young, and as a pleasurable means of engendering literary taste and culture. The social importance of the lyceum was widely recognized. On January 5, 1852, Governor Reuben Wood, in his annual message before the Ohio legislature on the condition of the state, requested that the General Assembly provide funds to promote the organization of lyceums and literary associations. Such a policy, declared the Governor, "would certainly have a tendency to prevent dissipation by the desertion of places tending to immoralities, and cause young men to store their minds with useful knowledge and elevate themselves in their own self-dignity and self-respect."[5]

In some communities where the literary or debating societies did not sponsor lectures, or the lyceums could not afford to hire speakers from abroad, lecture associations were established, either as permanent organizations or as temporary societies to furnish a course for a single winter's entertainment. The genesis of the lecture associations usually followed a familiar pattern. A public meeting would be called, a simple organization effected, and a list of subscribers obtained to protect the association against a financial deficit. Then the officers would

---

[4] *Daily Cincinnati Gazette,* December 21, 1850.
[5] Columbus *Daily Capital City Fact,* January 7, 1852.

be appointed, including a lecture committee to select the speakers, "a Secretary to invite them, a Treasurer to pay them, and a President to introduce them to the audience. The lecture then becomes the weekly excitement of the place; all local appointments make way for it, and it attracts people from long distances."[6]

The public was sometimes apathetic in its support of the lecture program, particularly in those communities where the citizens, accustomed to attending free lectures, were called upon to pay an admission fee. The newspaper editors were then given the responsibility of whipping up public interest. The editor of the *Hamilton Intelligencer* (November 3, 1853) complained that for three winters the lectures of the Hamilton Library Association "have been kept up under difficulties" because the "ranker excitements of political strife have usurped the place of sober intellectual culture." Hamilton's youth had not been interested in the lectures, and it was hoped "that in future our citizens will feel it a *duty* to attend them and take the elder members of their families."

Columbus lecture-goers, accustomed to the free lecture courses of the Franklin Lyceum, did not enthusiastically support the pay lectures of the newly founded Atheneum in 1853. The *Ohio State Journal* (January 19, 1853) warned the public that it "is better to spend money to educate our young men aright, than it is to be taxed to keep up a numerous night-police, to build jails and penitentiaries. Will our citizens think of those things, and act as becomes enlightened Christian men at the noon of the 19th century?"

In 1854 the lecture course of the Toledo Young Men's Association was a "complete failure," although the meetings "have been held in a part of the city, favored with good side-walks, in the midst of a literary and intelligent society." The chief reason for the failure was that

many believe they would go into faintings or fits, were they obliged to have their minds put into requisition for one hour in the week. To dance all night, to play games of chance or sit tippling or smoking for hours, is a very easy and delightful task, but to sit and listen to an hour's sober talk is pronounced "an intolerable bore."[7]

[6] Thomas Wentworth Higginson, "The American Lecture System," *Macmillan's Magazine*, XVIII (May, 1868), 49.
[7] Letter from "Horatius," *Daily Toledo Blade*, January 30, 1855.

Despite such difficulties as these, the lecture system in Ohio developed rapidly, and the market for Eastern lecturers steadily grew. In later years Western lecture associations learned to negotiate winter appointments with the Eastern orators during the months of summer and early fall. But until the lecture system became better organized, there was a scramble on the part of Ohio lyceums to catch the Easterners on the road. Such efforts usually failed, because the lecturers followed itineraries which allowed them little spare time for sudden appointments.

When Cleveland citizens observed in Eastern journals that Emerson was speaking in New York State in February, 1852, a lecture invitation was promptly dispatched to him at Buffalo, where he lectured on February 4. Emerson replied from Concord on February 26:

> Your letter I found on my road, but it offered me fruit which I could not eat, however fair. All my days were promised, for the Lyceums along the Albany and Buffalo road now act in concert, and when they send to us, eastern demagogues, arrange a series of engagements for us. Yet I was glad to be asked—glad to be remembered.[8]

The naïveté of the methods employed by inexperienced lecture committees is illustrated in the proposed course of the Dayton Library Association in 1854. At a meeting of the association's board of directors on November 30, 1854, the lecture committee presented for consideration a lecture course "which on motion was approved." The course listed precise dates for addresses by George W. Curtis, Bayard Taylor, Horace Greeley, Thomas Starr King, and John Pierpont.[9] None of these lecturers came. Some of them did not visit Ohio at all, and those who did had already arranged their itineraries.

But even such an unpromising plan as that of the Dayton Library Association revealed the desire of Western lecture-goers to see and hear the Eastern celebrities. If the lyceums and lecture associations were to elevate the minds of the people so that "the sounds of riot and debauchery would be heard no more in the streets," there would be a heavy responsibility for the cultured lecturers of the East. "So

---

[8] *Cleveland Herald*, March 2, 1852. This letter is not recorded in Rusk's *Letters of Ralph Waldo Emerson*.
[9] Manuscript "Minutes of the Dayton Library Association."

long as there is ignorance in the world," wrote the editor of the *Sandusky Commercial Register*, "there will be need of Emersons, Mitchels [*sic*], *et id omne genus*; and out West, where there is room for growth, we pray they may come."[10]

The prayers of Ohio's lecture enthusiasts were answered more and more frequently during the decade of the fifties, as the railroads spread westward across the Alleghenies. When Emerson visited Cincinnati in the spring of 1850, he had been obliged to journey southward from Sandusky, as Cleveland was not yet connected by rail with the "Queen of the West." However, in February, 1851, the Cleveland, Columbus and Cincinnati Railroad was completed, and the first important north-south route of the lecturers was established. After the 135-mile ride to Columbus, the traveler transferred to the cars of the Columbus and Xenia Railroad; at Xenia he changed to the Little Miami line for the final 67 miles of his trip to Cincinnati.[11]

In March, 1852, the opening of the Cleveland and Pittsburgh Railroad provided another connection between Lake Erie and the Ohio River. This line, which served lecturers journeying directly to or from Pittsburgh and the communities of northern Ohio, passed through Hudson, Ravenna, Alliance, and Wellsville. At Wellsville the traveler took a river packet to Pittsburgh. In November, 1852, the Lake Shore Railroad, joining Cleveland, Painesville, and Ashtabula, was extended to Erie in "the last link connecting Cleveland with all 'Down East' by a continuous railway." In reviewing the progress of the railroad builders, the *Cleveland Herald* (November 18, 1852) observed that

Three years since, at this season of the year, Cleveland was isolated. Cincinnati was four days distant; Pittsburgh was reached by two days journey through the mud; and New York was a far off city, cut off from us by four days staging and twenty six hours of railroading over

---

[10] November 14, 1853. Donald G. Mitchell, commonly known as Ik. Marvel, was widely known as a writer and lecturer. Especially popular were his *Reveries of a Bachelor* (1850) and *Dream Life* (1851). In 1856 he lectured in Ohio on "Pictures of Venice in Her Later Days." The materials of this lecture were gathered by Mitchell during his term as United States Consul at Venice. Mitchell was received with only moderate enthusiasm in Ohio.

[11] "Ohio Railroads," *American Railroad Journal*. Reprinted in the Columbus *Daily Ohio State Journal*, December 13, 1851.

a flat rail variegated with sundry snakeheads. Today we can breakfast in Cleveland and sup in Cincinnati, the same day finds us lodged at Leland's Metropolitan in New York.

Toledo was the last of the large cities in northern Ohio to obtain a railroad connection with the East. On December 4, 1852, the editor of the *Toledo Blade*, after noticing in the Cleveland newspapers that "among other lecturers, the Young Men's Association of that city, have engaged Hon. Horace Mann, Ralph Waldo Emerson, and E. Whipple," commented hopefully that, "On the completion of the Railroad, we ought to be able to secure the services of these lecturers in this city. It is on the highway to Chicago, and must necessarily be a point in their travels."

On January 24, 1853, the first passenger train of the Toledo, Norwalk and Cleveland Railroad traveled from Toledo to Cleveland. But apparently more than the railroad was needed to stimulate the lecture course of the Young Men's Association. A few weeks after the opening of the new road, the editor of the *Blade* (February 21, 1853) asserted that, although Toledo was now connected by railroad with all points of the compass and lecturers could be obtained with great convenience, "a pall seems to hang over the Association. No matter who the lecturer, however eminent, the meetings are thinly attended. . . . This is all wrong, and speaks sadly to the discredit of our city."

The chief lecture routes in Ohio were formed by the east-west line of the Lake Shore Railroad (which included the Toledo, Norwalk and Cleveland Railroad) extending through the principal cities and towns along the shores of Lake Erie; and the north-south line of the Cleveland, Columbus and Cincinnati Railroad. These two lines intersected at Cleveland to form a giant "T" that sprawled across the state.

During the expansion of Ohio's railroads, numerous short lines were constructed which provided railway facilities for communities inaccessible by the main routes. In September, 1851, the Cincinnati, Hamilton and Dayton Railroad was opened, and the entire run from Cincinnati to Dayton could be made in two hours. In January, 1851, the Sandusky, Mansfield and Newark Railroad was completed; this line intersected the Cleveland and Columbus Railroad at Shelby. In March, 1852, the Ohio and Pennsylvania Railroad, running through Salem, Alliance, and Canton, was completed from Pittsburgh to Massillon. Akron could be reached from Cleveland by the Akron Branch Railroad, opened in July, 1852. In 1853 Zanesville was five hours from Columbus by the Central Ohio Railroad, and Newark was a station en route. The Cincinnati, Wilmington and Zanesville Railroad reached Circleville and Lancaster in the spring of 1854 and was completed to Zanesville by November, 1855.

Thus the early fifties saw the passing of the stagecoach and the steamboat as the chief means of transportation between the populous communities of Ohio. The expansion of the railroads presaged a new era of commerce and industry in the state, and for the lecture system it promised a period of growth and popularity. Among the passengers on the new railroads were such eminent lecturers from abroad as Ralph Waldo Emerson; Henry Giles; Theodore Parker, the fighting minister of Boston's Twenty-Eighth Congregational Society; Henry Ward Beecher, the eloquent pastor of Brooklyn's Plymouth Church; Bayard Taylor, the world traveler and author; Edwin P. Whipple, one of America's foremost literary critics; and Park Benjamin and John G. Saxe, the popular humorous poets.

In their curiosity to see and hear the great men of the nation, some lecture sponsors were inclined to discount the importance of lectures by their townsmen. In 1853 the Sandusky Atheneum had no funds with which to procure the services of Eastern professional lecturers, and, as a consequence, the organization undertook no lecture course at all. Aroused by this lethargy on the part of the Atheneum, the editor of the *Commercial Register* (December 22, 1853) commented that Sandusky had home talent "which has made its mark in the pulpit, at the bar, in the lecture room." Was the city's cultural life to be impaired "because forsooth, we have no $500, or $300, with which to hire some broken down, hackney-horse lecturer from the *East*? It is a shame, an insult to our men of talent to be thrust aside, and we say it must *not* be."

During the early 1850's the chief objection to the lecture system was that it had developed into an organized profession which permitted traveling, "hackney-horse" lecturers—most of whom were from the East—to receive large profits from the reading of a single manuscript in dozens of different communities. Despite the growing desire of Western people to hear the Eastern celebrities, there were many complaints that these orators were in the field to make money rather than to disseminate knowledge. The *Cleveland Herald* (November 13, 1852) insisted that, "with some honorable exceptions, Lectures are humbugs. They have become a regular branch of business, a recognized method of obtaining a livelihood, and are hereafter to be ranked with Brandreth's Pills, Davis' Pain Killer, Vaughan's Lithontripiic and Jew David's Plaster." This journalist could recall the time when men like Benjamin Silliman gave free courses of lectures because they loved to spread truth and knowledge. But those days were past; instead, "a lecturing corps is organized, and the same prosy, commonplace and ill-digested ideas, is [*sic*] recited from Boston to New Orleans."

On January 25, 1853, three days after Emerson read his lecture on "Culture" before the Cleveland Library Association, the editor of the *Plain Dealer* attempted to "frame a receipt" to describe "the modern style of lecturing":

Take a gentleman (though this is not absolutely necessary)—one who has brains enough to *collate*; let him choose a subject, read extensively and carefully upon it, and, with a passable knowledge of it, pen some dozen or twenty pages of stuff, with here and there a flashing point to make the people stare, and a witticism to make the people laugh; stuff this in his pocket; give him a carpet bag, with a supply of linen; put him on the next train, and far over the land let him travel, delivering that same lecture in every city that is blessed with a Young Men's Association willing to guaranty *his price*. That we believe to be a true picture of the modern style of lecturing.

In summarizing the lecture season of 1853–54, the editor of the *Cleveland Herald* (March 17, 1854) observed that the ears of Clevelanders had often been tickled, but slight additions had been made to their stock of information. While the winter's lectures offered much transcendentalism, poetry, and sentimentalism, "everything but matter-of-factism," it seemed "remarkable that there have been few of a practical or instructive nature."

By 1854 the objections to the cultural lecture, the "intellectual feast," were not so numerous as the complaints against the commercialism of the lecture system. But later, when some of the novelty of seeing the Eastern cultural lecturers had worn away, those people who paid their quarters to hear and to be instructed were to demand practical, useful lectures with an insistence which was much more vehement than the grumbling against professionalism.

2. 1855–1856 *"All creation is scrambling up to the platform"*

BY THE mid-fifties the public lecture was an important part of the social organization in most of the communities in Ohio. In the major cities, lectures were sponsored by library associations, lyceums, mechanics' institutes, literary societies, churches, and charity groups. There were perhaps a hundred towns and villages where the weekly lectures before the local lyceums were the chief social events during the months from November to March. A town without an annual lecture course ran the hazard of being stigmatized a laggard in cultural taste and community pride. Ohioans had come to expect an annual lecture program "with the same matter-of-course manner in which they look for the approach of Christmas and Election-day."

In the towns where lecture associations or lyceums did not exist, there were frequent appeals for lectures. "Pomeroy, with all her wealth, refinement, and other advantages, has not been favored with a single lecture within the past three or four years," complained the editor of the *Meigs County Telegraph*.[12] The desire for a cultural form of entertainment was asserted in the *Mansfield Herald*: "Let us have lectures, by all means. Let us have a higher grade of entertainments, this winter, than negro minstrels and strolling mountebanks."[13] The familiar plea to save young men from evil appeared in the *Lancaster Ohio Eagle*: "At present our city cannot boast of a single place of public instruction, and amusement; and night after night may be seen hundreds of our young men lounging

---

[12] December 25, 1855. A course by Ohio University professors from Athens began on January 19, 1856.

[13] November 7, 1855. A course was immediately undertaken by the newly organized Mansfield Young Men's Library Association.

around hotels and saloons, who might if proper steps were taken, be allured from idleness and dissipation, and saved from a long train of evils flowing from frivolous amusements and baneful associations."[14] The editor of the *Highland Weekly News*, noticing in his exchanges that many towns smaller than Hillsboro were offering lectures, declared that "the reflection that we are apparently behind them in public spirit and enlightenment, is rather mortifying to our pride."[15]

The response to such editorial comments was usually the institution of a course of lectures delivered by home talent. There was no shortage of aspirants for the privilege of lecturing. Indeed there was no surer way for a man to impress his fellow citizens with his abilities than by demonstrating his eloquence and wisdom upon the lecture platform. The respect for the public lecturer which grew during the days of the early lyceum had by 1855 ripened into full-blown admiration. "The lecture room is fast becoming the great *popular* test of talent," wrote editor Thomas Brown of the *Cleveland Ohio Farmer*. "Whatever a man can do elsewhere, if he cannot stand on a pine board before a table and two candles and give an account of himself, he must wait for his fame in America."[16]

In addition to the many fledglings testing their powers before the local associations, there were swarms of independent lecturers traveling among the Western towns in search of fame and livelihood. "There are but few communities that are not visited by Temperance, and Anti-Slavery and Spiritual Rapping lecturers, and the representatives of all new things are perambulating the land in squadrons," asserted the correspondent of the *Marietta Intelligencer* (October 24, 1855). Equipped with a stock of conventional arguments, sketches of alcoholic horror, and pledge cards, many a young man attempted to emulate the phenomenal success of Gough. This was a period not only of temperance unions but of antislavery societies, and in the northern Ohio cities particularly the lecturer could be certain of an

---

[14] December 13, 1855. No course was established until 1860, when the Lancaster Literary Institute sponsored a lecture series.

[15] December 13, 1855. A course was undertaken by the Hillsboro Lyceum in December, 1856.

[16] "A Short Lecture on Lecturing," February 10, 1855. All other quotations from Thomas Brown are from this article.

audience to listen to the familiar platitudes about slavery's evils. But he was a brave orator who carried his message to the towns along the Ohio River; there was always the ominous possibility that his audience might contain an uninhibited delegation of citizens from Kentucky or Virginia. A substratum of itinerant charlatans squeezed an income from popular interest in current fads and superstitions. The spirit rappers found a ready audience for their ghostly exhibitions, and in their wake came a horde of debunking lecturers who looked under the spirit rapper's table and exposed the contrivances of his art. And finally there were the mesmerists, the phrenologists, the astrologists, the mathematical wizards, the female "physicians," and the fakirs, who, for a dime or a quarter, were eager to prove the truth of their testimonials by edifying and amusing the people. There was ample justification for Thomas Brown's succinct statement: "All creation is scrambling up to the platform."

This mania for hearing lectures denoted several things: that the people sought a new amusement, that they wanted to see and hear the famous men of the country, that they wished to add to their culture and education, and that, as Brown said, "they begin to suspect they cannot make a model republic out of a dozen conflicting nationalities, and untwist knots like slavery, national expansion, popular education and religion, without a little more knowledge than they now have."

These were the reasons which, in 1855 and 1856, accounted for the enormous demand among the Western lecture associations for the services of the professional lecturers from the East. In many of Ohio's smaller towns, lecture-goers who had once been content with the eloquence of their local clergymen and prominent citizens clamored for a view of the stars in the profession. The high fees charged by the celebrities had in former years discouraged the small lyceums from hazarding their slender lecture funds in a reckless venture. But the successful Western tour of Bayard Taylor in the spring of 1854 had awakened these associations to the high prospects of financial gain. Everywhere that Taylor had been, the lecture associations had profited handsomely. Two hundred patrons paying twenty-five cents each would provide the lecturer with his fifty dollars. Five or six dollars for the rent of a hall, and a few dollars more for a newspaper advertisement, some handbills and tickets—these were the only additional expenditures necessary. And what community could not attract two or three hundred lecture-goers to see and hear the great men of the nation? If the weather was good on lecture night, and the roads hard and dry, thirty, or fifty—perhaps a hundred—people would drive their carriages in from the surrounding farms. Thus with new-found confidence and temerity, Ohio's lecture associations wrote their invitations to the famous men of the East.[17]

And the lecturers came. John G. Saxe, Park Benjamin, Theodore Parker, Henry Giles, Bayard Taylor, Parke Godwin, Wendell Phillips, Henry Ward Beecher, Oliver Wendell Holmes, Edwin P. Whipple, Ralph Waldo Emerson, John Pierpont, Horace Greeley, Thomas Starr King, Frederick Douglass, Donald G. Mitchell, E. H. Chapin, Benjamin Silliman, George Sumner—these and many less renowned Eastern lecturers appeared on Ohio's lecture platforms during the years 1855–56. They followed a golden trail; Ohio's lecture associations spared no expense in their effort to satisfy the people's desire for culture and amusement.

As there was unusually keen competition for the services of lecturers for the season of 1855–56, a feeling developed among the smaller communities that the stars of the profession would desire to appear only in the major cities, where large fees were assured, and would tend to neglect those towns and villages which were not easily accessible by railroad or whose lecture associations could not afford to pay the highest prices. In October, 1855, the suggestion was made in the *Sandusky Commercial Register* that, if the associations in the northern and central Ohio towns would join forces in providing an attractive itinerary, some of the prominent orators might agree to furnish these towns with lectures at moderate cost.

The response was enthusiastic, and the first meeting of the lec-

---

[17] Ohio communities offering lectures by Eastern professionals in 1855–56 included Akron, Bucyrus, Canton, Chillicothe, Cincinnati, Circleville, Cleveland, Columbus, Dayton, Delaware, Elyria, Findlay, Glendale, Hamilton, Hudson, Kenton, Lima, Mansfield, Massillon, Milan, Newark, Norwalk, Oberlin, Painesville, Ravenna, Salem, Sandusky, Springfield, Steubenville, Tiffin, Toledo, Wilmington, Wooster, Xenia, Yellow Springs, and Zanesville.

ture associations was held in Sandusky on October 10. Delegates from
Sandusky, Toledo, Tiffin, Mansfield, Mt. Vernon, Zanesville, and
Adrian, Michigan, formed a society under the name of the Bryant
Association, "so named in honor of William Cullen Bryant, the Veteran Poet and Journalist."[18] In their resolutions the delegates expressed confidence that by association they could, "with certainty
and at fair rates, procure good Lectures for such Societies."[19]

At a second meeting, held in Sandusky on October 24, lecture associations "throughout Ohio and Indiana" were invited to participate. New delegates were present from Kenton, Springfield, Bucyrus,
Lima, and Findlay.[20] The Bryant Association completed its organiza-
ton, drew up a constitution, and proposed a course of twelve lectures
to be delivered before the member societies. The speakers included
Theodore Parker; Henry Giles; Parke Godwin of the *New York
Evening Post*; William T. Coggeshall, editor of the *Cincinnati
Genius of the West*; Reverend John Pierpont of New Bedford, Massachusetts, who was a preacher, poet, and grandfather of J. P. Morgan; and Reverend O. E. Daggett of Canandaigua, New York. In
most cases, member associations added local lecturers to complete
their courses.

Theodore Parker was the first of the Eastern lecturers to travel
the Bryant Association circuit. He was expected to deliver the opening lecture of the series on November 16, 1855, at Sandusky. An
audience of four hundred persons gathered at Norman Hall and
waited in vain for his appearance. He arrived "by the 'Slow Coach'
train from Cleveland, at one-quarter before nine," but his audience
had already gone home. This was the first of the numerous lecture

---

[18] Lecture associations represented were the Sandusky Young Men's Library
Association, the Toledo Young Men's Association, the Seneca Library Association (Tiffin), the Mansfield Young Men's Library Association, the Mt. Vernon
Literary Association, the Zanesville Atheneum, and the Adrian Library Association. A plan to present Bryant as a lecturer before the associations did not
materialize.

[19] *Sandusky Daily Commercial Register*, October 26, 1855.

[20] New associations represented were the Kenton Library Association, the
Springfield Irving Association, the Bucyrus Literary Association, the Lima Library Association, and the Findlay Literary Association. Some Bryant Association appointments were made also in Elyria, Norwalk, Circleville, and Milan.

cancellations that were to plague the association's speakers and audiences alike. Train service in the smaller Ohio communities was inadequate to meet the demands of the lecturers' schedules.

Almost from the time the Bryant Association lectures began, it was apparent that they would be a financial failure. In each of the communities represented in the association there were a few enthusiastic lecture-goers, but the majority of citizens, after one or two glimpses of the platform celebrities, showed little interest. People accustomed to free lectures did not readily spend two or three dollars for a course ticket; moreover, money was scarce, as the hard times preceding the Panic of 1857 had already begun. The lecture associations had little working capital, and stormy weather on one or two lecture nights would result in small audiences and financial losses that would wipe out the profits of more successful lectures. While the association's speakers were competent men and were highly regarded in the profession, they were not outstanding crowd-gatherers; they did not have the magnetic appeal of the world traveler Bayard Taylor or the abolitionist Wendell Phillips to draw the population from the farms and surrounding villages.

The Bryant Association was not revived after the lecture season of 1855–56. Most of the towns which had participated in its program returned to the system of free lectures by local talent. The citizens of these towns seemed to agree with the editor of the *Springfield Nonpareil* (November 13, 1856), who was "half inclined to believe that the old idea of *importing* mental pabulum for the public palate is an arrant humbug. It is a positive fact that many of those who have come to our city with splendid foreign reputations have come far short of giving that satisfaction to their audience which would have been given by some of our home orators."

A second co-operative society, the Massillon Association,[21] originated and managed by J. E. Wharton, editor of the *Massillon News*,

---

[21] The official name of this society, together with details of its organization, is probably contained in the columns of the *Massillon News*. The writer has been unable to discover any existing files of this newspaper, or of any other Massillon journal, for the years 1855–56. In this study, the society will be called the "Massillon Association." Information about the society comes from the *Canton Ohio Repository*, October 31, 1855.

was a "concert of action" by lecture associations in "towns along the
line of the Ohio and Pennsylvania and connecting Railroads." Its
purpose, like that of the Bryant Association, was to provide small
communities with first-class lectures at moderate cost.

In October, 1855, a meeting was held at Massillon by delegates
representing lecture associations in Massillon, Salem, Canton,
Wooster, Mansfield, Medina, Akron, Hudson, and Ravenna. On
this occasion "it was unanimously agreed, that $50 per lecture was
more than the community was able to pay, but that one half that sum
should be the maximum to be offered for the services of one individual."

The secretary of the association wrote a series of lecture invitations
and in late October reported that Theodore Parker, Ralph Waldo
Emerson, Parke Godwin, and Dr. William Elder of Philadelphia
"have acceded to the terms." The addition of John Pierpont and
O. E. Daggett gave the Massillon Association nearly the same staff
of Eastern lecturers as that provided by the Bryant Association.

The failure of the Massillon Association's lecture program came
quickly. The Wooster Library Association, after suffering a financial
loss on Parker's lecture, canceled Godwin's appointment and abandoned the course entirely. Cancellations were numerous, as the
itineraries furnished the lecturers were unsatisfactory. Emerson, who
was scheduled to travel the Massillon Association circuit during the
last week in January, 1856, lectured only at Akron and Hudson.
He then dissolved his relationship with the association because of the
failure of some of the member societies to fulfill their contracts with
the lecturers.[22]

The experience of the Bryant Association and the Massillon Association discouraged other lecture sponsors in the state from attempting the organization of such co-operative groups. The desire
for a successful lecture agency in the West was finally met in 1865
with the establishment of the Associated Western Literary Societies,
which furnished lecturers for hundreds of towns from western Pennsylvania to Iowa.

The financial problems of the Bryant Association and the Massillon Association were typical, for, except in the major cities, Ohio's

---

[22] Salem *Columbiana County Republican*, January 30, 1856.

lecture associations consistently lost money in the years 1855 and 1856. The Xenia Lyceum was deprived of its only opportunity to balance its deficit when Bayard Taylor failed to appear for his scheduled lecture.[23] The Hamilton Irving Club, according to the *Hamilton Intelligencer*, abandoned its lectures in January, 1856, "for the reason that the course was kept up thus far at a loss to their treasury of about fifty dollars." In announcing that John Pierpont would deliver his poem "The Scholar's Hope" before the Pickaway Lyceum, the correspondent of the *Circleville Herald* (February 29, 1856) sadly pointed out that "this closes the lectures of the season, and unless there is more hope of sufficient encouragement, doubtless closes them for the future." The annual report of the Dayton Library Association for 1856 contained the statement: "Our course of Lectures last season, while unexceptionable, perhaps, in point of ability, made nothing for the Association."[24]

The newspapers of Ohio provided numerous explanations for the poor patronage given the lecture associations by the public. The most persistent complaints were that the lecture system was infested with charlatans, that the lecture fees were exorbitant, that the lecture materials themselves were lacking in solid substance, and that the Eastern orators were an expensive and unsatisfactory luxury.

The editor of the *Cincinnati Enquirer* (December 5, 1856) lamented that "the lecture field, under the system *in vogue*, seems to be singularly adapted for indolent men of talent and fancy, or for superficial men of spirit and smartness, or for bold-faced and glib-tongued charlatans." At least it seemed that "these three classes are quite as likely to be successful as any other description of persons whatever."

The correspondent of the *Clevelander* (January 26, 1856) felt that the lecturing profession had "too many accessions of champions and too small an acquisition of talent." As a result, "the lecturer aims to secure the largest price possible for the smallest amount of information—and it is really surprising what sharp bargains some of them drive."

According to the Columbus *Ohio Statesman* (December 4, 1856)

[23] *Xenia Torch-Light*, January 9, 16, 1856.
[24] *Daily Dayton Journal*, January 16, 1857.

most of the lectures imposed upon the public were "little better than stump speeches at a political gathering." If they did not deal predominantly with politics, "and that of the fanatical order," they presented "a mixture of Millerism in religion, and of Fourierism in morals, and the mixture would puzzle a German Chemist to separate the various parts and discover their uses."

Since the Eastern lecturers had appeared in Ohio with conspicuous frequency during 1855 and 1856, newspaper critics associated the performances of these orators with the dwindling support of the lyceums. The general opinion was expressed in a letter signed "Modern" and published in the *Dayton Journal* (February 16, 1856):

Hitherto we have imported our lecturers, and for a while there was wonderful curiosity to hear Eastern Celebrities. One by one they came. Regularly our hall was crowded with hearers; and almost as regularly did they go home considerably humbugged. . . . Experience has proved that Eastern lecturers are no better than Western. They are certainly twice as expensive, and almost invariably disappoint our expectations.

The shortcomings of lectures by Eastern celebrities and the effect of these orations on the prestige of the lecture system were summarized by the editor of the *Sandusky Commercial Register* (October 24, 1855) who contended that the Eastern performers failed to instruct in any of the valuable branches of moral, physical, or political science. Instead, the star lecturer comes "as a beautiful speaker, who deals in pretty conceits, admirable rhetoric, witty or witless poetry." After giving his hearers an "intellectual treat" and "pocketing $50 or $75 for his service, he leaves town to give place for some other notable who proposes to talk for a like sum." Thus through the winter from $300 to $1000 is expended in every lectured city, the disappointed public becomes suspicious of the word *lecture*, "and a good book and an evening at home is determined upon rather than a profitless and expensive discourse in some crowded public room."

The necessity of restoring public confidence in the lecture system was apparent to the lyceums and to the press. Editor Thomas Brown called for a closer organization of the system by the consolidation of all the Young Men's Library Associations in America. He also believed that each lecturer should provide a sustained course of several lectures; the undesirable performers would thus be weeded out, as only the most capable speakers could hold the interest of a permanent audience. A few courses of that kind would be vastly better than "a series of brilliant essays from a dozen famous men whose exorbitant charges exhaust the whole literary fund of the place, and whose profound or startling productions leave only the impression of a spectacle on the majority who hear."

The correspondent of the *Cincinnati Gazette* (November 25, 1856) was of the opinion that the lecture system should be purged through the power of the public press. Too many audiences were compelled to endure "elegant stupidities, mechanical flippancies and stale platitudes." But the newspapers had the power of criticism and should exercise it. "Let the press once act on the hypothesis that the speaker's matter and manner, style and syntax, are legitimate subjects for criticism, and the new profession will undergo a speedy and much-needed purification."

When these critical suggestions were made, the lecture system was already undergoing the process of purification. In 1855 and 1856 Ohio's lyceums overreached themselves to satisfy the clamor for lectures, and through public reaction to the lecture program the associations learned that "just any lecturer" would not do. The method employed by the people of Ohio to insure the careful selection of their future lecturers was anticipated by Thomas Brown, who declared that "The sacred liberty of staying at home must drive off crowds of blatant stupidities that now vex the air of the lecture room, and weary good men into disgust at our new American Profession."

3. 1857–1860 *The Vogue of the Practical and Scientific*

THE OHIO market for Eastern lecturers was considerably curtailed in the late 1850's. Although lecture associations in most of the large cities had not been seriously affected by the financial problems of 1855–56, the Toledo Young Men's Association found it necessary the following year to be content with a course of home lectures;[25]

---

[25] The financial risk, as well as the opportunity for profit, in such a course was small. According to the treasurer's report for the year ending October 5, 1857, the total expenses for the Toledo course were $93.00, and the gross re-

and the directors of the Dayton Library Association, meeting on
October 10, 1857, "to take into consideration the subject of a course
of lectures" decided that "it was not . . . advisable to make any definite
arrangements for that purpose."[26]

Many of the smaller communities returned to the system of lectures by local speakers, and a few towns entirely abandoned a lecture program. At a public meeting on October 19, 1857, the people
of Springfield planned a course of free lectures. The secretary of the
lecture committee cautioned his fellow citizens that the town had
"annually paid to foreign lecturers some five or six hundred dollars,
which although not very large sums, were much larger than we
ought to send abroad, when we can procure lectures fully as valuable,
instructive and amusing at home and gratis."[27]

The Akron Young Men's Association did not sponsor a course
in 1857–58. A few private lectures were read by local residents, but
there was apparently a general willingness to forego "a succession of
sky-rocket brilliancies from the class, known as professional star lecturers."[28] In appealing for a lecture course on December 22, 1858, the
editor of the Akron *Summit County Beacon* declared that productions
by home talent would be "more instructive and more practically
beneficial to all, than most of the itinerant capital that wanders about
dispensing pleasant sentiments, graceful gestures, and rhetorical
flourishes, only when puffed and paid for."

Some communities, including Canton, Mansfield, Marietta, and
Sandusky, did not have lecture programs in 1857, and many towns
were to find their home courses unrewarding. Despite the efforts of
newspaper editors to praise the eloquence of their townspeople, the
local lecturers often held little attraction for audiences who had become accustomed to seeing and hearing the nation's celebrities. Many

---

ceipts were $158.50. *Daily Toledo Blade*, October 7, 1857. The Young Men's
Association continued the system of lectures by local talent until November 9,
1859, when John P. Hale delivered the opening lecture in a course featuring
Eastern professionals.

[26] Manuscript "Minutes of the Dayton Library Association."

[27] *Daily Springfield Nonpareil*, October 20, 1857.

[28] Akron *Summit County Beacon*, February 17, 1858.

people attended lectures because they were curious to look at famous men or because it was fashionable to be seen once a week in the presence of greatness.

It is doubtless true that many lyceums, after hearing a particularly uninteresting discourse by some Easterner, questioned the advantage of importing their orators from Boston or New York. But there were also disadvantages to a course by home talent. When the directors of the Dayton Library Association found it "inadvisable to resort to the Lecture system as a means of pecuniary profit" in 1858–59, a program of home lectures was not substituted for a professional course because, as the association's secretary declared:

The public having feasted so long upon lion's meat, have little or no taste for the flesh of inferior animals; but lion's meat is now, as heretofore, *fifty* dollars a meal, without the incidentals; and the hard times forbid all indulgence in such expensive luxuries.[29]

A pessimistic, though not uncommon, view of the home lecture system was taken by the correspondent of the *Mt. Vernon Republican* (December 6, 1860), who strongly opposed a lecture course of any kind. The town could not support "the high-priced stranger article" and the citizens would not be interested in a free course by local talent, "as it is notoriously true that people much prefer to *pay* for being bored by a stranger, rather than to be instructed and entertained by a neighbor, gratis."

Among the sponsors of professional lectures there was a determination to provide speakers selected on the basis of their power to attract large audiences and of the merits of their instruction. By this means the lyceums hoped to ensure their financial security by pleasing not only the people who came to see, but also those more serious patrons of the lecture who came to hear. "Let us hereafter have either great men from the east, whom we want to see for what they have done before," wrote the editor of the Columbus *Daily Ohio State Journal* (January 11, 1859), "or else let us have men as capable to instruct and entertain us, as a dozen people whom we nod to on the street every day."

The selection of lecturers on the basis of their drawing power was

[29] *Daily Dayton Journal*, January 12, 1859.

often decried during the late fifties by those journalists who realized
that the most attractive speakers were sometimes those who merely
entertained the fashionables and were motivated by no great desire
to "do good." But there was no returning to the noble aims of the
early cultural lecture. Rightly managed, the lecture system could
provide financial profit for its sponsors, and the lyceums were intent
on making the most of their opportunity. During the late fifties
they provided as many lectures as possible by the established favorites,
such as Taylor, Emerson, and Saxe; and later, when still larger
profits were sought, the lecture associations would send their invitations to the reformers, the politicians, the popular humorists, and
the polar explorers.

With the increasing complaints against the inutility of the cultural
lecture, there was a concomitant growth in the demand for practical
and scientific discourses. Lecture-goers complained that the elegant
productions by the cultural lecturers were remembered "as the flash
of the meteor, or the flight of the gorgeous cloud." Though brilliant
and often pleasing discourses, they were not useful.

The reception of cultural lectures was especially unenthusiastic in
those sponsoring organizations whose members were chiefly interested
in mechanical trades and who had little time or energy, at the end
of a twelve-hour working day, to pursue the study of literature or
philosophy. The annual report of the Ohio Mechanics' Institute for
1857 declared that most popular lectures offered little profit to persons engaged in mechanical enterprises. The organization's lecture
committee was advised to sponsor only practical discourses and to
"cease to strive after a display of brilliant oratory or attractive
humbug."[30]

In planning their lecture programs, lyceums could not afford to
disregard the tastes of the mechanics. Not only was their patronage
needed to support the financial burden of lecture courses, but the
education of the laboring class was felt to be of the utmost importance
in the making of a cultured society. In some cases, a special inducement was offered to the laborer by lecture associations. In announcing
its lectures for 1859–60, the Norwalk Whittlesey Academy advertised

[30] *Cincinnati Daily Gazette*, March 10, 1858.

course tickets for $1.50, and "The Proprietor or Foreman of a Machine Shop or Manufactory, taking two tickets at the first named rate the men in his employ will be supplied, each at $1.25."

The reaction of some lecture associations to the demand for useful and scientific lectures is typified by the following excerpt from the annual report of the Cleveland Library Association for 1859:

The Board wish to see a course of lectures, on practical scientific subjects, delivered by competent men, and illustrated by diagrams, models, apparatus and experiments. They believe that such a course would prove, from the novelty alone, much more attractive to the community than the majority of lectures which they have been accustomed to listen to; and from the amount of information which can be imparted in a pleasant manner, in a popular lecture on science, they believe that such a course would be a greater source of entertainment and benefit than any that has yet been delivered in Cleveland.[31]

The major obstacle to the offering of lectures on science was the scarcity of speakers who specialized in popular scientific discourses. The Ohio visits of Benjamin Silliman and his son, Benjamin Silliman, Jr.,[32] were infrequent. The Cincinnati astronomer O. M. Mitchel removed to the Dudley Observatory in Albany, New York, in 1859 and thereafter did most of his lecturing in the East. Louis Agassiz,[33] the nation's most famous scientist in the third quarter of the nineteenth century, delivered a few courses in the West, but his teaching at Harvard, his journeys with the Coastal Survey, and the great demand for his lectures in the Eastern cities compelled him to refuse most of his invitations to appear before Ohio's lyceums. The popular scientist most often heard in the West was Edward L. Youmans of

---

· [31] *Daily Cleveland Herald*, April 10, 1860. In December, 1860, the association offered three lectures on zoology by P. A. Chadbourne of Williams and Bowdoin Colleges.

[32] The younger Silliman continued his father's scientific activities, although his special interest was chemistry, rather than geology. He was a professor at Yale from 1837 to 1885. His infrequent lectures in the West were well received.

[33] A Swiss-born scientist and follower of Cuvier, Agassiz came to the United States in 1846. In 1848 he became a professor of natural history in the Lawrence Scientific School at Harvard, where he had great influence as a teacher. His most distinguished writing in America appeared in *Contributions to the Natural History of the United States* (4 vols.; 1857–63).

New York.[34] During the early 1850's his lecture courses were usually given privately, but with the growth of interest in scientific lectures during the middle and late fifties, he became a regular speaker before many of Ohio's lyceums. His lecture on "The Chemistry of the Sunbeam" was one of the favorite discourses of the time. Youmans enhanced the attractiveness of his lectures by illustrating them with simple scientific experiments on the platform. However, he did not attempt the sensational exhibitions which many of the popular scientists of the sixties employed to entertain and mystify their audiences. Youmans was a conscientious and competent lecturer, and the people of Ohio anticipated with considerable pleasure his almost annual visits to the West.

The prominence of scientific lectures in the late fifties is illustrated by a statement of the lecture fund for 1858–59 from the treasurer's book of the Cleveland Young Men's Christian Association. Four of the ten lectures were delivered by Youmans and Silliman and, according to the association's annual report for 1858, a lecture by O. M. Mitchel was scheduled in the course.[35] The discourse by Dr. John S. Newberry, a local lecturer, was apparently substituted when Mitchel was unable to meet the appointment. It will be observed that the fees of Silliman and Bayard Taylor were double those of such eminent lecturers as Josiah G. Holland, editor of the *Springfield* (Mass.) *Republican* and popular author using the pseudonym "Timothy Titcomb"; of John Lord of Boston, noted for his historical lectures; and of George Sumner of Massachusetts, abolitionist and brother of Senator Charles Sumner.

Paid door tender	$ 9.00
Melodeon 9 nights, 3 at $10, 6 at $12	102.00
Review bill, adv., etc.	20.25
Leader's Bill, adv., posters, etc.	25.50
Plain Dealer, adv.	8.50

---

[34] Youmans was a popular writer and promoter of scientific education. Among his publications were *A Class-Book of Chemistry* (1851), which was a standard textbook of the time, the *Chemical Atlas* (1854), and the *Hand-Book of Household Science* (1857). In 1872 he established the *Popular Science Monthly* (later called *Scientific Monthly*), for which he wrote many articles stressing the need of scientific education.

[35] *Cleveland Daily Leader*, February 26, 1859.

Herald	16.25
Prof. Youman's [*sic*] three lectures	132.00
Dr. Holland, one lecture	50.00
Rev. Mr. Hogarth, one lecture	50.00
B. Silliman, one lecture	100.00
Rev. Dr. Lord, one lecture	50.00
Geo. Sumner, one lecture	50.00
Bayard Taylor, one lecture	100.00
Expenses of Dr. John S. Newberry, lecture	23.50
Balance net proceeds course of ten lectures	343.13
	$1080.13[36]

4. 1861–1865 *The Wartime Lecture Market*

WITH THE outbreak of the Civil War, Ohio's young men's associations found their memberships considerably depleted by the demands of the army. The responsibility of arranging and supporting lecture programs was left to older citizens whose energies and enthusiasm were often not equal to the task. As the public mind was filled with the affairs of war and the fate of the Union, there was a general willingness to set aside the cultural education of society until the arrival of a more propitious time. The immediate problem of the men of Ohio was to fill the state's regiments with their quota of volunteers, and many fashionable ladies cheerfully forfeited their pleasant social meetings in the lecture hall to the necessity of providing woolen socks and underwear for the soldiers at the front.

During most of the war years a number of Ohio communities, including Akron, Dayton, Mansfield, and Zanesville, suspended their lecture courses. The *Dayton Journal* (November 18, 1862) regretted that the cessation of lecture activities left the city's residents with nothing more elevating than "bar-room clubs, surprise parties, and political plotting and mutual criminations, which culminate in the murderous spirit of the mob, by which peace, morality and public reputation are destroyed."

The most serious blows to the lecture system in Ohio came through the discontinuance of courses by the Columbus Atheneum and the Cincinnati Young Men's Mercantile Library Association. The com-

---

[36] *The Young Men's Christian Association of Cleveland* (Cleveland: J. B. Savage, 1900), p. 36.

munities of central and southern Ohio, accustomed to engaging the speakers selected by these two organizations, found their source of supply cut off. The editor of the Columbus *Daily Ohio State Journal* (October 30, 1862), lamenting the city's lack of a lecture program, asserted that "We have the requisite type of cultivated mind; we have the means and the will to invest; we have the best of halls and accommodations, and need *alone*, energetic *movers* in the cause." But no energetic movers appeared until 1866, when the Young Men's Christian Association sponsored a course.

As the Cincinnati Young Men's Mercantile Library Association was deeply in debt during the early sixties, its members did not desire to undertake the financial hazards of a full course of lectures. In 1861 the association sponsored only four lectures—one by Josiah G. Holland and three by James E. Murdoch—and at their conclusion the editor of the *Gazette* (February 1, 1861), recalling the long courses of former years, declared ruefully that "There are thousands in the city who will remember, with satisfaction, evenings spent in Smith & Nixon's Hall, listening to the lecturing stars of the country, under the auspices of the Association." The cautious attitude of the organization was reflected by this statement in the annual report for 1861: "Your Board have had several applications from professional lecturers, but have been averse to incurring the certain expense of engagements without a reasonable certainty of security from loss."[37]

Although the association's brief course in 1862 offered lectures by such luminaries as Bayard Taylor, James E. Murdoch, Wendell Phillips, and Artemus Ward, the net profits were only $41.92.[38] No course was given in 1863, but in February, 1864, the association sponsored a series of six scientific lectures by Reverend W. C. Richards. In December of that year, Reverend John S. C. Abbott, the popular author of historical books for children and of *The History of the Civil War in America*, was engaged to deliver two lectures. The editor of the *Gazette* (December 2, 1864) wrote that Cincinnatians "shall hail with delight the blue posters of the Y.M.M.L.A., assured

---

[37] *Cincinnati Daily Gazette*, January 8, 1862.
[38] "Annual Report of the Cincinnati Young Men's Mercantile Library Association for 1862," *Cincinnati Daily Gazette*, January 7, 1863.

that what may be done now will fully equal what was done in the olden time." But the lectures were poorly patronized, and this correspondent complained that only one hundred fifty people were present at Abbott's first performance on December 5. The lecture program for 1864 was "an utter failure" and resulted in a loss of $128.20.[39] Thoroughly discouraged by this experience, the Mercantile Library Association abandoned the lecture field.

The state's lecture system was most prosperous in the communities along the shores of Lake Erie. Cleveland was a key point on the railroad line connecting the Eastern cities with Detroit and Chicago, and, as this was the most traveled lecture route through the West during the war, the Cleveland Library Association superseded the Cincinnati Young Men's Mercantile Library Association as Ohio's most important sponsor of professional lectures. Sharing the success of Cleveland's wartime lecture program were lyceums in the northern Ohio communities of Oberlin, Norwalk, Toledo, and Warren. Ambitious lecture associations in towns which were situated far from the northern route were obliged to content themselves with local speakers or an occasional visit from one of the star performers.

The problem of obtaining lecturers was complicated by the fact that many of the Eastern orators were so occupied with war affairs that they were unable to make speaking tours in the West. In 1863 the Salem Lecture Association sent invitations to a large number of Eastern celebrities, including Phillips, Taylor, George W. Curtis, and Oliver Wendell Holmes, but none of these orators appeared. Even the Cleveland Library Association had difficulty acquiring the services of the most desirable lecturers. In arranging a course for the season of 1862–63 the association attempted unsuccessfully to employ Louis Agassiz, Holmes, Curtis, Henry Ward Beecher, Thomas Bailey Aldrich, and George Henry Boker, the eminent Philadelphia author of romantic dramas. The organization's annual report of April 13, 1863, complained that the lecture committee "were in a measure compelled to take such lecturers as the Lake cities generally secured." No efforts had been spared to secure the

---

[39] "Annual Report of the Cincinnati Young Men's Mercantile Library Association for 1864," *Cincinnati Daily Gazette*, January 4, 1865.

best talent in every department of literature and learning, "but owing to the peculiar state of the times, few of those most sought after could be induced to leave the immediate sphere of their home duties."[40]

The most important change in the cultural taste of Ohio's lecture public during the war was evinced by the increased demand for political and reform addresses. A new nation was in the making, and if that nation was to survive and flourish, its political and social structure would have to be as stalwart as a mountain. Western minds were thirsty for the theories and opinions of the country's prominent statesmen and social critics. These principles were especially welcome on the lyceum platform if they were enforced by patriotic oratory. While politics and reform acquired a new significance, literature and philosophy lost their attraction. As a result the scholar was crowded from the boards, and in his place appeared the orator.

The altered taste of the times is reflected in the Cleveland Library Association's report of April 13, 1863. In reviewing the lecture program of 1862–63, which yielded the association a net profit of $505.41, the lecture committee declared that the lectures were "mostly of a popular and patriotic stamp," as "literary men seemed to be at a discount and political addresses demanded." Because of the state of the public mind "incident to the mutations and calamities of civil war," the association believed that only political lectures "would have proved popular or been patronized."

Ohio's lyceums attempted to satisfy the public interest in politics and reform by requesting lectures from such orators as Charles Sumner of Massachusetts; Schuyler Colfax, speaker of the United States House of Representatives; William G. Brownlow, the fiery Tennessee advocate of the Union; Anna E. Dickinson of Philadelphia; Frederick Douglass; Daniel S. Dickinson of New York; Theodore Weld, the abolitionist; Major General Cassius M. Clay of Kentucky; and Wendell Phillips. Other lecturers who were in demand because of their patriotic eloquence or their interest in the moral state of the Union included James E. Murdoch, John B. Gough, Josiah G. Holland, and Theodore Tilton, editor of the *New York Independent*.

---

[40] *Daily Cleveland Herald*, April 14, 1863.

A decreasing respect for the dignity of the lecture platform is revealed in the immense popularity of William G. Brownlow. "Parson" Brownlow, as he was usually called, was an itinerant Methodist preacher who achieved notoriety as editor (1849–61) of the *Knoxville Whig*, the most influential newspaper in Tennessee. An unconditional advocate of the preservation of the Union, Brownlow was forced to flee to the mountains on the North Carolina border in November, 1861. Arrested and charged with treason, he was released a month later and went to Ohio, where he was popularly acclaimed as a patriot and was much sought after as a lecturer.

The audiences that gathered to hear Brownlow did not expect polite or cultural discourses; they anticipated high-spirited, angry condemnations of Southern institutions. After hearing "the Hero of East Tennessee" lecture on "The Rebellion," the editor of the *Toledo Blade* (October 11, 1862) commented that Brownlow's impulsive speech revealed "a vindictive spirit in his bosom that is unquenchable except by the cold hand of death, or the complete overthrow and destruction of those who inaugurated secession."

When he spoke to "a tremendous house" in Cleveland on January 1, 1863, "Mr. Brownlow said that he had been announced to deliver a lecture before the Association; but he called it a stump speech." In the course of his bitter attack on the Confederacy, Brownlow asserted that better men than the South's leaders could be found in Northern penitentiaries or in the depths of hell. If any Universalist preachers were present, "he hoped they would forego advocating the *no hell* question until this rebellion is over." In reviewing this oration, the correspondent of the *Plain Dealer* (January 2, 1863) declared that Brownlow's audience, while "intensely interested," was "disgusted and shocked at some of his low and vulgar expressions." It seemed doubtful that there was "another man in America who could make use of such vulgarities during a public address without being hissed down at once."

If there was no man in America who could match Brownlow's powers of vituperation, there was a woman—Anna E. Dickinson, the most eloquent of the female reform lecturers in the sixties. Her oratorical powers were discovered in 1860, when, at a meeting of

Progressive Friends, she delivered an impromptu address on "Woman's Rights and Wrongs." In 1861, while working at the United States Mint in Philadelphia, Miss Dickinson was discharged by her employer because of a speech made at Winchester in which she attributed the Union defeat at Ball's Bluff to the treason of General McClellan. After this experience she entered upon a lecturing career, speaking usually on antislavery, woman's rights, or the political aspects of the Civil War.

Described by Wendell Phillips as "the young elephant sent forward to try the bridges to see if they were safe for the older ones to cross," Miss Dickinson was frequently called upon to campaign for the Republican party in the East. J. B. Pond relates that "The Democrats gave her the credit of changing Vermont from a Democratic to a Republican State."[41]

Although Miss Dickinson achieved her greatest platform triumphs in the late sixties, she was much in demand as a lecturer before Western lyceums during the war years. During an antislavery speech in Cincinnati on February 16, 1864, she demonstrated her powers of denunciation as well as her impatience with Democratic sympathizers:

> She had no manuscript or notes, and evidently spoke for the most part extemporaneously; for being interrupted two or three times, once by a hiss, during general applause, she with a spirit and point rebuked the intrusion. If there were any Democrats (so-called) present, they evidently felt they had got into the wrong church.[42]

The ascendancy of emotionalism and political fervor over the culture and dignity formerly associated with the public lecture is illustrated in this reviewer's final remarks: "At the close of the lecture three cheers were given for the fair speaker, which, though well enough after an electioneering stump speech, we thought out of character on such an occasion."

After arriving from Chicago on March 3, 1864, Miss Dickinson delivered a political lecture in Toledo. The *Blade* reported that "The

---

[41] "The Lyceum," *Cosmopolitan*, XX (April, 1896), 602. In his description of Miss Dickinson's platform eloquence, Pond declares that "In vituperation and denunciation, she had no rival among living orators."

[42] *Cincinnati Daily Gazette*, February 17, 1864.

demand for reserved seats was such, that within half an hour after
the sale commenced there were very few desirable locations to be
had." On this occasion Miss Dickinson was "laboring under a severe
cold, seriously affecting her voice and making utterance very laborious." Nevertheless, "in many portions of her address the hearer
was able to see the distinctness, earnestness and power which dis-
tinguish her speaking and make her the leading oratress of the
country."

According to the *Blade* (March 4, 1864) the audience was not
altogether pleased with either "the manner or spirit of her treatment
of the Administration":

... the lecturer's treatment of President Lincoln and Secretary
Seward was not distinguished by that justice to which they are en-
titled. We were not only pained, but shocked, to hear her speak of
Mr. Seward as the "man behind the President"—meaning clearly that
he controlled that office—and in the next breath declare that he (Mr.
S.) would be a fit associate for traitors like Mason, Slidell, &c.

Like many of the political and reform lecturers of the time,
Frederick Douglass usually spoke for the benefit of charity organizations such as the Freedmen's Aid Society. He was chiefly concerned
with the future of the Negro in the social and economic spheres of
American life. Even when he lectured in the communities of northern
Ohio, Douglass' discourses did not often receive much attention
from journalists. The editors of Democratic newspapers were inclined
to ignore his orations entirely, and Republican reviewers, realizing
that many Ohioans looked upon the Negro reformer as a curiosity
whose notions were radical or impracticable, usually gave his performances only a passing notice. As public opinion on the Negro
problem was not coherent, editors were reluctant to take a stand for
or against Douglass' views on Negro citizenship and suffrage.

This wariness of the press is illustrated by the following announcement in the *Sandusky Commercial Register* (March 16, 1864):

The celebrated, and to those who hate him, the notorious, Fred.
Douglass, lectures to-night at Norman Hall, on the "Mission of the
War." We have no doubt there will be a crowded house. Those who go
to hear him will not be disappointed in hearing well-considered and
decided opinions, eloquently and forcibly uttered. Whatever men may

allow their prejudices and passions to induce them to say of him, if
they will hear him calmly, they will be compelled to confess both his
ability as a man and his superiority as an orator.

This journalist found the lecture, "both as to matter and manner,"

worthy of the speaker's reputation as one of the first orators in our
country. It evidenced logical thought, abounded in nice points, well
put, and was delivered in most choice and chaste language, and with
an air of ease and dignity which belongs to the graver debates in the
Senate chamber, but which is too rarely seen there or elsewhere.
All may not be able to agree with him in all his conclusions, but
all will be forced to admit he makes a strong case for according man-
hood and its responsibilities to the colored man.

The reputation of Daniel S. Dickinson, the United States Attorney
General in 1861, as "a statesman of extensive experience in the
counsels of the nation, an orator of great power, and one of the
noblest, purest patriots in the land" made his performances extremely
attractive to Western lecture-goers. His delivery of "The Union"
at Cleveland was described in the *Herald* (November 20, 1863) as
"a beautiful word-chaplet woven for the Goddess of Liberty, and
studded with gems, that glistened and sparkled in every link."
Dickinson "scored the traitors in arms and their sympathizers most
unmercifully, and held them up to the scorn and execration of an
outraged and betrayed civilization." His words were such as made
"the heart of every true Union man and woman beat truer and
steadier for the glorious cause of human liberty throughout the
world, which could only be vouchsafed by the preservation of the
American Union."

The *Toledo Blade* (November 21, 1863) praised Dickinson's
lecture on "The Citizen, His Relative Rights and Duties" as a
finished, instructive discourse. As Dickinson spoke with "his wonted
vigor and brilliancy," the audience "sat for nearly two hours eagerly
drinking in every word," and many were satisfied that it was the
best lecture ever read before the Young Men's Association.

A similar success was scored at Warren, where Dickinson delivered
"The Union" on December 9, 1863. The *Western Reserve Chronicle*
(December 16, 1863) reported the lecture to be "sublime in thought,

irresistible in the force of its logic, and radiant and fragrant with the choicest flowers of rhetoric."

Theodore Weld of Massachusetts, a pioneer abolitionist who had visited Ohio as early as the 1830's, lectured in the West in 1863. At Cleveland, where he delivered "The Great Uprising of the Nineteenth Century," he pleased a large audience with his attack upon "the false issues and lying pretexts of the present rebellion." Weld attempted to expose the falsity of the arguments "used by traitors to justify their course, proving the design and effect of the Constitution to be to establish a consolidated government, instead of a league of separate sovereignties."[43]

Another and more famous abolitionist, William Lloyd Garrison, appeared in Ohio in the fall of 1865. His delivery of "The Past, Present, and Future of Our Country" on November 30 was enthusiastically applauded by his Cincinnati audience. "We have scarcely ever heard a more agreeable or forcible speaker," wrote the editor of the *Gazette* (December 1, 1865). "Mr. Garrison is sixty years old, his head white, but with shoulders erect, he stands before his audience and extemporizes with the ease and skill of the professional debater."

With his usual antipathy for abolitionists, the editor of the *Enquirer* (December 1, 1865), a Democratic journal, described Garrison as "The Author of the Sentiment: 'The Union a League with Hell; the Constitution a Covenant with Death.'" As for the lecture, this writer declared that in it, Garrison "communicates the true spirit and feelings of that class of politicians at the North who have been called radicals, but whose better designation would be malignants or infernals."

The attendance at Garrison's second Cincinnati lecture, "The Claims of the Freedmen," was small, as "the subject of slavery and the negro, was too late in the rapidly changing condition of the public mind at the present period to absorb the attention of our people." Since slavery was now "nominally an obsolete institution, our sympathy for the negro, its subject, has greatly diminished, as we have imagined him to occupy the position of a free American citizen like

---

[43] *Cleveland Herald*, March 13, 1863.

the rest of us."[44] It is apparent that by 1865 lecture-goers had been surfeited with discourses on the slavery problem and were curious to hear opinions on other topics. The lectures of men like Douglass and Garrison were a much-needed stimulus to a Northern public which too easily turned aside the complexities involved in assimilating a vast Negro population that was ill-fitted to participate in a competitive society.

The lecture activities of Major General Cassius M. Clay of Kentucky, who had been a favorite performer before the Cincinnati Young Men's Mercantile Library Association in the 1850's, were considerably restricted by his responsibilities as an officer in the Union army. His opportunities to visit Ohio were rare, although he managed to deliver a few antislavery speeches in other parts of the West. Some Democratic journalists were incensed by Clay's activities as both lecturer and soldier. On November 18, 1862, the *Cleveland Plain Dealer* reprinted with hearty approval the following opinions from the *Madison* (Wis.) *Patriot*:

This Abolition agitator is drawing a Major General's pay, and in the name of God, we ask, can the Government put him to no better service than making abolition speeches at some $300 or $500 per month? Are we poor cusses to be taxed to support a crowd of Abolition agitators? Have we not already had enough of them? Is the country not already ruined by these evil geniuses?

A more popular genius in the West was James E. Murdoch, who during the war years contributed thousands of dollars to the Union cause. His great reputation as a tragedian combined with his fame as a patriot to make him one of the most acclaimed lyceum performers in the West. Newspapers of the day devoted numerous columns to describing the wonderful power of his voice "over which he exercises a complete mastery—modulating it to every form and style of expression, elevating it to the highest compass or modulating it to the lowest key; and yet never for a moment suffering it to break the harmony and beauty of nature."[45]

On March 19, 1863, "the talented and brilliant elocutionist"

[44] *Cincinnati Daily Gazette*, December 2, 1865.
[45] *Cleveland Plain Dealer*, November 20, 1862.

delivered a program of patriotic selections in Cleveland "for the purpose of strengthening and increasing the patriotism of his audience." As Murdoch's emotions caught fire "the words of fervid patriotism seemed to burn and glow as they issued from his lips. The tones thrilled the audience, until every one present felt ready to leap forward at the impassioned appeal of Marco Bozzaris, and every one echoed Longfellow's glorious Apostrophe to the Union."[46]

The people of Cincinnati revealed their gratitude for Murdoch's benevolences in behalf of the Union by sponsoring a testimonial performance on October 31, 1864. The balconies and the stage were draped with flags, and "the elite of the city gathered beneath their folds to do honor to the man whose name is linked with every one of the many noble charities to which the war has given birth." On this occasion Murdoch gave the first public reading of the famous war poem, "Sheridan's Ride." "Thomas Buchanan Read's exquisite lines entitled 'Drifting' was followed by a new poem—and we think one of his best—by the same gentleman, called 'Sheridan's Ride,' which was written yesterday."[47]

Another important contributor to Union charities was John B. Gough. During the early sixties he entertained Ohio audiences with his temperance orations and with his observations on London, where he had conducted a successful lecture tour in 1857–60. Occasionally he delivered "Eloquence and Orators," a series of passages from famous historical speeches. As Gough's attraction on the lecture platform lay chiefly in his magic powers of declamation, his temperance speeches, which gave full scope to these powers, were usually more popular than his discourses on other topics.

One of Gough's most ambitious charity ventures was undertaken in January, 1863, at Cincinnati, where he delivered twelve lectures. Despite the capacity audiences that applauded "Eloquence and Orators," "Lights and Shadows of London Life," "London by Night," and the temperance discourses, the elaborate lecture series was a financial failure. Gough was paid $2000.00, while the owner

---

[46] *Daily Cleveland Herald*, March 20, 1863. The net profits of this lecture, sponsored by the Soldiers' Aid Society, were $264.50. *Ibid.*, March 21, 1863.
[47] *Cincinnati Daily Gazette*, November 1, 1864.

of the Opera House, S. N. Pike, received the fantastic sum of $2100.00. When accused of depriving war charities of their just profits, Pike defended himself by asserting in the city's newspapers that, to make the hall available for Gough, he was obliged to pay $175.00 nightly to a dramatic company which had contracted for the use of the Opera House. The loss to the sponsors of Gough's lectures was $1,032.45.[48]

In October, 1863, Gough delivered four lectures in Cincinnati for the benefit of the Christian Commission, the Storrs Association, and the Theological Association. The net profits of these lectures were $155.21. A great triumph for Union charity was his lecture on October 26, 1863, in behalf of Ohio's 7th Regiment. An immense audience of patriotic Cincinnatians contributed net proceeds of $774.07.[49]

In the midst of the perplexing problems of the war, Ohio's lecture enthusiasts were comforted by the optimistic, and sometimes senti- mental, views of the nation set forth by Josiah G. Holland and Theodore Tilton. In his lecture on "The National Heart," Holland contended "the Heart of the Nation was all right, and he founded his reasons for such belief upon the unanimity of the people when the National life was assailed by traitors."[50] The theme of this lecture was thus stated in the *Western Reserve Chronicle* (December 23, 1863):

When the culture of the heart fails to keep pace with the culture of the head, then will it breed corruptions. With a pure popular heart, even if the government should be overthrown, the nation would live. But if love of God, home and country were to cease then the nation would be lost.

At Cincinnati, where Theodore Tilton delivered "The State of the Country" on January 10, 1865, the *Gazette* described the New York journalist as a man of youthful appearance, smoothly shaven, and with long hair "in keeping with his tall and graceful form. He has a full, melodious voice, and seemed to speak extemporaneously,

---

[48] *Ibid.*, February 19, 1863.
[49] *Ibid.*, November 5, 1863.
[50] *Daily Toledo Blade*, December 5, 1863.

though it was evident his sentences were well studied." In presenting his hopeful view of the country Tilton concluded that "The Nation stands upon a higher and nobler moral plane than ever before."

The evils of the Reconstruction period were to provide a bitter refutation of the cheerful sentiments of Holland and Tilton. Perhaps a nearer approximation of the condition of the country and of the spirit of Northern statesmen was to be found in the vindictive criticism of Anna Dickinson and Wendell Phillips.

During the war years, humorous lecturers attained a prominence second only to that of the politicians and reformers. In earlier days, popular humorists were rarely invited to speak before Ohio's lecture associations; as long as the dissemination of culture and knowledge was the main function of the lecture system, the popular humorist was obliged to keep his place with the bell ringers and minstrels. Indeed, he was a representative of those "frivolous amusements" whose influence the serious lecture was expected to counteract.

But the wartime relaxation of cultural taste, which removed the political speaker from his accustomed stump and dignified him with a lecture-desk upon the lyceum platform, supplied a cordial welcome for the popular humorist whose laugh-getting had heretofore been confined chiefly to noisy, Saturday night performances in Ohio's less expensive halls and opera houses. He gave variety to lyceum programs overburdened with the patriotic effusions of political orators and provided diversion for lecture-goers whose lives were often darkened by the anxieties of war, its costly campaigns, and its inevitable casualty lists.

Charles F. Browne—or Artemus Ward, as he was usually called —was the first important humorist to invade Ohio's lyceum plat-forms.[51] During the 1860's Browne had worked as a journeyman printer in Cincinnati, Toledo, and other communities in the West, but his fame as a humorist was established in 1857–59, when he was a regular contributor to the columns of the *Cleveland Plain Dealer*. The imaginary adventures of "A. Ward" and his traveling puppet

---

[51] Next in popularity to Browne during the early sixties were R. J. De Cordova of New York and A. Miner Griswold, "The Fat Contributor," of Ohio.

show, related with numerous misspellings and comic incidents, afforded much amusement to the people of the West. The success of his contributions to *Vanity Fair* resulted in his removal to New York in 1859 to join the editorial staff of that magazine.

Browne's lecture career began in the East in 1861, when he successfully delivered "Babes in the Wood," a collection of satirical witticisms and humorous anecdotes which had nothing to do with either babes or woods.[52] In 1862 he read this lecture in the West, where he attracted large audiences. At Springfield, where he "spoke his piece" on January 28, the correspondent of the *Republic* could "not remember to have seen, in a long time, so large an assembly gathered there, for any purpose."

On the following evening Browne appeared before the Cincinnati Young Men's Mercantile Library Association. The *Gazette* (January 30, 1862) described the lecturer as being about thirty years old, of medium height, light complexion and hair, and wearing a heavy mustache. "This appendage, however, rather takes from the humorous expression of his features, which are quite grave for a humorist."

This writer declared that Browne's discourse "is called a lecture while it partakes of little in common with that peculiarly American institution. Perhaps 'The Children in the Wood' should be called, more properly an entertainment, for such it really is." Browne's style "reminds one of Timothy Titcomb's [Josiah G. Holland's] in his letters and essays, yet it lacks the depth and thought shown in them." The lecture, or entertainment, "was heartily enjoyed and applauded throughout."

At Cleveland, where Browne read "The Children in the Wood" for the benefit of the Soldiers' Aid Society, 1,531 people crowded the city's Academy of Music and contributed proceeds of $275.10.[53] "This is probably a larger audience than ever assembled in Cleveland to hear a lecture," reported the *Herald* (February 3, 1862). In reviewing the lecture, the correspondent of the *Plain Dealer* (February 1, 1862) observed that "the affected seriousness, the

---

[52] This lecture was frequently announced as "The Children in the Wood."
[53] "Weekly Report of the Cleveland Soldiers' Aid Society," *Daily Cleveland Herald*, February 10, 1862.

pauses here and there to be followed by something immensely ridiculous and comical, all combined to make it irresistable [*sic*]."

When Browne read "The Children in the Wood" before the Toledo Young Men's Association, he made these introductory remarks:

The lecture field has been plowed, planted and dug; mowed and reapt; and cultivated indeed, in so many ways, that I suppose a man of very able mind might not feel too sure of offering you any thing strikingly novel or brilliant. Oblige me, then, by overlooking the short-comings of a person who has no such thing as an able mind. I have tried, however, to make these paragraphs cheerful in the main; some of them, indeed, may border on the farcical, but I make no apology for that. The fool with his cap and bells often deals Folly its deadliest blows.[54]

The discourse, which Browne described to his audience as "nothing more than a collection of humorous sentences and funny stories," was not much admired by the *Blade's* editor, who associated the public lecture with a higher level of instruction and entertainment:

There was nothing offered by the lecturer which could in the least atone for the manifest feeling of the audience that they were *sold* or raffled off, in the most ludicrous manner. The audience, however, were in the best possible humor, and enjoyed the *sell* as thoroughly as the lecturer could desire, but we think there were very few, if any, who felt disposed to award Mr. Brown [*sic*] much credit for his production.

On January 10, 1863, the Columbus Atheneum "was densely crowded with the beauty, fashion and chivalry of our city" for Browne's reading of "Sixty Minutes in Africa." The *Ohio State Journal* (January 12, 1863) characterized the lecture as "a bully thing," praised Browne for "the instruction as well as amusement," and expressed regret that "the school children could not have been universally present."

At Cleveland, Browne's large audience "laughed consumedly" at the "good humored fun, jokes, and sarcasms" of "Sixty Minutes in Africa"; and at Sandusky the hall "was one guffaw of laugh'n gas—Artemus furnished the gas and the audience the laugh."[55] On March 17, 1864, while commenting on R. J. De Cordova's humorous lecture

[54] *Daily Toledo Blade*, February 3, 1862.
[55] *Sandusky Daily Commercial Register*, April 17, 1863.

"Our First Baby," this reviewer declared that "It was almost as foolish as 'Artemus Ward's' Lecture on Africa, and seemed to have excited laughter—doubtless for the same reason—its foolishness. Verily, 'popular lectures' are fast running into the ground."

In 1863–64 Browne lectured extensively in the Far West. In Utah and Nevada he visited the Mormons, whose way of life so interested him that he made a careful study of their habits. His impressions were revealed in his lecture, "Artemus Ward Among the Mormons," which was read with great success in both East and West. The discourse was advertised as a panorama and, like many historical and travel lectures of the day, was illustrated with numerous colorful paintings.

"Artemus Ward Among the Mormons," with its tickets which would "admit a gentleman and one wife," was delivered in Cincinnati on March 6 and 7, 1865. The lecture was apparently more serious than some of Browne's hearers anticipated, and "Men who went only to laugh were surprised to find themselves not sadder but wiser men, as the panorama and accompanying remarks yield an immense amount of information in regard to Mormon life."[56]

The lecturer's discourse was well received, although "Mr. Browne has the bad habit of allowing a part of his voice to straggle into his nose." Browne's kinship with the popular stage entertainers of the time was evidenced by his use of a musical accompaniment for portions of his lecture. Commenting on this aspect of the program, the *Gazette's* editor declared that "We must protest against the musical part of the entertainment. A third rate piano, out of tune, with poor selections badly performed certainly admits of improvement."

In 1866 Browne visited England, where he died the following year. In his short lecturing career he established himself as the foremost humorist of the day. On Ohio's lecture platforms his popularity was unrivaled until the emergence of Mark Twain. Browne's chief influence on the lecture system was to foster the acceptance of humorous entertainment. But in doing so, he joined the political orators in furthering the estrangement of the lyceum system from

---

[56] *Cincinnati Daily Gazette*, March 7, 1865.

the serious cultural purposes which its New England founders had
envisioned for it.

5. 1866–1870   *Postwar Revival and Decline*

BETWEEN 1865 and 1868 Ohio's lecture system enjoyed unprecedented
prosperity. With the return of peace the state's lyceums regained
their large memberships, and the Eastern lecturers once more resumed their journeys to the West. Money was plentiful; lecture-
goers willingly paid admission fees of fifty cents, or seventy-five
cents if they desired reserved seats. The two-dollar course ticket now
cost from three to five dollars, and the demand was such that the
lyceums were assured sufficient revenue to pay the lecture fees of
two hundred dollars exacted by Henry Ward Beecher, John B.
Gough, and Anna E. Dickinson.

The system of acquiring lecturers by direct invitation or by application to a speaker's personal agent was generally superseded by the
method of selecting an entire corps of orators from the published
circulars of large lecture agencies. These organizations annually provided lists of lecturers and their prices, and, for five or ten per cent
of the lecture fee, arranged speaking schedules for orators throughout
the country. The chief lecture bureau in the West was the Associated
Western Literary Societies, which was established in 1865.[57] Other
agencies founded during the late sixties included the American
Literary Bureau, the Williams Lecture and Musical Bureau, and
the Redpath Lyceum Bureau.

The railroad line extending through the Lake Erie communities
continued to be the state's most traveled lecture route, and lyceums
in Akron, Ashtabula, Cleveland, Mansfield, Norwalk, Oberlin, Sandusky, Toledo, and Warren attracted the most popular speakers in
the land. An example of the renewed interest in lectures occurred
at Sandusky, where the financial prospects of lecture courses had
never been auspicious. The *Commercial Register* reported on November 6, 1866, that "A prominent lecturer East recently addressed one

---

[57] For a history of the Associated Western Literary Societies see Hubert H.
Hoeltje, "Notes on the History of Lecturing in Iowa," *Iowa Journal of History
and Politics*, XXV (January, 1927), 120–131.

of our leading citizens to know if he would be warranted in coming here and received the reply, if he had a puppet show or minstrels, to come along; otherwise it wouldn't pay for him to venture." But in 1867 the Young Men's Christian and Library Association undertook a course "to revive our taste for the intellectual, to cultivate in our young men and women an appreciation of something higher and better than negro minstrelsy and simpering nonsense generally."[58] And at the conclusion of this project the city's residents could look back with pleasure upon "the first financially successful lecture course Sandusky has ever had."[59]

The financial prosperity of the Cleveland Library Association was measurably increased by the postwar revival. According to the organization's annual report of May 1, 1866, the course for 1865–66, which yielded net receipts of $2,209.80, was the most profitable in the city's lecture annals.[60] In the following year the association reported a balance of $1,052.41 in the lecture fund after all expenses were paid.[61] In 1867–68 the lectures in the association's seventeenth annual course were given in newly constructed Case Hall, with its 1800 seats, including "1240 luxurious Opera Chairs." The annual report of May 5, 1868, declared that "The total receipts for the course were $4,018.80; the total expenses, $2,517.30; leaving a net profit of $1,501.50."[62]

In central Ohio the most important lecture sponsor was the Columbus Young Men's Christian Association, although many of the nation's leading orators appeared also in Delaware, Springfield, and Zanesville. At Cincinnati a succession of sponsors provided lecture courses during the late sixties, the most pretentious being managed by a private citizen, William F. Phillips, and supported by subscription. The Young Men's Mercantile Library Association did not revive its elaborate lecture courses of former years. In 1867

---

[58] *Sandusky Daily Commercial Register*, December 12, 1867.

[59] *Ibid.*, March 4, 1868.

[60] *Morning Cleveland Herald*, May 3, 1866.

[61] *Ibid.*, May 8, 1867.

[62] *Ibid.*, May 7, 1868. Since there were ten lectures in the course, the average expense of each performance was about $250.00, a much greater financial risk than lyceums were required to take in the prewar period.

"Letters of invitation and inquiry were directed to most of those gentlemen possessing favorable reputations as lecturers. Declinations, refusals and delays were so general that we were forced to relinquish the project."[63] The association's annual report for the following year stated that "The Board have made no effort to arrange for a course of lectures during the present winter, the experience of former years having convinced them that any attempt in that direction would result unsatisfactorily in a pecuniary point of view."[64]

The flourishing state of the lecture system was not marked by renewed interest in cultural discourses. Writing in 1868, Thomas Wentworth Higginson declared that "With us, poetry and science have almost left the field. The popular lecture is coming to be a branch of that national institution 'the stump.' Politics, long excluded by common consent, now threaten to exclude everything else. The long slavery agitation, and the war for the Union, very properly brought this element in, and it shows no symptoms of going out."[65] As the lyceums of the West were well aware of the financial profits to be gained by catering to the public taste, the lecture programs were heavily weighted with political and reform addresses by such speakers as Phillips, Anna E. Dickinson, Douglass, Gough, Horace Greeley, Colfax, and Susan B. Anthony, the eminent woman suffragist.

Besides this great enthusiasm for politics and reform, there was a broadening interest in popular humor and novel forms of diversion on the platform. "A year or two after the war, when over a million of men had returned from military strife to civil pursuits having been through four years of excitement that rendered it next to impossible to settle quietly down, there came an unprecedented demand for entertainments and amusements."[66] But despite the attractive market for humorous discourses, only a few were delivered between 1865 and 1868. Mark Twain (Samuel L. Clemens), Josh

[63] "Annual Report of the Cincinnati Young Men's Mercantile Library Association for 1867," *Cincinnati Daily Gazette*, January 8, 1868. This experience of the association suggests the disadvantage of dealing directly with speakers whose schedules were arranged by the lecture bureaus.

[64] *Cincinnati Daily Gazette*, January 6, 1869.

[65] "The American Lecture System," *Macmillan's Magazine*, XVIII (May, 1868), 52.

[66] J. B. Pond, "The Lyceum," *Cosmopolitan*, XX (April, 1896), 596.

Billings (H. W. Shaw), and Petroleum V. Nasby (D. R. Locke) appeared briefly in 1868, but these entertainers achieved their fame on Western lyceum platforms in later years. Popular amusement was frequently provided by such lecturers as Captain C. F. Hall, the Arctic explorer; P. B. Du Chaillu, the African traveler; or G. B. Winship of Boston, "the strongest man in the world," who demonstrated his prowess by carrying sacks of wheat upon the stage. The desire for novelty was sometimes met by the performances of musicians or other entertainers. When Horace Greeley lectured at Cincinnati on February 14, 1868, the program managers provided, as an added attraction, a thirteen-year-old wonder, Miss Etta Soule, "The Temperance Morning Star," who wrenched the emotions of her audience with the recital of a poem entitled "The Drunkard's Death."

The interest in popular science was partially satisfied through the lectures of Edward L. Youmans. Cultural lecturers were not much in demand. Edwin P. Whipple, Josiah G. Holland, and other less-renowned orators occasionally appeared in Ohio, but the cultural lecturer who was most often invited to speak before the state's lyceums was Emerson.

The clamor for political and reform lectures continued unabated through the late sixties. The antislavery agitators who had dominated the platform during the war now turned their energies to the problems of equal rights and suffrage for the Negro. The advocates of woman's rights also appeared in increasing numbers. The feminist's cause was strengthened by the support of such able orators as Phillips and Tilton and by a gradual decrease in the popular prejudice against female lecturers. The widespread popularity of Anna Dickinson's wartime lectures had been particularly effective in winning a secure place on the lyceum stage for "female radicals" such as Susan B. Anthony, Elizabeth Cady Stanton, and Lucy Stone.

Newspaper protests against the submersion of the cultural lecture in a flood of political and reform discourses were increasingly rare. The following appeal was conspicuously at odds with the pattern of popular taste:

Now that the Lecture Season has arrived, we hope efforts will be made to bring to our City this winter some of the ablest men of the country to Lecture before our citizens on purely literary and scientific subjects. The mere political lecturers of the country, who stir up bad blood among the people, instead of exciting pleasurable emotions, should be discountenanced. The object of all lectures should be to "raise the genius and to mend the heart"—to improve the morals and to cultivate the intellects of the people.[67]

Chief among the lecturers whose attraction was owing to their fame as statesmen were Senator Charles Sumner of Massachusetts and Schuyler Colfax of New York, Speaker of the United States House of Representatives. Sumner made one of his rare Ohio appearances on November 7, 1867, at Toledo. His subject, "Are We a Nation?" was discussed "with the masterly manner for which the distinguished speaker has gained a world wide reputation." Sumner's "ably prepared discourse, the clear heavy voice and fine personal appearance of the orator, made this entertainment one of great interest to the public and success to the Association."[68]

Colfax's Ohio lectures were not on political subjects, although it is evident that his political reputation was the source of much of his popularity. On November 8, 1866, he read "Across the Continent" before the Toledo Library Association. His "beautifully written" description of a trip to the Pacific coast in 1865 attracted cash receipts of $250.00, exclusive of the income from season tickets, a success which the *Commercial* (November 9, 1866) termed "a good beginning for the Association in the series of lectures they are to furnish our citizens this winter."

On the next evening Colfax, whose "remarkable public career has given him a position in the affections and confidence of the people not surpassed by any man in the country," lectured in Cleveland. "Across the Continent" was read "in a masterly and eloquent manner, giving entire satisfaction, judging from the immense applause that greeted many of its most effective points."[69]

When Colfax appeared in Akron the public desire to see and hear

[67] *Mt. Vernon Democratic Banner*, November 4, 1865. No course was undertaken in response to this appeal.
[68] *Toledo Daily Commercial*, November 8, 1867.
[69] *Morning Cleveland Herald*, November 10, 1866.

him was so great that his audience was swelled by "a large number from Middlebury, Tallmadge, Springfield, and other neighboring towns, and a number from Ravenna, and other adjoining counties."[70] "Across the Continent" was received with "interest and delight" by his hearers.

In 1867 Horace Greeley joined the reform lecturers in Ohio with a discourse entitled "The Issues and Lessons of Our Civil War." At Cincinnati Greeley "started out with the assurance that his theme was not an entertaining one, nor himself an entertaining man." But the *Commercial* (January 3, 1867) insisted that "his lecture *was* entertaining in the highest and largest sense. Contrary to tradition he was neatly dressed, and his benevolent face and manner lent a charm to his delivery, that compensated for all defects of elocution."

When the editor of the *New York Tribune* read "Self-Made Men" in Zanesville on February 12, 1868, the *Courier* reported that, as a reader, Greeley "is slow, deliberate, distinct and, semi-occasionally, rattles over a clause quicker than double-geared lightning." Many were disappointed that he "did not feel at liberty to speak of some of the self-made men of modern times," but as for drawing a large audience "he excels anything we have had for some time; knocking the wind out of a nigger show; filling Music Hall, and drawing half dollars by the hundred out of the pockets of our citizens, thus setting a tight money market at defiance."

The Cleveland audience which heard Greeley's lecture on "Abraham Lincoln" anticipated that the speaker, "availing himself of his personal acquaintance with the great statesman," would give a vivid, authentic account of Lincoln's life and character. "Instead of this, however, we had inflicted upon us a tedious *melange* of political disquisition." The lecture was pronounced by the *Leader* (March 2, 1868) "the least interesting of the year." Greeley's long-winded readings from the "Rebellion Record" were more than his hearers could bear. "A great number left the hall under the infliction, and those who perseveringly sat it out were terribly bored."

During the late sixties Frederick Douglass persistently appealed for the social acceptance of his race. The reviews of Ohio's editors

---

[70] Akron *Summit County Beacon*, April 25, 1867.

stressed his vigorous eloquence but infrequently ventured a judgment of his views on equal rights for the Negro. Occasionally there
is evidence of the public prejudice against the lecturer or against the
large number of Negroes who attended his addresses. When Douglass
appeared in Cincinnati, the *Commercial* (January 14, 1867) revealed
that many citizens tried "to exclude the colored people from the
parquette" and "compel them to occupy the galleries." This correspondent considered it "a short-sighted policy to draw such lines when
the center of attraction is himself of the tabooed."

At Douglass' reading of "Self-Made Men" in Cincinnati on March
17, 1868, the large audience was "composed perhaps about equally
of representatives of both sexes of the Caucasian and the African
race." According to the *Commercial* (March 18, 1868) the audience
gathered "as much for the purpose of finding out what Mr. Douglass
could say as for any expectation that his lecture would be instructive
and entertaining." Douglass' realization that he was viewed as something of a curiosity is revealed in his introductory remarks, adapted
from Dr. Samuel Johnson's comment about female preachers, that

he made his appearance under great advantages, one of which was that
very little was expected of him, and where little was expected no one
could be disappointed. "Men come to hear Fred. Douglass speak," said
he, "as the boy is amused with his dog when he stands on his hind
legs—not because he stands well, but because he stands at all."

Douglass was announced to deliver "Self-Made Men" in Cadiz
on February 3, 1869, "but Fred wished to practice 'William the
Silent,' as he is to deliver that lecture in Cincinnati, and so the
audience listened in patience for over two hours to a rehearsal of the
history of the Netherlands." The *Republican* (February 5, 1869)
observed that "the soul of the theme was the progress of humanity
under the inspiration of liberty," and added that "No lecturer speaks
purer English, nor more eloquently—not a word suggestive of Southern pronunciation, emphasis or manner." The editor of the *Sentinel*
(February 10, 1869) attempted to satisfy his readers' curiosity concerning the lecturer's appearance with the statement that "Douglass
has none of the features of the negro, but the tinge of color. The
judges of elections in Cadiz township would pronounce him, without

waiting to hear a word of argument, a 'White Male Citizen of the United States.' "

The postwar lectures of Anna E. Dickinson, which dealt usually with the problems of Negro suffrage or woman's rights, earned for her the title of "Queen of the Platform." Despite her lecture fees of $200.00 she was much sought after by Western lyceums, as the prospect of hearing her eloquence and strong logic consistently drew large audiences. After hearing her delivery of "Home Thrusts" the editor of the *Toledo Commercial* (February 8, 1866) wrote that "as the eloquent pleader for the rights of humanity, with her womanly enthusiasm, tenderness and instinctive perception of justice, she is an ornament of the American forum. Her voice is clear and ringing, her diction elegant and her language well selected."

Miss Dickinson's independence and flair for showmanship were demonstrated at Cincinnati, where, in preparation for her discourse on "The Assassination and the Suicide," a lecture-desk had been prepared with lights on either side in addition to footlights, "accommodations generally required by professional lecturers." All these trappings Miss Dickinson had removed, "whereat the audience applauded, and she stepped to the fore part of the stage untrammeled by manuscripts or notes of any kind."[71]

In her popular woman's rights lecture, "Something to Do," Miss Dickinson related to many Ohio audiences how "she earned her first money by scrubbing the pavements for two shillings, to pay her way to one of Wendell Phillips' lectures."[72] When this discourse was read at Warren, the *Western Reserve Chronicle* (April 24, 1867) commended Miss Dickinson as "a brave woman and a powerful advocate of the rights of her sex. Her thoughts are fresh, clear and bold; her words fitly chosen and charmingly uttered. She is at times severely denunciatory, but her condemnation always seems fitly applicable to the point of criticism." The lecturer was pronounced "one of the few who having the ability dares to grapple with social wrongs and evils of great magnitude."

Occasionally Miss Dickinson and her forthright views on woman's

---

[71] *Cincinnati Daily Gazette*, April 5, 1866.
[72] *Ibid.*, April 16, 1867.

proper position in society encountered journalistic censure. The editor of the *Steubenville Herald* (March 25, 1870) saw in the lecturer none of that pink-cheeked feminine beauty "which reminds one of roses sopped in silver dew," but rather "a woman ungraceful in appearance of form, with no semblance of beauty, a square decided face, not a subject of flattery, a true type of the strong-minded woman, simply this and nothing more." This writer's parting lament was that "the pants are likely to be worn by a few of the Dickinson converts before the vexed question is laid."

The prevalent interest in woman's rights during the decade of the sixties brought a deluge of lectures in the West from such ardent feminists as Elizabeth Cady Stanton, Susan B. Anthony, and Lucy Stone. Mrs. Stanton and Miss Anthony were early convinced by their unenthusiastic reception as temperance and antislavery lecturers that only through equal rights could women perform useful social service in America. Frequently appearing together on the same platform, they lectured throughout the nation on the necessity of woman suffrage. At the organization of the National Woman Suffrage Association in 1869, Mrs. Stanton was elected its first president and Miss Anthony its vice-president.

When these two suffragettes lectured in Cincinnati on November 28, 1867, they were introduced to an audience of four hundred by the eccentric English reformer George Francis Train, who appeared "in black pantaloons, white vest and blue coat with brass buttons." The *Commercial* (November 29, 1867) described Mrs. Stanton as a handsome woman of fifty, a dignified figure with her luxuriant gray hair and graceful manner. Her audience listened closely as she spoke "in a low, gentle voice" of such clarity that it could be distinctly heard throughout the hall.

Miss Anthony was "tall and commanding in appearance" and "rather thin in face and person." In the more eloquent parts of her address she emphasized her words by tapping the floor with her foot. She used more inflection than Mrs. Stanton, although her voice occasionally grew monotonous. "She frequently stumbles over her words, but always corrects herself immediately. She commands the close attention of an audience."

Lucy Stone, a pioneer feminist in America, graduated in 1847 from Oberlin College, where she was considered a dangerous radical. In 1850 she headed the first call for a woman's rights convention and figured prominently in the resultant meeting at Worcester, Massachusetts. Though she married in 1855 she insisted on retaining her maiden name as a matter of principle. Like Mrs. Stanton and Miss Anthony, Miss Stone lectured frequently in the West. After hearing her speak in Cincinnati the editor of the *Commercial* (January 27, 1869) wrote this review:

Those who had come expecting to be lectured about the pre-eminent excellences of the sex, and the unbearable brutalities to which they were subjected at the hands of the august "lords of creation," by the traditional female of blue stocking proclivities, of a severe and venerable aspect—and we have no doubt such apprehensions were entertained by many—were agreeably disappointed on being presented to a lady pleasing in appearance and agreeable in voice, whose utterances, marked as they were by the evidence of refined thought and culture, and delivered in a manner singularly natural and engaging, commanded the undivided attention of the audience.

Another important female lecturer in the late sixties was Clara Barton, organizer of the American Red Cross, who performed so many invaluable services for Union soldiers and their families during the Civil War. Her lectures usually comprised vivid accounts of her wartime experiences. When Miss Barton lectured in Cleveland, the reporter for the *Herald* (February 26, 1867) confessed that "He did not intend to stay over fifteen minutes, but remained an hour":

And for one time, to the credit of a Cleveland audience, everybody that entered the hall remained an *hour* also. They couldn't go away. They wanted to hear *one* more instance of the valor of the bravest and best men that ever marched under the banner of any land beneath the sun. . . . no one went away until the last syllable was uttered, and then with regret, because time and circumstances would not permit a longer stay. Miss Barton has made a good impression, and for her devotion to the soldiers of the Republic she is entitled to a nation's gratitude.

Few reform lecturers in the West met with as much success as Theodore Tilton, the learned editor of the *New York Independent*. In 1866 he frequently read "The Corner Stone of Reconstruction," in which he maintained that "*perfect equality before the law, without*

*regard to race or color, and impartial suffrage for all American citi-
zens, was the true basis of re-construction."*[73]

After listening to this discourse the editor of the Warren *Western
Reserve Chronicle* (December 5, 1866) praised Tilton as "an earnest,
ardent, eloquent speaker, animating his theme with 'thoughts that
breathe and words that burn.'" Without benefit of notes or manuscript Tilton spoke with "an ease, freedom, eloquence and fervor
that captivates and draws his audience into full sympathy with him."

On January 11, 1869, Tilton read "The American Woman" before Columbus' Hannah Neil Mission. "He spoke as the master of
his subject, confidently, seeming to understand just when to strike
a heavy blow, just when to have attitude and face and voice, have
most power in grand utterances, and just when to take the audience
with a random shot."[74]

A week later this discourse was given in Canton. Tilton "spoke of
that part of creation last given, that doubled our joys and quadrupled
our expenses." He did not consider woman "an angel," but believed
it was "the want of the ballot that lowered woman, who did not receive from man those political rights she deserved."[75]

Tilton's habit of deliberately attacking the prejudices of his audience was resented by the local editor in Tiffin, where Tilton appeared
on March 16, 1869. "His whole effort was devoted to ridiculing our
city and western people generally.—He is an egotistical donkey, un-
worthy the todyism [*sic*] betowed upon him. We hope the practice
of employing eastern lecturers to puff up eastern interests in the west
will soon 'play out.'"[76]

The eloquent discourses of Gough and Murdoch continued to be
popular during the years after the war. When Gough attracted a
large audience in Toledo, the *Commercial* (January 12, 1866) called
it a great pity "that his eloquence cannot be heard by all the poor
besotted creatures who revel their lives away in the drinking hells
of our cities, for it would seem that none, however degraded and
debauched, could resist it."

[73] Akron *Summit County Beacon*, December 6, 1866.
[74] Columbus *Ohio State Journal*, January 12, 1869.
[75] *Canton Repository and Republican*, January 21, 1869.
[76] Tiffin *Seneca Advertiser*, March 18, 1869.

Gough returned to Toledo on November 16, 1866, and this correspondent lamented that he could not report the lecture, as he "would as soon attempt to write down the revolutions of the wings of a wind-mill in a hurricane, or count the puffings of a steam-engine going at the rate of a mile a minute." The discourse was "filled with good, solid advice, humorous and pathetic anecdotes and flights of imagination, such as only Gough has ever given in the lecture field."

In "Eloquence and Orators," given at Cincinnati on March 17, 1868, Gough presented "highly entertaining imitations of some of the most noted speakers and pulpit orators on both sides of the Atlantic." The orator attempted "to prove that no particular rules could be laid down or followed in order to make eloquence effective." His theory was that "when a speaker feels his subject he will make his audience feel, and never otherwise."[77]

During this lecture Gough, in illustrating a Negro sermon he had heard, happened to say, "An thar is brudder Jones stuck in de mud, an thar is brudder Johnson stuck in de mud." The audience, thinking immediately of the troubles of President Andrew Johnson, who was then being threatened with impeachment, "made the hall resound with shouts of laughter, and kept up for some seconds prolonged applause. A. J.'s predicament, thus unintentionally indicated, became the most entertaining illustration of the evening."

On the evening of January 14, 1867, Brainard's Hall in Cleveland "was packed, . . . the occasion being a lecture by James E. Murdoch, one of the most renowned of American tragedians, on 'Shakespeare and the Drama—his relations to Plays, to Acting, and the Stage,' interspersed with readings from Romeo and Juliet, Hamlet, Henry the Fourth, and As You Like It." For its "beauty of composition and the manner of its delivery" this lecture was acclaimed by the *Herald* (January 15, 1867) "one of the most enchanting productions ever delivered to the Association."

At Murdoch's reading of "An Evening with Sir Walter Scott" in Cincinnati on March 5, 1867, his sponsors, the managers of Bryant, Stratton and DeHan's Commercial College, plastered the stage and proscenium with posters advertising the college, "in the violation of good taste and the customary propriety of the lecture room." The

---

[77] *Cincinnati Commercial*, March 18, 1868.

Commercial (March 6, 1867) commented that "In voice and gesture Mr. Murdoch is still the same charming and graceful recitation-
ist he was when years dealt more kindly with his genial face."

One of Murdoch's most popular lectures at this time was "Recollections of Abraham Lincoln." In this discourse, given in Cincinnati
on November 10, 1868, Murdoch related the circumstances of his
first meeting with Lincoln at Springfield in 1860. Lincoln attended
Murdoch's reading one night, and the next day the two men enjoyed a visit of several hours. Murdoch "was particularly struck with
the intelligence and justness of Mr. Lincoln's criticisms on literary
and dramatic characters and with his comprehensive views of the
political situation at that time."[78]

Despite the success of many of these postwar lectures, the prosperity of Ohio's lecture system was of brief duration. Between 1868
and 1870 there was increasing evidence in the account books of the
state's lyceums to indicate that public support of the lecture programs
was dwindling. At Cleveland the decline came quickly; the Library
Association's course in 1867–68 had yielded a net profit of $1,501.50,
but, the following year, "the lecture course was not a financial success, realizing but a small sum above expenses."[79] After losing $134.80
on its first three lectures in 1868–69 and emerging with a deficit at
the end of the course, the Ravenna Lecture Association suspended
activities.[80] During the same lecture season the Springfield Young
Men's Christian Association reported proceeds of $844.25, expenses
of $847.05, and a lingering hope of recovering $20.00 from the sale
of course tickets which had not been paid for.[81] At Zanesville two
scientific lectures by the popular Edward L. Youmans in February,
1868, resulted in a loss of $63.00, although the Young Men's Chris-
tian Association paid Youmans the comparatively low fee of $80.00
per lecture.[82]

On December 8, 1869, the Canton Young Men's Christian Association opened its course with a lecture by James E. Murdoch. Two

[78] *Ibid.*, November 11, 1868.
[79] "Annual Report of the Cleveland Library Association, May 4, 1869,"
Cleveland Morning Herald, May 5, 1869.
[80] Ravenna *Portage County Democrat*, April 21, 1869.
[81] *Springfield Daily Republic*, April 6, 1869.
[82] *Zanesville Daily Courier*, February 25, 1868.

days later the *Repository and Republican* informed the public that "The Murdoch reading on Wednesday last lost about $75. With this sample of encouragement the society does not feel warranted in providing a course of lectures for the winter." The Lancaster Young Men's Christian Association suffered a more humiliating experience. At the inauguration of its lecture series on December 6, 1869, no audience appeared to hear the travel discourse of George Kennan of Norwalk. This course was discontinued.

The reactions of Ohio's journalists to the poor patronage of the lecture system often echoed familiar themes. The editor of the Tiffin *Seneca Advertiser* (January 14, 1869) wrote these comments:

It appears that an entertainment of a beneficial and instructive character, does not meet with the patronage it should. Why is it? Were a Negro Minstrel Troup [*sic*] to come along the hall would be crowded. A "Sleight of Hand performer," would fill his pockets with filthy lucre, but a good, sensible lecture, for the benefit of a worthy object, is left to languish.

The correspondent of the *Painesville Telegraph*, appealing on November 25, 1869, for a course of home lectures, declared that "Past experience furnishes little encouragement to renew the effort to sustain a course at the outrageously high prices paid for the professional lecturers." Moreover, there was no advantage in "paying such high prices for *imported* goods, when as good or better can be made nearer home."

The decline in the fortunes of Ohio's lyceums made necessary some alterations in the lecture programs. While many of the smaller communities either discontinued their courses or turned to the system of home lectures, the lyceums in most of the major cities attempted to sustain public interest by offering various forms of entertainment on the platform. An alternative procedure, the presentation of a short series of lectures by established favorites, was undertaken in 1870–71 by the Young Men's Christian Association in Columbus, where lectures by Gough, Phillips, and Anna Dickinson, together with a concert by the Boston Quintette Club, earned net proceeds of $1,000.00.[83]

---

[83] Columbus *Daily Ohio State Journal*, March 22, 1871.

The straining after novelty which typified the lyceum programs made inevitable the decline in importance of the cultural lecture and the growth of humorous and sensational entertainment. Indeed, since the end of the war, newspaper editors had habitually put lecture advertisements in the "Amusements" column rather than in the more dignified "Special Announcements" department. And in publicizing their courses, lyceums referred with increasing frequency to their annual "Course of Lectures and Entertainments." The public-spirited editor of the Chillicothe *Scioto Gazette* announced on December 1, 1869, that the city ought to have, in addition to a skating rink and a gymnasium, a "Lecture Association" and an "unobjectional Ten Pin Alley." In the fall of 1870 a course was organized by the Chillicothe Musical and Lecture Association.

The changed character of the lyceum programs is illustrated by the lecture series offered by the Cleveland Library Association in 1869–70. The lecturers included J. W. Powell, "the Colorado explorer"; P. B. Du Chaillu, "the African traveler"; Captain C. F. Hall, "the Arctic explorer," who introduced an Eskimo family on the stage; Moses T. Brown of Tufts College, a dramatic reader; Mrs. H. M. Smith, "the matchless soprano"; and W. C. Richards, the popular scientist, who was advertised to produce "Vivid Flashes of Lightning! Magnificent Aurora Coruscations! Dazzling Chemical Lights! Singing Flames!" The most successful of these lectures, the discourse of Captain Hall, made a profit of three dollars for the association. All the others resulted in financial losses. Total receipts for the course were $2,118.04; expenses amounted to $2,904.05. The lecture deficit of $786.01 was the greatest loss ever suffered by the association.[84]

The increased demand for amusement on the platform was met in part by the performances of some of the nation's leading humorists. In announcing Mark Twain's "The American Vandal Abroad," given before the Cleveland Library Association on November 17, 1868, the *Leader* declared that "Cleveland will be honored with the first lecture delivered by Mr. Clemens on the Atlantic slope." The hall was "early filled" with an audience "prepared to criticise closely this new candidate for their favor." Expecting merely amuse-

---

[84] *Cleveland Morning Herald*, May 4, 1870.

ment, Clevelanders were surprised to be carried "on the wings of his redundant fancy away to the ruins, the cathedrals, and the monuments of the old world." Twain was to be congratulated for "having conclusively proved that a man may be a humorist without being a clown. He has elevated the profession by his graceful delivery and by recognizing in his audience something higher than merely a desire to laugh."[85]

When Twain read this lecture in Toledo on January 20, 1869, "White's Hall was crowded" and "a more delighted audience never occupied those seats." The originality and pungency of his wit gave it "a relish to the most cultivated minds." Twain was never "gross and coarse in his utterances," and the "humor is so interwoven with facts and incidents collected by many weary months of travel in the East that the wit serves to drive the truths deeper into the mind."[86]

Petroleum V. Nasby (D. R. Locke), editor of the *Toledo Blade*, whose humorous accounts of the adventures of the "postmaster at Confederate x roads" were familiar to Ohioans, received numerous invitations to speak before the state's lyceums. When Nasby lectured in Springfield on March 12, 1868, he was described by the editor of the *Republic* as "a portly gentleman of dark complexion and comfortable aspect" and having "the air rather of a prosperous farmer than of a celebrated satirical writer." According to this journalist, Nasby's "Cussed be Canaan" was delivered "in a straightforward, unambitious, yet not ungraceful manner, distinctly, somewhat rapidly, but on the whole with a more successful elocution than that of many public speakers of larger oratorical pretension."[87] To those who expected that the lecture "might be simply funny and grotesque," it was "an agreeable disappointment." In the serious portions of his discourse Nasby called for revision of the principles of the Republican party in regard to the Negro, and appealed for equal suffrage.

When Nasby appeared in Athens the *Messenger* (February 24,

---

[85] *Ibid.*, November 18, 1868.

[86] *Toledo Daily Commercial*, January 21, 1869.

[87] March 13, 1868. The title of Nasby's lecture, "Cussed be Canaan," was taken from Genesis 9:25: "Cursed be Canaan; a servant of servants shall he be unto his brethren." This declaration of Noah had been frequently quoted by Confederate sympathizers as a Biblical justification for slavery.

1870) observed that the audience came to be amused and were not
disappointed. Nasby concealed many "pungent witticisms" amidst
his "drapery of elegant verbiage." At the conclusion of this discourse
he gave what this correspondent described as "one of the most grand,
beautiful and eloquent tributes to woman which it has ever been our
fortune to listen to."

Josh Billings (H. W. Shaw), who had been famous as a cracker-
box philosopher since the publication of *Josh Billings, His Sayings*
(1865), lectured occasionally in Ohio in the late sixties. After he appeared before "a full house" in Tiffin, the editor of the *Seneca Advertiser* (December 17, 1868) commented that "We are creditably
informed that a peck of buttons were gathered up from the floor on
cleaning the hall this week. 'Josh' is a funny man, says some humorous things, and makes some pointed hits."

When Billings performed before the Alpha Nu Society in Newark
on December 30, 1870, the *Advocate* made some passing remarks
about the discourse and some significant comments about public
taste:

Wallace's Opera House was filled on Friday night to hear "Josh
Billings" on Milk. The lecture caused a great deal of merriment, though
part of its wit could not be classed with what is exactly refined or
elegant. Had the lecturer been Motley, Bancroft, or some celebrity in
science, philosophy or travels, the audience would have been one half
smaller. Even S. S. Cox's lecture a year ago, drew but $47.50, a trifle
less than his charge for delivering it. Billings, on the contrary, made a
handsome dividend for his employers. Our people like sensation and
fun.[88]

By 1870 Ohio's once-prosperous lecture system was falling into a
state of decadence from which it was powerless to rise. This failure
is illustrated by the experiences of the Cincinnati Young Men's
Mercantile Library Association and the Cleveland Library Association. In the spring of 1870 Cincinnatians were informed that "After
years of quiet on the part of the Young Men's Mercantile Library
Association, they have again entered the lecture field, and propose

---

[88] January 6, 1871. The references are to John Lothrop Motley and George
Bancroft, the eminent American historians of the nineteenth century. S. S. Cox
was a prominent Columbus journalist and one of Ohio's best known lecturers
in the fifties and sixties.

to give this spring a short course, preparatory to a regular one contemplated next fall."[89] The first lecture of the series, a discourse by I. J. Allen, "the late United States Consul at Hon [sic] Kong," was attended by a decidedly slim audience. The *Gazette* (April 8, 1870) testily remarked that "the speaker and his theme merited a full house, and there are cities in this land where he would have had it."

At the association's next lecture, read by Robert Collyer of Chicago, "A fine audience was present, but there was room for a couple more just such audiences, and a pity it is they staid away."[90] The effect of this brief venture is reflected in the association's annual report of January 3, 1871:

It has not seemed wise to prepare a series of lectures during the winter, although many inquiries were made as to when they would commence. The expense of lectures, advertising, rent of hall, is so great we thought it advisable to give up the hope.[91]

Although the Cleveland Library Association, in preparing its course for 1869–70, had attempted "to cut loose entirely from the old stock lecturers who had made lecturing a mere trade, and of whom the public were heartily tired," the program was a serious financial failure. In the association's annual report of May 3, 1870, the lecture committee made this statement:

The conclusion to which the committee have arrived is, that for the present the lecture feature of the Association should be suspended. Abstinence may restore the appetite of the public for them, but at present lectures are not in request.[92]

Thus Ohio's most important sponsor of professional lectures joined the Northern communities of Ravenna, Painesville, Ashtabula, and Warren in abandoning the field. While lecture courses were to be continued with varying degrees of success by lyceums in Oberlin, Sandusky, Toledo, Norwalk, Columbus, and other cities, the state's lecture system had by 1870 lost the public support which could restore it to prominence.

---

[89] *Cincinnati Daily Gazette*, April 7, 1870.
[90] *Ibid.*, April 22, 1870.
[91] *Ibid.*, January 4, 1871.
[92] *Cleveland Morning Herald*, May 4, 1870.

The rapid growth of professionalism after 1850 served to make the strength of the lecture system increasingly dependent upon the condition of its financial structure. After the Civil War, particularly, the social importance of the system diminished, and the function of the lyceum in the cultural life of the community was often subordinated to the purposes of popular amusement and the striving after increased financial gain. And when, in the late sixties, many lyceums did not realize their anticipated profits, they curtailed or abandoned their lecture programs.

There were numerous reasons why the account books of the lecture associations showed inadequate receipts. In many communities the success of the lecture program was dependent upon the number of course tickets which the public would purchase. And yet public resistance to the course ticket was such that some sponsoring organizations, including the Cleveland Library Association, dispensed with the entire principle of the "course" of lectures and substituted the plan of selling single admissions to individual lectures. The result was that the profits of successful lectures were sometimes wiped out by the public's refusal to patronize the discourse of some speaker whom they did not choose to hear and whose failure was not indemnified by the income from course tickets. The main objection to the course ticket was that subscribers had "to pay for good and bad alike." Competition for lecturers' services sometimes left the lyceum program with two or three attractive speakers and half a dozen "Jacks upon occasion." And the people resented the obligation of paying for lectures which they did not wish to attend.

In accounting for the financial debacle of 1869–70 the Cleveland Library Association's annual report of May 3, 1870, concluded:

The real secret of the failure lay in the apathy of the public. They had been fed to nausea with lectures of little or no merit; were weary of discourses in which infinitessimal [sic] ideas were beaten out to cobweb thinness in order to cover the customary hour or hour and a half, and could not be brought to believe that a better article had been provided them. They would not listen to the lecturers with whom they had been familiar, for too much familiarity had bred contempt. Nor would they venture on lecturers with whom they were not familiar, lest they too might prove to be humbugs. Hence they stayed at home.

When the Warren Polemics Club ceased its lecture activities in 1868, the editor of the *Western Reserve Chronicle* (December 23, 1868) reviewed the club's experiences of the past four years, and, in doing so, pointed out the common problems of lyceums throughout the state:

During the four winters the principal lecturers in the United States had visited us, and besides Mr. Gough and Miss Dickinson, there were but two or three others who attracted full and paying houses. . . . Having seen the "lions" of the lecture-field once or twice, that class of persons, whom there are more or less in every community, who go to see the lecturer, rather than to hear his discourse, cannot be expected to patronize the course unless the rostrum is occupied by a different set of lecturers, whom the sight seeing patrons have heard sufficiently of to induce them to come out and stare at until they have gratified their curiosity to the amount of the admission fee. There is also a considerable class who will patronize only the sensational or the humorous lecture. There are also quite a number of pretentious persons who are always blowing up the lecture committees because, in each instance, what they call "first class" lecturers are not secured, and find it more congenial with their dispositions to belittle the lectures and berate the committee than to give a single word of encouragement.

Observing that the courses of the Delaware Young Men's Christian Association and the Ohio Wesleyan University Lecture Association did not prosper in 1869–70, the *Gazette* (February 18, 1870) offered this explanation:

We think the thinness of the audiences has been due in a great measure to an increasing indifference to this class of entertainments. They appear to be growing a little stale, and the time seems to have passed by when a lecture by *anybody* can be regarded as much of a sensation. The truth is, the world is lectured, as well as governed, too much. It has become, as it were, lecture hardened. If we could have two or three winters' respite, our Associations would no doubt be gladdened again by crowded houses. Something of the old novelty would return, and good literary digestion would tread the heels of appetite. But just now there seems to be a prevailing surfeit, and it wouldn't be a bad idea for Messieurs and Mesdames, the lecturers, to relieve it by a few brilliant flashes of silence.

J. B. Pond, who during the sixties arranged the speaking schedules of some of the nation's leading orators, attributed the decline of the lecture system to the scarcity of good lecturers.[93] He noted that, by

[93] "The Lyceum," *Cosmopolitan*, XX (April, 1896), 597.

the mid-seventies, Charles Sumner had died, Emerson was "worn out," Curtis was busy as editor of *Harper's Weekly*, Gough's voice had failed him, Douglass had become United States Minister to Haiti, the reputations of Beecher and Theodore Tilton were being destroyed by a scandal involving the alleged adultery of Beecher and Tilton's wife, and Anna Dickinson had deserted the lecture platform for the stage. In addition, the ratification in 1870 of the Fifteenth Amendment, granting Negro suffrage, ended the many discussions of that favorite topic of reform lecturers in the North. Finally, declared Pond, there was a diminishing interest in the declamations of the woman's rights lecturers, who "had said all there was to say on the subject."

Still another view of the lecture decline was given by Josiah G. Holland, who observed in 1871 that "There is a general complaint this year, throughout that portion of the country in which the 'lecture system' has become an institution, that the usual courses of lectures and of intellectual entertainments grouped with lectures have been unremunerative."[94] As the lecture bureaus which sprang up after the war demanded ten per cent of the speaker's fee, the lecturer, objecting to a payment "so out of proportion to the service rendered . . . is at once moved to get a part of it back from the associations to which he is sent." The action of lecturers in raising their fees reduced the prospect of gain by the lyceums, and, in many cases, forced them to discontinue their annual lecture courses.

Holland also blamed the lecture bureaus for "the introduction into the lecture field of great numbers of men and women who have nothing to say,—'dead weights' all of them,—who never would have found their way to a platform but for the help of a bureau." On the rolls of the bureaus, the great names in the lecture profession were found "associated in a common column with literary jesters and mountebanks, readers, singers, etc.,—men who, outside of a lecture course, would not draw auditors enough to pay for the rent of their audience rooms."

By 1871 Ohio's declining lecture system provided abundant evidence of the truth of Holland's statement that "The good lecturers

---

[94] "Lecture Brokers and Lecture-Breakers," *Scribner's Monthly* (Century), I (March, 1871), 560–561.

have been cheapened by association with their inferiors in gifts and aims, and the 'lecture system' has degenerated into a string of entertainments that have no earnest purpose, and minister to no manly and womanly want." At various intervals during the seventies and after, some of the state's major cities were to support the "Star Courses" of the lecture bureaus; but the people of these communities were rarely to hear a cultural lecturer whose merits were comparable to those of Emerson, Henry Giles, or Edwin P. Whipple. The cultural function of the lyceum was to remain subordinated to the purposes of popular amusement. The musical performer, the political orator, the humorist, the explorer, and the foreign celebrity were to satisfy the public demand for novelty and diversion.

In most of Ohio's towns and villages, where the people were to find it impossible to afford the high fees of Redpath's "Star" performers, the occasional lecture was to supersede the courses of former years. With the passing of the lecture associations and pending the emergence of the Chautauqua movement, the opera house, with its acted dramas, its minstrels, its comedians, and its troupes of musical entertainers, was to secure the place once proudly held by the lyceums in the social organization of Ohio's communities.

APPENDIX B

The Ohio Lecture Schedules of Fifteen
Eastern Orators

The schedules in this appendix give, wherever possible, the date, place, sponsor, title, and financial results of the Ohio lectures of fifteen prominent Eastern orators. The bibliographies of lectures list references in newspapers, manuscripts, periodical articles, books, and pamphlets. Dates of newspaper issues giving extensive criticism or reportage of lectures are marked with an asterisk (*). Lectures which were announced, but for which there is no proof of delivery, are marked with a dagger (†). In cases where the sponsor was not announced, the most probable sponsor is usually indicated. The contents of newspaper reviews have been used at times to determine the probable title of lectures whose subjects were not announced. Lecture fees and other financial data are given immediately before the sources of the information. In the bibliographies the following abbreviations are used:

CPL—Concord Public Library.

Hastings—Louise Hastings, "Emerson in Cincinnati," *New England Quarterly*, XI (September, 1938), 443–469.

HCL—Harvard College Library.

Hayes Diary—*Diary and Letters of Rutherford Birchard Hayes*, ed. Charles R. Williams. 5 vols. Columbus: Ohio State Archaeological and Historical Society, 1922.

MHS—Massachusetts Historical Society.

Rusk—*The Letters of Ralph Waldo Emerson*, ed. Ralph L. Rusk. 6 vols. New York: Columbia University Press, 1939.

AMOS BRONSON ALCOTT

Alcott's discourses are all "Conversations" unless otherwise noted.

November 11, 1853. Cincinnati. Private. "Chaos." Manuscript Journals (CPL).
November 12, 1853. Cincinnati. Private. "Paradise." Manuscript Journals (CPL).

November 17, 1853. Cincinnati. Private. "The Fountain." Manuscript Journals (CPL).

November 21, 1853. Cincinnati. Private. "The Seminary." Manuscript Journals (CPL).

November 23, 1853. Cincinnati. Private. "The Mart." Manuscript Journals (CPL).

November 26, 1853. Cincinnati. Private. "The Altar." Net receipts for the six Cincinnati conversations: $209.00. Manuscript Journals (CPL).

December 7, 1853. Cleveland. Private. "The Individual." Manuscript Journals (CPL).

December 9, 1853. Cleveland. Private. "The Family." Manuscript Journals (CPL).

December 10, 1853. Cleveland. Private. "The Garden." Manuscript Journals (CPL).

December 12, 1853. Cleveland. Private. "The School." Manuscript Journals (CPL).

December 13, 1853. Cleveland. Private. "The State." Manuscript Journals (CPL).

December 14, 1853. Cleveland. Private. "The Church." Net receipts for the six Cleveland conversations: $50.00. Manuscript Journals (CPL).

December 30, 1857. Cleveland. Private. "Intellect and Its Organs." Manuscript Journals (CPL).

December 31, 1857. Cleveland. Private. "Hearts, or the Affections." Net receipts for the two Cleveland conversations: $18.00. Manuscript Journals (CPL).

January 11, 1858. Cincinnati. Private. "Heads, or Intellect." *Cincinnati Daily Gazette*, January 11, 15. *Cincinnati Daily Commercial*, January 11, 15. Manuscript Journals (CPL).

January 12, 1858. Cincinnati. Private. "Hearts, or the Sentiments." *Cincinnati Daily Gazette*, January 11, 15. *Cincinnati Daily Commercial*, January 11, 15. Manuscript Journals (CPL).

January 14, 1858. Cincinnati. Private. "Hands, or Conduct." Manuscript Journals (CPL).

January 15, 1858. Cincinnati. Private. "Oversights." *Cincinnati Daily Commercial*, January 16. Net receipts for the four Cincinnati conversations: $60.00. Manuscript Journals (CPL).

January 18, 1858. Cleveland. Private. "The Family." Manuscript Journals (CPL).

January 19, 1858. Cleveland. Private. "Friendship." Manuscript Journals (CPL).

January 20, 1858. Cleveland. Private. Subject not announced. Net receipts for the three Cleveland conversations: $40.00. Manuscript Journals (CPL).

January 24, 1859. Cincinnati. Private. "Fate." *Cincinnati Daily Gazette*, January 24, 25. *Cincinnati Daily Enquirer,* January 25*. Manuscript Journals (CPL).

January 26, 1859. Cincinnati. Private. "Fascination." *Cincinnati Daily Enquirer,* January 27*. Manuscript Journals (CPL).

January 28, 1859. Cincinnati. Private. "Recreation." *Cincinnati Daily Enquirer,* January 29. Manuscript Journals (CPL).

January 31, 1859. Cincinnati. Private. "Worship." *Cincinnati Daily Enquirer,* February 1*. Net receipts for the four Cincinnati conversations: $25.25. Manuscript Journals (CPL).

February 5, 1859. Cleveland. Private. "Fascination." Manuscript Journals (CPL).

February 7, 1859. Cleveland. Private. "Recreation." Manuscript Journals (CPL).

February 9, 1859. Cleveland. Private. "Worship." Manuscript Journals (CPL).

February 10, 1859. Cleveland. Private. "Social Life." Manuscript Journals (CPL).

February 12, 1859. Cleveland. Private. "Genesis." Manuscript Journals (CPL).

February 13, 1859. Cleveland. Private. "Marriage and Social Life." Net receipts for the six Cleveland conversations: $50.00. Manuscript Journals (CPL).

March 8, 1866. Cincinnati. Private. "New England Men and Women." Net receipts: $33.00. Manuscript Journals (CPL).

March 11, 1866. Cincinnati. Free Congregation Church. "The New Church, Its Faith and Forms" (Lecture). Fee: $25.00. Manuscript Journals (CPL).

December 1, 1869. Cleveland. Private. "New England Authors." *Cleveland Morning Herald*, December 2. *Cleveland Daily Leader,* December 2*. Odell Shepard (ed.), *The Journals of Bronson Alcott* (Boston: Little, Brown and Company, 1938), pp. 403–404. Manuscript Journals (CPL).

December 6, 1869. Cleveland. Private. "Manners and Conversation." Manuscript Journals (CPL).

December 8, 1869. Cleveland. Private. "Temperament and Descent." Manuscript Journals (CPL).

December 9, 1869. Cleveland. Private. "Woman." Manuscript Journals (CPL).

December 10, 1869. Cleveland. Private. "Beauty." Net receipts for the five Cleveland conversations: $60.00. Manuscript Journals (CPL).

December 12, 1869. Toledo. Independent Society. "The Coming Church" (Lecture). Manuscript Journals (CPL).

December 13, 1869. Toledo. Woman's Suffrage Association. Subject not announced (Lecture). *Toledo Daily Commercial,* December 13. Manuscript Journals (CPL).

December 13, 1869. Toledo. Radical Club. "Genesis." Manuscript
Journals (CPL).

December 18, 1869. Elyria. Private. "New England Authors." *Elyria
Independent Democrat*, December 22*. Manuscript Journals
(CPL).

December 20, 1869. Elyria. Private. "Health." *Elyria Independent
Democrat*, December 22. Manuscript Journals (CPL).

December 21, 1869. Elyria. Private. "Social Life." *Elyria Independent
Democrat*, December 22. Manuscript Journals (CPL).

December 27, 1869. Elyria. Private. "Temperament and Descent."
Manuscript Journals (CPL).

December 28, 1869. Elyria. Private. "Culture." Net receipts for the
five Elyria conversations: $54.00. Manuscript Journals (CPL).

December 29, 1869. Tiffin. Private. Subject not announced. Manuscript
Journals (CPL).

December 30, 1869. Tiffin. Private. "Health and Temperance." Manuscript Journals (CPL).

December 31, 1869. Tiffin. Private. "Social Life." Net receipts for the
three Tiffin conversations: $30.00. Manuscript Journals (CPL).

HENRY WARD BEECHER

July 2, 1854. Cleveland. Plymouth Church. Morning and evening
sermons. *Cleveland Herald*, July 1, 3*. *Cleveland Daily Plain
Dealer*, July 3*.

July 4, 1854. Painesville. Independence Day address. *Painesville Telegraph*, July 7. *Cleveland Herald*, July 3, 5. *Cleveland Daily Plain
Dealer*, July 5.

October 22, 1855. Cincinnati. E. S. Wells. Probably "Patriotism." Fee:
$125.00. *Cincinnati Daily Gazette*, October 23*; November 15*.

October 23, 1855. Columbus. E. S. Wells. "Beauty." Columbus *Daily
Ohio State Journal*, October 24. Fee: $125.00. Gross receipts:
$14.50. Columbus *Daily Capital City Fact*, October 18, 23, 24*.
Cincinnati Daily Gazette, November 15.

October 24, 1855. Cleveland. E. S. Wells. "Patriotism." *Cleveland
Herald*, October 22, 23, 24, 25*, 27*. *Cleveland Daily Plain Dealer*,
October 25*. *Cleveland Morning Leader*, October 24; November 9.
Fee: $125.00. *Daily Clevelander*, in *Sandusky Daily Commercial
Register*, October 24. *Cincinnati Daily Gazette*, November 15*.

November 15, 1856. Cincinnati. First Orthodox Congregational Society.
"The Ministry of the Beautiful." *Cincinnati Daily Gazette*, October
29; November 15, 17*. *Cincinnati Daily Commercial*, November
17*.

November 16, 1856. Cincinnati. Seventh Street Congregational Church.
Morning sermon: "Cast Your Care upon Him." Evening sermon.
Cincinnati Daily Gazette, November 15, 17. *Cincinnati Daily Com-*

mercial, November 15, 17*. *Cincinnati Daily Enquirer*, November 18*.

November 17, 1856. Cincinnati. First Orthodox Congregational Society. "Patriotism." *Cincinnati Daily Gazette*, October 29; November 18*, 19. *Cincinnati Daily Commercial*, November 18*, 19*.

October 20, 1857. Cleveland. Cleveland Library Association. "The Beautiful." *Daily Cleveland Herald*, October 20, 21*. *Cleveland Daily Plain Dealer*, October 21.

October 21, 1857. Cleveland. Cleveland Young Men's Christian Association. "The Christian Commonwealth." *Daily Cleveland Herald*, October 21, 22*.

February 26, 1862. Cleveland. Cleveland Young Men's Christian Association. "The Results of the Past and Our Policy for the Future." *Daily Cleveland Herald*, February 27. *Cleveland Morning Leader*, February 27*. Sponsor's profit: $118.80. *The Young Men's Christian Association of Cleveland* (Cleveland: J. B. Savage, 1900), p. 42.

PARK BENJAMIN

January 3, 1852. Cleveland. Forest City Lyceum. "Fashion" (Poem). *Cleveland Herald*, January 2, 3, 5. *Cleveland Daily Plain Dealer*, January 3, 5.

January 5, 1852. Cleveland. Forest City Lyceum. "Modern Society." *Cleveland Herald*, January 5, 6. *Cleveland Daily Plain Dealer*, January 6.

January 6, 1852. Columbus. Franklin Lyceum. "Fashion." Columbus *Daily Ohio State Journal*, January 5, 7.

January 7, 1852. Columbus. Franklin Lyceum. "Money: a Love" (Poem). Columbus *Daily Ohio State Journal*, January 7, 8.

January 9, 1852. Cleveland. Forest City Lyceum. "Intellectual and Popular Amusements." *Cleveland Herald*, January 8, 10. *Cleveland Daily Plain Dealer*, January 10. Cleveland *Morning Daily True Democrat*, January 10.

January 10, 1852. Cleveland. Forest City Lyceum. "The Stage, Before and Behind the Curtain." *Cleveland Daily Plain Dealer*, January 10, 12.

January 12, 1852†. Cleveland. Forest City Lyceum. "Matrimony." *Cleveland Herald*, January 12.

January 13, 1852†. Cleveland. Private. "Money: a Love." *Cleveland Daily Plain Dealer*, January 13.

November 19, 1852. Toledo. Toledo Young Men's Association. "The Stage, Before and Behind the Curtain." *Daily Toledo Blade*, November 17, 20.

November 20, 1852. Toledo. Toledo Young Men's Association. "Matrimony." *Daily Toledo Blade*, November 17, 22*, 23, 24.

November 22, 1852†. Toledo. Toledo Young Men's Association. "Society" (Poem). *Daily Toledo Blade*, November 17, 22.

November 23, 1852. Cleveland. Forest City Lyceum. "Music and Musical Entertainments." *Cleveland Herald*, November 23. *Cleveland Daily Plain Dealer*, November 24.

November 26, 1852. Ohio City (Cuyahoga County). Ohio City Young Men's Association. "Age of Gold." *Cleveland Daily Plain Dealer*, November 26, 27.

November 30, 1852. Cincinnati. Cincinnati Young Men's Mercantile Library Association. "Intellectual and Popular Amusements." *Daily Cincinnati Gazette*, November 30; December 1*.

December 2, 1852. Cincinnati. Cincinnati Young Men's Mercantile Library Association. "Fashion." *Cincinnati Gazette*, December 2, 3.

December 4, 1852. Dayton. Private. "Fashion." *Daily Dayton Journal*, December 1, 3, 6.

December 6, 1852. Cincinnati. Private. "Money: a Love." *Daily Cincinnati Gazette*, December 4, 6, 7.

December 8, 1852†. Cincinnati. Private. "Society." *Daily Cincinnati Gazette*, December 8.

December 9, 1852. Dayton. Private. "Money: a Love." *Daily Dayton Journal*, December 6, 11.

December 10, 1852†. Cincinnati. Private. "Fashion." *Daily Cincinnati Gazette*, December 9.

November 8, 1855. Cincinnati. Cincinnati Young Men's Mercantile Library Association. "Americanisms." *Cincinnati Daily Gazette*, November 7, 9*. *Cincinnati Daily Commercial*, November 9.

November 10, 1855. Cincinnati. Cincinnati Young Men's Mercantile Library Association. "True Independence" (Poem). *Cincinnati Daily Gazette*, November 7, 12*. *Cincinnati Daily Commercial*, November 17*.

November 16, 1855. Dayton. Dayton Library Association. "Americanisms." Fee: $50.00. *Daily Dayton Journal*, November 14, 17; January 16, 1857.

November 17, 1855. Glendale. American Female College. "Americanisms." *Cincinnati Daily Gazette*, November 16, 20.

November 20, 1855. Springfield. Private. "Americanisms." *Daily Springfield Nonpareil*, November 20; December 1.

November 26, 1855. Circleville. Pickaway Lyceum. Probably "Americanisms." *Circleville Watchman*, November 22, 29.

November 27, 1855. Dayton. Dayton Library Association. "True Independence." Daily Dayton Journal, November 27, 28. *Dayton Daily Gazette*, November 29*.

November 28, 1855. Columbus. Columbus Atheneum. "Americanisms." Columbus *Daily Ohio State Journal*, November 28, 29. Columbus *Daily Capital City Fact*, November 29.

November 29, 1855†. Hamilton. Hamilton Irving Club. "Americanisms." *Hamilton Intelligencer*, November 29.

December 1, 1855. Springfield. Private. "Fashion." *Daily Springfield Nonpareil*, December 1, 3.

December 3, 1855. Cleveland. Cleveland Orphan Asylum. "Americanisms." Fee: $50.00 and expenses. *Cleveland Herald*, November 30; *Cleveland Daily Plain Dealer*, December 4.

December 7, 1855. Sandusky. Private. "Americanisms." *Sandusky Daily Commercial Register*, December 7, 8.

November 26, 1857. Cincinnati. Private. "Hard Times" (Poem). *Cincinnati Daily Gazette*, November 26, 27*; December 10, 12. *Cincinnati Daily Commercial*, November 27.

November 28, 1857. Cincinnati. Private. "Hard Times." *Cincinnati Daily Gazette*, November 28, 30; December 2*, 10*, 12*.

November 30, 1857. Cincinnati. Cincinnati Home of the Friendless. "Fashion." Fee: $55.00. Sponsor's profit: about $60.00. *Cincinnati Daily Gazette*, December 1, 10*, 12*.

ORESTES A. BROWNSON

February 17, 1852. Cincinnati. Cincinnati Young Men's Mercantile Library Association. "Non-Intervention." *Daily Cincinnati Gazette*, February 17, 18*, 25*, 26*.

February 13, 1854. Cleveland. Private. "Civil and Religious Liberty." *Cleveland Herald*, February 11, 13, 14*. *Cleveland Daily Plain Dealer*, February 14. Cleveland *Daily Forest City Democrat*, February 15.

January 25, 1858. Cincinnati. Cincinnati Young Men's Catholic Literary Institute. "Popular Objections to the Church." *Cincinnati Daily Gazette*, January 25, 26. *Cincinnati Daily Commercial*, January 26*.

February 4, 1858. Cincinnati. Cincinnati Young Men's Catholic Literary Institute. "Charity and Philanthropy." *Cincinnati Daily Gazette*, February 3, 5. *Cincinnati Daily Commercial*, February 5.

February 8, 1858. Cleveland. Private. "Popular Objections to the Church." *Cleveland Herald*, February 8, 9.

February 9, 1858. Cleveland. Cleveland Catholic Library Society. "Charity and Philanthropy." *Cleveland Herald*, February 9. *Cleveland Daily Plain Dealer*, February 10.

February 10, 1858. Columbus. Private. "Misguided Benevolence." Columbus *Daily Ohio State Journal*, February 9, 11. Columbus *Daily Ohio Statesman*, February 12. *Columbus Gazette*, February 12.

GEORGE WILLIAM CURTIS

December 15, 1853. Toledo. Toledo Young Men's Association. "Young America." *Daily Toledo Blade*, December 14, 16*.

December 16, 1853. Cleveland. Cleveland Library Association. "Young America." *Cleveland Herald*, December 15, 16, 17.

December 5, 1854. Cincinnati. Cincinnati Young Men's Mercantile Library Association. "Success." *Daily Cincinnati Gazette*, December 4, 6. *Cincinnati Daily Commercial*, December 6*.

December 6, 1854. Zanesville. Zanesville Astronomical Society. "Success." *Zanesville Gazette*, December 5, 12*.

December 7, 1854. Cleveland. Cleveland Library Association. "Success." *Cleveland Herald*, December 6, 8*.

December 8, 1854. Dayton. Dayton Library Association. "Success." *Daily Dayton Journal*, December 7, 11.

December 1, 1860. Toledo. Toledo Young Men's Association. "The Policy of Honesty." *Daily Toledo Blade*, December 1, 3.

December 3, 1860. Cleveland. Cleveland Library Association. "The Policy of Honesty." *Daily Cleveland Herald*, December 3, 4*. *Cleveland Daily Plain Dealer*, December 4*. *Cleveland Morning Leader*, December 4*.

RALPH WALDO EMERSON

May 16, 1850. Cleveland. Cleveland Library Association. "England." *Cleveland Herald*, May 16, 18. *Daily Cleveland Plain Dealer*, May 16. Cleveland *Daily True Democrat*, May 18. Manuscript Account Book (HCL). Rusk, IV, 203.

May 20, 1850. Cincinnati. Cincinnati Literary Club. "Natural Aristocracy." *Daily Cincinnati Gazette*, May 20, 22*. *Daily Cincinnati Commercial*, May 21. *Cincinnati Daily Chronicle and Atlas*, May 22. Cincinnati *Columbian and Great West*, June 1*. *Weekly Cleveland Plain Dealer*, May 29. Hayes Diary, I, 299. Fee for the series of five Cincinnati Literary Club lectures: $560.00. *The Literary Club of Cincinnati, 1849–1903* (Cincinnati: n.p., 1903), pp. 15–16. Hastings, pp. 443–451. Manuscript Account Book (HCL). Rusk, IV, 204.

May 22, 1850. Cincinnati. Cincinnati Literary Club. "Eloquence." *Daily Cincinnati Gazette*, May 24*. *Daily Cincinnati Commercial*, May 23. *Cincinnati Daily Chronicle and Atlas*, May 24. Cincinnati *Columbian and Great West*, June 1*. *Weekly Cleveland Plain Dealer*, May 29. Hayes Diary, I, 301. *The Literary Club of Cincinnati, 1849–1903* (Cincinnati: n.p., 1903), pp. 15–16. Hastings, pp. 443–451. Manuscript Account Book (HCL). Rusk, IV, 204.

May 24, 1850. Cincinnati. Cincinnati Literary Club. "The Spirit of the Times." *Daily Cincinnati Gazette*, May 30. Cincinnati *Columbian and Great West*, June 1*. *The Literary Club of Cincinnati, 1849–1903* (Cincinnati: n.p., 1903), pp. 15–16. Hastings, pp. 443–451. Manuscript Account Book (HCL). Rusk, IV, 204.

May 27, 1850. Cincinnati. Cincinnati Literary Club. "England." *Daily Cincinnati Gazette*, May 30*. Cincinnati *Columbian and Great West*, June 1. *The Literary Club of Cincinnati, 1849–1903* (Cincinnati: n.p., 1903) pp. 15–16. Hastings, pp. 443–451. Manuscript Account Book (HCL). Rusk, IV, 204.

May 28, 1850. Cincinnati. Cincinnati Literary Club. "Books." *Daily Cincinnati Gazette*, May 30. *The Literary Club of Cincinnati, 1849–1903* (Cincinnati: n.p., 1903), pp. 15–16. Hastings, pp. 443–451. Manuscript Account Book (HCL). Rusk, IV, 204.

May 30, 1850. Cincinnati. Private. "The Natural History of Intellect." *Daily Cincinnati Gazette*, May 29; June 3. *Cincinnati Daily Times*, in *Cincinnati Daily Chronicle and Atlas*, June 1. Hastings, pp. 443–451. Manuscript Account Book (HCL). Rusk, IV, 205.

May 31, 1850. Cincinnati. Private. "The Identity of Thought with Nature." *Daily Cincinnati Gazette*, May 29; June 3. Hayes Diary, I, 309. Hastings, pp. 443–451. Manuscript Account Book (HCL). Rusk, IV, 205.

June 3, 1850. Cincinnati. Private. "Instinct and Inspiration." *Daily Cincinnati Gazette*, May 29; June 5. Hastings, pp. 443–451. Manuscript Account Book (HCL). Rusk, IV, 205.

December 7, 1852. Cincinnati. Cincinnati Young Men's Mercantile Library Association. "The Anglo-Saxon." *Daily Cincinnati Gazette*, December 7, 8. *Daily Cincinnati Commercial*, December 8*. *Cincinnati Daily Enquirer*, December 9. *Cincinnati Daily Times*, December 8*. Hastings, pp. 452–453. Fee for the series of six Cincinnati lectures: $362.00. Manuscript Account Book (HCL). Rusk, IV, 328.

December 9, 1852. Cincinnati. Private. "Power." *Daily Cincinnati Gazette*, December 9, 10*. Hastings, p. 454. Rusk, IV, 328.

December 11, 1852. Cincinnati. Private. "Wealth." *Daily Cincinnati Gazette*, December 11, 13. Hastings, pp. 454–455. Rusk, IV, 328.

December 13, 1852. Cincinnati. Private. "Economy." *Daily Cincinnati Gazette*, December 14*. *Cincinnati Dollar Weekly Commercial*, December 16. Hastings, p. 455. Rusk, IV, 328.

December 15, 1852. Dayton. Private. "The Anglo-Saxon." *Daily Dayton Journal*, December 15, 17. *Dayton Daily Empire*, December 15, 17. Rusk, IV, 328.

December 16, 1852. Cincinnati. Private. "Fate." *Daily Cincinnati Gazette*, December 16, 18. Hastings, p. 455. Rusk, IV, 328.

December 20, 1852. Cincinnati. Private. "Worship." *Daily Cincinnati Gazette*, December 20. Hastings, p. 455. Rusk, IV, 328.

January 20, 1853. Cleveland. Cleveland Library Association. "The Anglo-Saxon." *Cleveland Herald*, January 19, 20, 21. Cleveland *Morning Daily True Democrat*, January 21. Manuscript Memorandum Book for 1853 (HCL). Fee for the two Cleveland lectures: $60.00. Manuscript Account Book (HCL).

January 22, 1853. Cleveland. Cleveland Library Association. "Culture." *Cleveland Herald*, January 20, 22. Cleveland *Morning Daily True Democrat*, January 24. Manuscript Account Book (HCL). Rusk, IV, 343.

February 11, 1854. Toledo. Toledo Young Men's Association. "Wealth and Economy." *Daily Toledo Blade*, February 9, 11, 13. Manuscript Memorandum Book for 1854 (HCL). Fee: $30.00. Manuscript Account Book (HCL). Rusk, IV, 428.

February 12, 1854. Toledo. Sponsor not announced. Sermon: "Worship and Faith." *Daily Toledo Blade*, February 13. Rusk, IV, 428.

January 23, 1856. Cleveland. Cleveland Library Association. "Beauty." *Daily Cleveland Herald*, January 23, 24. *Cleveland Daily Plain Dealer*, January 24*. *Cleveland Morning Leader*, January 24. Cleveland *Ohio Farmer*, February 2*. Manuscript Memorandum Book for 1856 (HCL). Fee: $50.00. Manuscript Account Book (HCL). Rusk, V, 9.

January 24, 1856. Columbus. Columbus Atheneum. "Beauty." Columbus *Daily Ohio State Journal*, January 24, 25*. Columbus *Daily Ohio Statesman*, January 24, 26. Columbus *Daily Capital City Fact*, January 25. Manuscript Memorandum Book for 1856 (HCL). Fee: $50.00. Manuscript Account Book (HCL). Rusk, V, 9.

January 25, 1856. Akron. Probably Akron Young Men's Association. "Beauty." Akron *Summit Beacon*, January 23, 30*. Manuscript Memorandum Book for 1856 (HCL). Fee: $25.00. Manuscript Account Book (HCL).

January 26, 1856. Hudson. Probably Western Reserve College. Probably "Beauty." Manuscript Memorandum Book for 1856 (HCL). Fee: $25.00. Manuscript Account Book (HCL).

January 19, 1857. Columbus. Columbus Atheneum. "The Conduct of Life." Columbus *Daily Ohio State Journal*, January 19, 20, 21*, 23, 24, 27, 28, 29, 31. *Columbus Gazette*, January 23. Manuscript Memorandum Book for 1857 (HCL). Fee: $40.00. Manuscript Account Book (HCL). Rusk, V, 57.

January 20, 1857. Columbus. Columbus Atheneum. "Poetry." Columbus *Daily Ohio State Journal*, January 20, 21. *Columbus Gazette*, January 23. Manuscript Memorandum Book for 1857 (HCL). Fee: $40.00. Manuscript Account Book (HCL). Rusk, V, 57.

January 27, 1857. Cincinnati. Cincinnati Young Men's Mercantile Library Association. "The Conduct of Life." *Cincinnati Daily Gazette*, January 27, 28*. *Cincinnati Daily Commercial*, January 27, 28*. *Cincinnati Daily Enquirer*, January 28. *Cincinnati Daily Times*, January 28*. Hastings, pp. 457–459. Manuscript Memorandum Book for 1857 (HCL). Fee: $100.00. Manuscript Account Book (HCL). Rusk, V, 59.

January 28, 1857. Sandusky. Cosmopolitan Art Association. "Beauty." *Sandusky Daily Commercial Register*, January 26, 28, 29*. Manu-

script Memorandum Book for 1857 (HCL). Fee: $50.00. Manu-
script Account Book (HCL). Rusk, V, 61.
January 29, 1857. Cleveland. Cleveland Library Association. "The
Conduct of Life." *Daily Cleveland Herald*, January 28, 29, 30*,
31. *Cleveland Daily Leader*, in Cleveland *Ohio Farmer*, February
7*. Manuscript Memorandum Book for 1857 (HCL). Fee: $50.00.
Manuscript Account Book (HCL). Rusk, V, 59.
January 31, 1857. Cincinnati. Private. "Beauty." *Cincinnati Daily
Gazette*, January 31; February 2. *Cincinnati Daily Commercial*,
January 31; February 2. *Cincinnati Daily Enquirer*, February 1.
Cincinnati Daily Times, February 2. Hastings, p. 459. Manuscript
Memorandum Book for 1857 (HCL). Emerson's proceeds from
the four private lectures in Cincinnati: $330.00. Manuscript Account
Book (HCL). Rusk, V, 59.
February 2, 1857. Cincinnati. Private. "Poetry." *Cincinnati Daily Com-
mercial*, February 3. *Cincinnati Daily Times*, February 3. Hastings,
p. 460. Manuscript Memorandum Book for 1857 (HCL). Manu-
script Account Book (HCL). Rusk, V, 59.
February 4, 1857. Cincinnati. Private. "Works and Days." *Cincinnati
Daily Commercial*, February 3. *Cincinnati Daily Times*, February
5. Hastings, p. 460. Manuscript Memorandum Book for 1857
(HCL). Manuscript Account Book (HCL). Rusk, V, 59.
February 6, 1857. Cincinnati. Private. "The Scholar." *Cincinnati Daily
Enquirer*, February 7. *Cincinnati Daily Times*, February 7. Hast-
ings, pp. 460–461. Manuscript Memorandum Book for 1857 (HCL).
Manuscript Account Book (HCL). Rusk, V, 59.
January 20, 1859. Cleveland. Cleveland Library Association. "The Law
of Success." *Cleveland Daily Herald*, January 20, 21. *Cleveland
Daily Plain Dealer*, January 20, 21*. *Cleveland Morning Leader*,
January 20, 21. Cleveland *Ohio Farmer*, January 29*. Manuscript
Memorandum Book for 1859 (HCL). Fee: $50.00. Manuscript
Account Book (HCL). Rusk, V, 131.
January 30, 1860. Toledo. Toledo Young Men's Association. "Man-
ners." *Daily Toledo Blade*, January 30, 31; February 1. Manuscript
Memorandum Book for 1860 (HCL). Fee: $50.00. Manuscript
Account Book (HCL). Rusk, V, 193.
February 1, 1860. Yellow Springs. Antioch College. "Manners." Manu-
script Memorandum Book for 1860 (HCL). Fee: $50.00. Manu-
script Account Book (HCL).
February 2, 1860. Cincinnati. Cincinnati Young Men's Mercantile
Library Association. "Manners." *Cincinnati Daily Gazette*,
February 2, 3*. *Cincinnati Daily Commercial*, February 1, 3, 4*.
Cincinnati Daily Enquirer, February 1, 3. *Cincinnati Daily Times*,
February 1, 3. Hastings, pp. 463–467. Manuscript Memorandum
Book for 1860 (HCL). Fee: $100.00. Manuscript Account Book
(HCL).

February 3, 1860. Cincinnati. Private. "Success." *Cincinnati Daily Gazette*, February 4*. *Cincinnati Daily Commercial*, February 6*. *Cincinnati Daily Enquirer*, February 4. Hastings, pp. 467–468. Manuscript Memorandum Book for 1860 (HCL). Emerson's proceeds: $50.00. Manuscript Account Book (HCL).

February 21, 1860. Zanesville. Zanesville Young Men's Literary Association. "Manners." *Zanesville City Times*, February 25. Manuscript Memorandum Book for 1860 (HCL). Fee for the two Zanesville lectures: $100.00. Manuscript Account Book (HCL). Rusk, V, 203.

February 22, 1860. Zanesville. Zanesville Young Men's Literary Association. "The Conduct of Life." *Zanesville City Times*, February 25. Manuscript Memorandum Book for 1860 (HCL). Manuscript Account Book (HCL). Rusk, V, 203.

July 4, 1860. Oxford. Miami University Literary Societies. "Thought and Originality." *Cincinnati Daily Gazette*, July 6*. *Cincinnati Daily Commercial*, July 6*. Edward L. Taylor, "Ralph Waldo Emerson," *Ohio Indians and Other Writings* (Columbus: F. J. Heer, 1909), pp. 299–309. Fee: $100.00. Manuscript Account Book (HCL).

January 14, 1863. Cleveland Library Association. "The Third Estate in Literature." *Daily Cleveland Herald*, January 13, 14, 15. *Cleveland Daily Plain Dealer*, January 13, 15. *Cleveland Morning Leader*, January 17. Manuscript Memorandum Book for 1863 (HCL). Fee: $50.00. Manuscript Account Book (HCL). Rusk, V, 307.

January 18, 1865. Warren. Warren Polemics Club. "Social Aims in America." Warren *Western Reserve Chronicle*, January 25. *Cleveland Morning Leader,* January 21. Manuscript Memorandum Book for 1865 (HCL). Fee: $50.00. Manuscript Account Book (HCL).

January 19, 1865. Cleveland. Cleveland Library Association. "Social Aims in America." *Morning Cleveland Herald*, January 17, 19, 20. *Cleveland Daily Plain Dealer*, January 20. *Cleveland Morning Leader*, January 21*. Manuscript Memorandum Book for 1865 (HCL). Fee: $50.00. Manuscript Account Book (HCL). Rusk, V, 401.

January 12, 1866. Oberlin. Oberlin College Societies Library Association. "Social Manners." Oberlin *Lorain County News*, January 10, 17. Manuscript Memorandum Book for 1866 (HCL). Fee: $50.00. Manuscript Account Book (HCL). Rusk, V, 449.

February 5, 1866. Toledo. Toledo Library Association. "Table Talk." *Daily Toledo Blade*, February 5. *Toledo Daily Commercial*, February 5, 6. Manuscript Memorandum Book for 1866 (HCL). Fee: $75.00. Manuscript Account Book (HCL). Rusk, V, 457.

February 6, 1866. Cleveland. Cleveland Library Association. "Resources." *Morning Cleveland Herald*, February 5, 7. *Cleveland Daily Plain Dealer*, February 7. *Cleveland Daily Leader*, February 6, 7. Manuscript Memorandum Book for 1866 (HCL). Fee: $75.00. Manuscript Account Book (HCL).

January 10, 1867. Cleveland. Cleveland Library Association. "The Man of the World." *Morning Cleveland Herald*, January 9, 11. *Cleveland Daily Plain Dealer*, January 11. *Cleveland Daily Leader*, January 9, 11. Manuscript Memorandum Book for 1867 (HCL). Fee: $75.00. Manuscript Account Book (HCL). Rusk, V, 489.

March 14, 1867. Cincinnati. William F. Phillips. "Social Life in America." *Cincinnati Daily Gazette*, March 12, 15. *Cincinnati Daily Commercial*, March 15*. *Cincinnati Daily Enquirer*, March 14, 15. Hastings, p. 469. Manuscript Memorandum Book for 1867 (HCL). Fee: $100.00. Manuscript Account Book (HCL).

March 15, 1867. Marietta. Addison H. Siegfried. "Social Life in America." *Marietta Times*, March 7, 21*. *Marietta Register*, March 14, 21*. Manuscript Memorandum Book for 1867 (HCL). Fee: $50.00. Manuscript Account Book (HCL).

March 16, 1867. Marietta. Private. "The Man of the World." *Marietta Register*, March 21. Manuscript Memorandum Book for 1867 (HCL). Manuscript Account Book (HCL).

March 17, 1867†. Marietta. Unitarian Church. "Immortality." (Sermon). Manuscript Memorandum Book for 1867 (HCL).

December 4, 1867. Cleveland. Cleveland Library Association. "Eloquence." *Morning Cleveland Herald*, December 5, 6. *Cleveland Daily Plain Dealer*, December 4. *Cleveland Daily Leader*, December 4, 5. Manuscript Memorandum Book for 1867 (HCL). Fee: $100.00. Manuscript Account Book (HCL). Rusk, V, 541.

December 6, 1867. Painesville. Painesville Young Men's Christian Association. "American Culture." *Painesville Telegraph*, December 12*. Manuscript Memorandum Book for 1867 (HCL). Fee: $100.00. Manuscript Account Book (HCL). Rusk, V, 542.

December 28, 1867. Steubenville. Steubenville Young Men's Christian Association. "Society in America." *Steubenville Weekly Herald*, December 27; January 3, 1868. Manuscript Memorandum Book for 1867 (HCL). Fee: $100.00. Manuscript Account Book (HCL).

December 30, 1867. Columbus. Columbus Young Men's Christian Association. "American Culture." *Columbus Morning Journal*, December 31. Columbus *Daily Ohio Statesman*, December 31. *Columbus Gazette*, December 27; January 3, 1868. Edward L. Taylor, "Ralph Waldo Emerson," *Ohio Indians and Other Writings* (Columbus: F. J. Heer, 1909), pp. 299–309. Manuscript Memorandum Book for 1867 (HCL). Fee: $100.00. Manuscript Account Book (HCL).

HENRY GILES

February 18, 1851. Cincinnati. Cincinnati Young Men's Mercantile Library Association. "Conversation." *Daily Cincinnati Gazette*, February 6, 11, 19.

February 20, 1851. Cincinnati. Private. "The Life and Genius of Cervantes." *Daily Cincinnati Gazette*, February 17, 24. *Cincinnati Daily Enquirer*, February 23.

February 24, 1851. Cincinnati. Private. "The Scope and Spirit of the Story of *Don Quixote*." *Daily Cincinnati Gazette*, February 17, 26.

February 27, 1851†. Cincinnati. Private. "The Censorship in the Library, or Literary Fame." *Daily Cincinnati Gazette*, February 17, 27.

March 2, 1851. Cincinnati. Unitarian Church. "By Wisdom We Know Not God" (Sermon). *Daily Cincinnati Gazette*, March 3.

March 3, 1851†. Cincinnati. Private. "Dulcinea, or Womanhood." *Daily Cincinnati Gazette*, February 17; March 3.

March 6, 1851†. Cincinnati. Private. "Sancho Panza, or the Worldling." *Daily Cincinnati Gazette*, February 17; March 6.

March 10, 1851†. Cincinnati. Private. "Don Quixote." *Daily Cincinnati Gazette*, February 17; March 10.

March 13, 1851. Cincinnati. Private. "The Hebrew Man, or the Man of Faith." *Daily Cincinnati Gazette*, March 7, 14, 18*.

March 16, 1851†. Cincinnati. Unitarian Church. Sermon. *Daily Cincinnati Gazette*, March 15.

March 18, 1851†. Cincinnati. Private. "The Greek Man, or the Man of Culture." *Daily Cincinnati Gazette*, March 7, 18.

March 20, 1851†. Cincinnati. Private. "The Roman Man, or the Man of Law." *Daily Cincinnati Gazette*, March 7.

March 25, 1851. Cincinnati. Private. "The Medieval Man, or the Man of Force." *Daily Cincinnati Gazette*, March 7, 27*.

March 27, 1851†. Cincinnati. Private. "The Modern Man, or the Man of Money." *Daily Cincinnati Gazette*, March 7, 27.

April 3, 1851. Cleveland. Cleveland Library Association. "The Modern Man, or the Man of Money." *Cleveland Herald*, March 31; April 4. Cleveland *Daily True Democrat*, April 5, 7*.

April 8, 1851. Cleveland. Cleveland Library Association. "Enthusiasm." *Cleveland Herald*, April 5, 8. Cleveland *Daily True Democrat*, April 7. *Daily Cleveland Plain Dealer*, April 8, 9*.

November 24, 1852. Cleveland. Cleveland Young Men's Mercantile Library Association. "The Irish Character." *Cleveland Herald*, November 24. *Daily Cleveland Plain Dealer*, November 26.

November 26, 1852. Cleveland. Cleveland Young Men's Mercantile Library Association. "The Worldling." *Cleveland Herald*, November 24, 27. Cleveland *Daily True Democrat*, November 29.

December 22, 1853. Cincinnati. Cincinnati Young Men's Mercantile Library Association. "The Genius and Immortality of Shakespeare." *Daily Cincinnati Gazette*, December 22, 23.

December 13, 1854. Cincinnati. Cincinnati Young Men's Catholic Literary Institute. "The Comic Powers of Shakespeare." *Daily Cincinnati Gazette,* December 12. *Cincinnati Daily Commercial,* December 14.

December 19, 1854. Columbus. Columbus Atheneum. "The Comic Powers of Shakespeare." Columbus *Daily Ohio State Journal,* December 16, 20. Columbus *Daily Ohio Statesman and Democrat,* December 20. Columbus *Daily Capital City Fact,* December 20.

December 20, 1854†. Cincinnati. Cincinnati Young Men's Catholic Literary Institute. "The Worldling Character." *Daily Cincinnati Gazette,* December 19.

December 22, 1854. Dayton. Dayton Library Association. "The Comic Powers of Shakespeare." *Daily Dayton Journal,* December 22, 23. *Dayton Daily Gazette,* December 23.

January 2, 1855. Dayton. Private. "The Comic Powers of Shakespeare." *Daily Dayton Journal,* January 1, 3.

January 5, 1855. Zanesville. Zanesville Astronomical Society. "The Worldling Character." *Zanesville City Times,* January 6. Fee: $50.00. *Zanesville Gazette,* October 23.

January 8, 1855. Chillicothe. Chillicothe Popular Lecture Association. "The Comic Powers of Shakespeare." Chillicothe *Daily Scioto Gazette,* January 8, 9*.

December 11, 1855. Elyria. Probably Elyria Lyceum. Probably "False and Extravagant Eulogy in Oratory." *Elyria Independent Democrat,* December 12.

December 12, 1855. Sandusky. Sandusky Young Men's Library Association. "False and Extravagant Eulogy in Oratory." Fee: $30.00. Gross receipts: $26.74. *Sandusky Daily Commercial Register,* December 12, 13; February 16, 1856.

December 13, 1855†. Milan. Sponsor not announced. Probably "False and Extravagant Eulogy in Oratory." *Sandusky Daily Commercial Register,* December 1.

December 14, 1855†. Tiffin. Seneca Library Association. Probably "False and Extravagant Eulogy in Oratory." Tiffin *Seneca Advertiser,* December 14.

December 15, 1855. Kenton. Kenton Library Association. "False and Extravagant Eulogy in Oratory." Kenton *Hardin County Republican,* December 14, 21.

December 17, 1855. Circleville. Pickaway Lyceum. "False and Extravagant Eulogy in Oratory." *Circleville Watchman,* December 13, 20.

December 19, 1855†. Mansfield. Mansfield Young Men's Library Association. "False and Extravagant Eulogy in Oratory." *Mansfield Herald,* December 12.

December 20, 1855. Springfield. Springfield Irving Club. "False and Extravagant Eulogy in Oratory." *Daily Springfield Nonpareil,* December 20, 21.

December 21, 1855†. Lima. Probably Lima Library and Reading Room Association. Probably "False and Extravagant Eulogy in Oratory." *Sandusky Daily Commercial Register*, December 1.

December 24, 1855. Toledo. Toledo Young Men's Association. "The *Worldling.*" *Daily Toledo Blade*, December 24, 26.

December 26, 1855. Norwalk. Whittlesey Academy. "False and Extravagant Eulogy in Oratory." *Norwalk Reflector*, January 1, 1856.

December 27, 1855†. Bucyrus. Bucyrus Literary Association. Probably "False and Extravagant Eulogy in Oratory." *Sandusky Daily Commercial Register*, December 1.

December 31, 1855†. Chillicothe. Chillicothe Popular Lecture Association. "False and Extravagant Eulogy in Oratory." Chillicothe *Daily Scioto Gazette*, December 31.

January 4, 1856. Cincinnati. Ohio Mechanics' Institute. "False and Extravagant Eulogy in Oratory." *Cincinnati Daily Gazette*, January 4, 5.

January 10, 1856†. Akron. Akron Young Men's Association. "False and Extravagant Eulogy in Oratory." Akron *Summit Beacon*, January 9.

January 15, 1856. Salem. Salem Popular Lecture Association. "False and Extravagant Eulogy in Oratory." Salem *Columbiana County Republican*, January 16.

March 23, 1856. Cincinnati. New Jerusalem Church. Sermon. *Daily Cincinnati Gazette*, March 25.

January 8, 1859. Cincinnati. Cincinnati Young Men's Mercantile Library Association. "Charlotte Brontë." *Cincinnati Daily Gazette*, January 8, 10. *Cincinnati Daily Commercial*, January 10*. *Cincinnati Daily Enquirer*, January 9*.

February 5, 1866. Zanesville. Zanesville Lecture Association. "The Jew in History." (Delivered by Louisa L. Giles.) *Daily Zanesville Courier*, February 2, 6.

PARKE GODWIN

November 23, 1854. Columbus. Columbus Atheneum. "Manifest Destiny." Columbus *Daily Ohio State Journal*, November 22, 24. Columbus *Daily Ohio Statesman and Democrat*, November 24.

November 27, 1854. Steubenville. Steubenville Atheneum. Probably "Manifest Destiny." *Steubenville American Union*, November 29.

January 9, 1855. Cincinnati. Cincinnati Young Men's Mercantile Library Association. "The Future Republic." *Daily Cincinnati Gazette*, January 8, 10*.

January 11, 1855. Chillicothe. Chillicothe Popular Lecture Association. "The Future Republic." Chillicothe *Daily Scioto Gazette*, January 11, 12.

January 12, 1855. Zanesville. Zanesville Astronomical Society. "The

Future Republic." Fee: $50.00. *Zanesville Gazette*, January 9, 16*; October 23.

January 15, 1855†. Newark. Probably Newark People's Lecture Association. Probably "The Future Republic." Chillicothe *Daily Scioto Gazette*, January 12.

December 1, 1855. Canton. Canton People's Lecture Association. Probably "The Future Republic." Canton *Stark County Democrat*, December 5. Canton *Ohio Repository*, November 28.

December 4, 1855. Elyria. Probably Elyria Lyceum. "The Future Republic." *Elyria Independent Democrat*, December 5.

December 5, 1855. Sandusky. Sandusky Young Men's Library Association. "The Future Republic." Fee: $30.00. Gross receipts: $21.88. *Sandusky Daily Commercial Register*, December 5; February 16, 1856.

December 6, 1855. Norwalk. Whittlesey Academy. Probably "The Future Republic." *Norwalk Reflector*, December 11.

December 7, 1855. Tiffin. Seneca Library Association. "The Future Republic." Tiffin *Seneca Advertiser*, December 7, 14.

December 8, 1855. Kenton. Kenton Library Association. "The Future Republic." Kenton *Hardin County Republican*, November 30; December 14.

December 10, 1855. Springfield. Springfield Irving Club. "The Future Republic." *Springfield Weekly Nonpareil*, December 11, 13. *Springfield Weekly Republic*, December 14.

December 11, 1855. Zanesville. Zanesville Atheneum. "American Social Life." *Zanesville Gazette*, December 18. *Zanesville Aurora* in *Sandusky Daily Commercial Register*, December 24.

December 12, 1855. Mansfield. Mansfield Young Men's Library Association. "The Future Republic." *Mansfield Herald*, December 12, 19*.

December 13, 1855†. Bucyrus. Bucyrus Literary Association. Probably "The Future Republic." *Sandusky Daily Commercial Register*, December 1.

December 14, 1855. Toledo. Toledo Young Men's Association. "American Journal Life." *Daily Toledo Blade*, December 12, 15.

February 28, 1856. Sandusky. Cosmopolitan Art Association. "The Dignity and Influence of Art." *Zanesville Gazette*, March 4.

February 29, 1856. Elyria. Elyria Lyceum. "The History and Progress of the Nineteenth Century." *Elyria Independent Democrat*, March 5.

OLIVER WENDELL HOLMES

September 4, 1855. Cincinnati. Cincinnati Young Men's Mercantile Library Association. "Byron and Moore." *Cincinnati Daily Gazette*, September 5*. *Cincinnati Daily Commercial*, September 5. *Cincinnati Daily Enquirer*, September 5.

September 5, 1855. Cincinnati. Cincinnati Young Men's Mercantile Library Association. "Lectures and Lecturing." *Cincinnati Daily Gazette,* September 1, 6*. *Cincinnati Daily Commercial,* September 6*. *Cincinnati Daily Enquirer,* September 6, 7*.

September 6, 1855. Cincinnati. Cincinnati Young Men's Mercantile Library Association. "Physical Life in New England." *Cincinnati Daily Gazette,* September 1, 7*. *Cincinnati Daily Enquirer,* September 7.

September 7, 1855. Cincinnati. Cincinnati Young Men's Mercantile Library Association. "The Poetry of Keats." *Cincinnati Daily Gazette,* September 1, 8*. *Cincinnati Daily Commercial,* September 8*.

HERMAN MELVILLE

January 11, 1858. Cleveland. Cleveland Library Association. "Statues in Rome." *Cleveland Daily Herald,* January 11, 12*. *Cleveland Morning Leader,* January 12. Cleveland *Ohio Farmer,* January 23*. George Kummer, "Herman Melville and the Ohio Press," *Ohio State Archaeological and Historical Quarterly,* XLV (January, 1936), 34–36. Fee: $50.00. Raymond M. Weaver, *Herman Melville, Mariner and Mystic* (New York: George H. Doran Company, 1921), p. 370.

February 2, 1858. Cincinnati. Cincinnati Young Men's Mercantile Library Association. "Statues in Rome." *Cincinnati Daily Gazette,* February 2, 3*. *Cincinnati Daily Commercial,* February 3*. *Cincinnati Daily Enquirer,* February 3. George Kummer, "Herman Melville and the Ohio Press," *Ohio State Archaeological and Historical Quarterly,* XLV (January, 1936), 34–36. Fee: $50.00. Raymond M. Weaver, *Herman Melville, Mariner and Mystic* (New York: George H. Doran Company, 1921), p. 370.

February 3, 1858. Chillicothe. Chillicothe Gymnasium and Library Association. "Statues in Rome." Chillicothe *Weekly Scioto Gazette,* February 2, 9. *Chillicothe Advertiser,* February 5*. George Kummer, "Herman Melville and the Ohio Press," *Ohio State Archaeological and Historical Quarterly,* XLV (January, 1936), 34–36. Fee: $40.00. Raymond M. Weaver, *Herman Melville, Mariner and Mystic* (New York: George H. Doran Company, 1921), p. 370.

THEODORE PARKER

November 5, 1852. Cincinnati. Private. "The Progress of Mankind." *Daily Cincinnati Gazette,* November 3, 4, 6. *Cleveland Herald,* November 9*.

November 6, 1852†. Cincinnati. Private. "The False and True Idea of a Gentleman." *Daily Cincinnati Gazette,* November 3, 6.

November 7, 1852. Cincinnati. Unitarian Church. Morning and evening sermons. *Daily Cincinnati Gazette,* November 6, 9, 10*, 11*.

November 9, 1852. Cleveland. Cleveland Young Men's Mercantile Library Association. "The False and True Idea of a Gentleman." *Cleveland Herald,* November 6, 9, 10. Cleveland *Morning Daily True Democrat,* November 11*.

January 12, 1854. Cleveland. Cleveland Library Association. "The Progress of Mankind." *Cleveland Herald,* January 12, 13. Fee: $50.00. Manuscript Lyceum Diary (MHS).

January 13, 1854. Toledo. Toledo Young Men's Association. "The False and True Idea of a Gentleman." *Daily Toledo Blade,* January 10, 14*, 16*. Fee: $30.00. Manuscript Lyceum Diary (MHS).

October 11, 1854. Cleveland. Probably Cleveland Library Association. "The Condition, Character and Prospects of America." *Cleveland Herald,* October 9. Fee: $50.00. Manuscript Lyceum Diary (MHS).

October 13, 1854. Toledo. Toledo Young Men's Association. "The Condition, Character and Prospects of America." Fee: $30.00. Manuscript Lyceum Diary (MHS).

October 14, 1854. Yellow Springs. Antioch College. "The Condition, Character and Prospects of America." Fee: $40.00. Manuscript Lyceum Diary (MHS). Maria L. Moore, Manuscript Diary (Antioch College Library).

October 16, 1854. Cincinnati. Ohio Mechanics' Institute. "The Relation of the Anglo Saxon Tribe to the Other Nations of the Earth." *Daily Cincinnati Gazette,* October 14. *Cincinnati Daily Commercial,* October 17*. Fee for the series of four Cincinnati lectures: $205.15. Manuscript Lyceum Diary (MHS).

October 17, 1854. Cincinnati. Ohio Mechanics' Institute. "The Condition, Character and Prospects of America." *Daily Cincinnati Gazette,* October 14. *Cincinnati Daily Commercial,* October 18*. Manuscript Lyceum Diary (MHS).

October 19, 1854. Cincinnati. Ohio Mechanics' Institute. "The Condition, Character and Prospects of American Slavery." *Daily Cincinnati Gazette,* October 19. *Cincinnati Daily Commercial,* October 20. Manuscript Lyceum Diary (MHS).

October 21, 1854. Cincinnati. Ohio Mechanics' Institute. "The Function of the Beautiful in the Development of Mankind." *Daily Cincinnati Gazette,* October 21. *Cincinnati Daily Commercial,* October 23*. Manuscript Lyceum Diary (MHS).

October 23, 1854. Dayton. Probably Dayton Library Association. "The Progress of Mankind." *Daily Dayton Journal,* October 23. Fee: $30.00. Manuscript Lyceum Diary (MHS).

November 7, 1855. Hudson. Western Reserve College. "The False and True Idea of a Gentleman." Akron *Summit Beacon,* October 24. Fee: $25.00. Manuscript Lyceum Diary (MHS). Minutes of the Phi Delta Literary Society (Western Reserve University Library).

November 8, 1855. Ravenna. Probably Ravenna Literary Association. "The Progress of Mankind." Ravenna *Portage Sentinel,* November 10. Fee: $25.00. Manuscript Lyceum Diary (MHS).

November 9, 1855. Salem. Salem Popular Lecture Association. "The Progress of Mankind." Salem *Columbiana County Republican,* November 14*. Fee: $25.00. Manuscript Lyceum Diary (MHS).

November 10, 1855. Massillon. Probably Massillon People's Lecture Association. "The Progress of Mankind." Fee: $25.00. Manuscript Lyceum Diary (MHS).

November 12, 1855. Canton. Canton People's Lecture Association. "The False and True Idea of a Gentleman." Canton *Ohio Repository,* October 31. Fee: $25.00. Manuscript Lyceum Diary (MHS).

November 13, 1855. Wooster. Probably Wooster Library Association. "The Progress of Mankind." Wooster *Wayne County Democrat,* November 15. Fee: $25.00. Manuscript Lyceum Diary (MHS).

November 14, 1855. Mansfield. Mansfield Young Men's Library Association. "The False and True Idea of a Gentleman." Mansfield *Richland Shield and Banner,* November 14. Fee: $25.00. Manuscript Lyceum Diary (MHS).

November 15, 1855. Akron Young Men's Association. "The False and True Idea of a Gentleman." Akron *Summit Beacon,* November 14, 21. Fee: $25.00. Manuscript Lyceum Diary (MHS).

November 17, 1855. Toledo. Toledo Young Men's Association. "The Progress of Mankind." *Daily Toledo Blade,* November 16, 19*. *Toledo Daily Times* in *Sandusky Daily Commercial Register,* November 21. Fee: $15.00. Manuscript Lyceum Diary (MHS).

November 18, 1855. Toledo. "False Rules of Action and False Guides of Conduct" (Morning Sermon). "Overruling Providence" (Evening Sermon). *Daily Toledo Blade,* November 19*.

WENDELL PHILLIPS

November 30, 1854. Cleveland. Cleveland Library Association. "The Lost Arts." *Cleveland Herald,* November 30; December 1.

December 1, 1854. Zanesville. Zanesville Astronomical Society. "The Lost Arts." Fee: $50.00. *Zanesville Gazette,* November 28; December 5*; October 23, 1855.

December 2, 1854. Cincinnati. Ohio Mechanics' Institute. Antislavery lecture. *Cincinnati Daily Commercial.* December 2, 4*.

December 4, 1854†. Cleveland. Private. Antislavery lecture. *Cleveland Herald,* December 2.

November 6, 1855. Cincinnati. Cincinnati Young Men's Mercantile Library Association. "The Lost Arts." *Cincinnati Daily Gazette,* November 6, 7*. *Cincinnati Daily Commercial,* November 7.

November 8, 1855†. Elyria. Probably Elyria Lyceum. Probably "The Lost Arts." *Elyria Independent Democrat,* November 7.

November 29, 1856. Salem. Probably private. "The Lost Arts." Salem *Columbiana County Republican*, November 26; December 3.

November 30, 1856. Salem. Probably private. Morning and afternoon antislavery lectures. Salem *Columbiana County Republican*, December 3.

December 1, 1856. Columbus. Columbus Atheneum. "The Lost Arts." Columbus *Daily Ohio State Journal*, December 1, 2.

December 2, 1856. Cincinnati. Cincinnati Young Men's Mercantile Library Association. "The Philosophy of Reform." *Cincinnati Daily Gazette*, December 2, 3*. *Cincinnati Daily Enquirer*, December 3*.

March 23, 1862. Cincinnati. First Congregational Church. "The Democracy of Christianity." *Cincinnati Daily Commercial*, March 22, 24.

March 24, 1862. Cincinnati. Cincinnati Branch of the United States Sanitary Commission. "Slavery and the War." Sponsor's profit: $114.88. *Cincinnati Daily Gazette,* March 24, 25*, 26*, 28. *Cincinnati Daily Commercial*, March 25*. *Cincinnati Daily Enquirer*, March 25*. Edward L. Taylor, "Wendell Phillips," *Ohio Indians and Other Writings* (Columbus: F. J. Heer, 1909), pp. 315–325. Moncure Daniel Conway, *Autobiography, Memories and Experiences* (2 vols.; Boston and New York: Houghton, Mifflin and Company, 1905), I, 353–354. Oscar Sherwin, *Prophet of Liberty: A Biography of Wendell Phillips* (Abridgment of a dissertation, New York University, 1943), pp. 13–14. Carlos Martyn, *Wendell Phillips: The Agitator* (New York: Funk and Wagnalls Company, 1890), pp. 325–326. Lorenzo Sears, *Wendell Phillips, Orator and Agitator* (New York: Doubleday, Page and Company, 1909), p. 234. Charles Edward Russell, *The Story of Wendell Phillips: Soldier of the Common Good* (Chicago: Charles H. Kerr and Company, 1914), p. 95. *Liberator*, April 4, 11, 1862.

April 9, 1862. Cleveland. Cleveland Young Men's Christian Association. "Slavery and the War." *Daily Cleveland Herald*, April 9, 10. *Cleveland Daily Plain Dealer*, April 10*. *Cleveland Morning Leader*, April 11*. Sponsor's profit: $72.00. *The Young Men's Christian Association of Cleveland* (Cleveland: J. B. Savage, 1900), p. 42.

April 10, 1862. Toledo. Toledo Young Men's Association. "Toussaint L'Ouverture." *Daily Toledo Blade*, April 10, 11.

April 17, 1867. Toledo. Toledo Library Association. "The Lost Arts." Selections from "The Perils of the Hour." *Daily Toledo Blade*, April 17, 18*. *Toledo Daily Commercial*, April 18*.

April 18, 1867. Cincinnati. William F. Phillips. "The Times." *Cincinnati Daily Gazette*, April 19*. *Cincinnati Daily Commercial*, April 19*. *Cincinnati Daily Enquirer*, April 18, 19*.

April 19, 1867. Cleveland. Cleveland Young People's Christian Association. "The Perils of the Hour." *Morning Cleveland Herald*,
April 18, 20*. *Cleveland Daily Leader*, April 20.

February 17, 1868. Warren. Warren Polemics Club. "The Times."
Warren *Western Reserve Chronicle*, February 12, 19.

February 18, 1868. Cleveland. Cleveland Young Men's Christian Association. "The Times." Fee: $200.00 *Morning Cleveland Herald*,
February 18, 19*, 27. *Cleveland Daily Leader*, February 19*.

February 19, 1868. Ashtabula. Ashtabula Citizens' Lecture Committee.
"The Times." *Ashtabula Telegraph*, February 22.

February 20, 1868. Oberlin. Oberlin Young Men's Christian Association. "The Times." Oberlin *Lorain County News*, February 19,
26*.

February 24, 1868. Sandusky. Sandusky Young Men's Christian and
Library Association. "The Lost Arts." *Sandusky Daily Commercial Register*, February 24, 25.

February 25, 1868. Cleveland. Cleveland Library Association. "The
Lost Arts." Fee: $200.00. *Morning Cleveland Herald*, February
25, 27. *Cleveland Daily Leader*, February 26*.

February 26, 1868. Delaware. Ohio Wesleyan University Lecture Association. "The Times." *Delaware Gazette*, February 28*. *Delaware
Herald*, February 20; March 5. Edward L. Taylor, "Wendell Phillips," *Ohio Indians and Other Writings* (Columbus: F. J. Heer,
1908), pp. 315–325.

February 27, 1868. Columbus. Columbus Young Men's Christian As-
sociation. "Daniel O'Connell." Fee: $150.00. Columbus *Daily Ohio
State Journal*, February 27, 28*. Columbus *Daily Ohio Statesman*,
February 28*.

February 28, 1868. Cincinnati. William F. Phillips. "The Lost Arts."
Cincinnati Daily Gazette, February 28, 29. *Cincinnati Daily Commercial*, February 29. *Cincinnati Daily Enquirer*, February 29.

March 2, 1868. Cincinnati. William F. Phillips. "Impeachment." *Cincinnati Daily Gazette*, March 3*; December 18*. *Cincinnati Daily
Commercial*, March 3*. *Cincinnati Daily Enquirer*, March 2, 3.

March 19, 1868. Columbus. Private. "The Times." Columbus *Daily
Ohio State Journal*, March 16, 20. Columbus *Daily Ohio Statesman*, March 19, 20.

JOHN GODFREY SAXE

February 22, 1853. Cincinnati. Cincinnati Young Men's Mercantile
Library Association. "Yankee Land" (Poem). *Daily Cincinnati
Gazette*, February 21, 23*. *Cincinnati Daily Commercial*, Febru-
ary 23*.

February 23, 1853. Columbus. Private. "Yankee Land." Columbus
Daily Ohio State Journal, February 22, 23, 25*. Columbus *Daily

Capital City Fact, February 24. Columbus *Daily Ohio Statesman*, February 25.

February 24, 1853. Cleveland. Cleveland Library Association. "Yankee Land." *Cleveland Herald*, February 19, 24, 25*. *Cleveland Daily Plain Dealer*, February 25.

February 25, 1853. Toledo. Toledo Young Men's Association. "Yankee Land." *Daily Toledo Blade*, February 21, 26.

March 2, 1853. Cleveland. Cleveland Library Association. "Progress" (Poem). "The Proud Miss McBride" (Poem). *Cleveland Herald*, February 25. *Cleveland Daily Plain Dealer*, March 2. Cleveland *Morning Daily True Democrat*, March 4.

March 3, 1853. Sandusky. Sandusky Atheneum. "Yankee Land." *Sandusky Daily Commercial Register*, March 3, 4.

March 4, 1853†. Ohio City (Cuyahoga County). Probably Ohio City Young Men's Association. Probably "Yankee Land." Cleveland *Morning Daily True Democrat*, March 4.

February 6, 1854. Akron. Akron Young Men's Lyceum. "Yankee Land." Akron *Summit Beacon*, January 18; February 8.

February 7, 1854. Zanesville. Zanesville Popular Lecture Association. "Yankee Land." *Daily Zanesville Courier*, January 18; February 3, 8. *Zanesville Gazette*, February 14.

February 8, 1854. Columbus. Columbus Atheneum. "Poets and Poetry." "The Proud Miss McBride." Columbus *Daily Ohio State Journal*, February 7, 9*. Columbus *Daily Ohio Statesman*, February 9. Columbus *Daily Capital City Fact*, February 9. Columbus *Swan's Elevator*, February 11.

February 9, 1854. Cleveland. Cleveland Library Association. "Poets and Poetry." "The Proud Miss McBride." *Cleveland Herald*, February 9, 10. *Cleveland Daily Plain Dealer*, February 10. Cleveland *Daily Forest City Democrat*, February 11.

February 10, 1854. Norwalk. Whittlesey Academy. "Yankee Land." *Norwalk Reflector*, February 7, 14.

February 11, 1854. Sandusky. C. L. Derby. "Poets and Poetry." "The Proud Miss McBride." *Sandusky Daily Commercial Register*, February 11, 13.

February 12, 1855. Chillicothe. Chillicothe Popular Lecture Association. "Yankee Land." Chillicothe *Daily Scioto Gazette*, February 12, 13*.

February 14, 1855†. Xenia. Xenia Lyceum. "Yankee Land." *Xenia Torch-Light*, February 14.

February 15, 1855. Delaware. Delaware Library Association. "The Money-King" (Poem). "The Proud Miss McBride." Delaware *Olentangy Gazette*, February 9, 16.

February 16, 1855. Sandusky. Probably Independent Lecture Committee. "The Money-King." *Sandusky Daily Commercial Register*, February 17*.

October 11, 1855. Delaware. Private. "The Press" (Poem). Delaware *Olentangy Gazette*, September 28; October 19.

October 25, 1855. Mansfield. Mansfield Female College. "Yankee Land." *Mansfield Herald*, October 24, 31. Mansfield *Richland Shield and Banner*, October 31.

November (8?) 1855. Oberlin. Oberlin College Societies Library Association. Probably "Yankee Land." Sponsor's profit: $00.30. Manuscript Account Book of the Oberlin College Societies Library Association (Oberlin College Library).

January 29, 1856. Dayton Library Association. "The Money-King." Selections from "Yankee Land." Fee: $50.00. *Daily Dayton Journal*, January 29, 30; January 16, 1857.

February 7, 1856. Cincinnati. Cincinnati Young Men's Mercantile Library Association. "The Money-King." Selections from "The Press." *Cincinnati Daily Gazette*, February 6, 7.

March 17, 1857. Cleveland. Cleveland Library Association. "The Press." Selections from "Yankee Land." *Daily Cleveland Herald*, March 17. *Cleveland Daily Plain Dealer*, March 18*. Cleveland *Ohio Farmer*, March 28*.

February 17, 1859. Cincinnati. Cincinnati Young Men's Mercantile Library Association. "Love" (Poem). *Cincinnati Daily Gazette*, February 17, 18. *Cincinnati Daily Enquirer*, February 18*.

February 19, 1859. Cincinnati. Cincinnati Young Men's Mercantile Library Association. "Love." *Cincinnati Daily Gazette*, February 19, 21. *Cincinnati Daily Enquirer*, February 20.

February 18, 1860. Toledo. Toledo Young Men's Association. "Love." *Daily Toledo Blade*, February 18, 21.

February 20, 1860. Cleveland. Cleveland Young Men's Christian Association. "Love." *Daily Cleveland Herald*, February 20, 21. *Cleveland Daily Plain Dealer*, February 21. *Cleveland Morning Leader*, February 21.

February 21, 1860. Cleveland. Cleveland Young Men's Christian Association. "Yankee Land." *Daily Cleveland Herald*, February 21, 22. *Cleveland Morning Leader*, February 22.

January 16, 1861. Oberlin. Oberlin Irving Lecture Association. "Yankee Land." "The Proud Miss McBride." Oberlin *Lorain County News*, January 16, 23*.

January 22, 1861. Medina. Medina Lecture Association. "Love." "The Proud Miss McBride." *Medina Gazette*, January 17, 24.

December 27, 1865. Zanesville. Zanesville Young Men's Literary Association. "Yankee Land." *Zanesville Daily Courier*, December 27, 28.

February 9, 1866. Cincinnati. Private. "Yankee Land." "The Proud Miss McBride." *Cincinnati Daily Gazette*, February 8, 10.

October 15, 1866. Cleveland. Cleveland Young People's Christian Association. "Poetry and Poets." "The Proud Miss McBride." Selections from "The Press." *Morning Cleveland Herald,* October 15, 16. *Cleveland Daily Plain Dealer,* October 16. *Cleveland Daily Leader,* October 16.

January 19, 1867. Marietta. Addison H. Siegfried. "Love." "The Proud Miss McBride." *Marietta Times,* January 10, 24*.

January 23, 1867†. Warren. Warren Polemics Club. "Love." "The Proud Miss McBride." Warren *Western Reserve Chronicle,* January 23.

October 25, 1867. Oberlin. Oberlin Young Men's Christian Association. "Poetry and Poets." Oberlin *Lorain County News,* October 23, 30.

December 15, 1868. Ravenna. Ravenna Lecture Association. "Yankee Land." Sponsor's profit: $35.00. Ravenna *Portage County Democrat,* December 16, 23.

January 20, 1869†. Ashtabula. Ashtabula Young Men's Christian Association. "Yankee Land." *Ashtabula Telegraph,* January 9.

December 16, 1869. Canton. Canton Young Men's Christian Association. "Yankee Land." "The Proud Miss McBride." *Canton Repository and Republican,* December 24.

BAYARD TAYLOR

March 20, 1854. Toledo. Toledo Young Men's Association. "The Arabs." *Daily Toledo Blade,* March 20, 21.

March 21, 1854. Sandusky. C. L. Derby. "Japan and the Japanese." *Sandusky Daily Commercial Register,* February 13, 23, 27; March 22*.

March 22, 1854. Cleveland. Private. "The Arabs." *Cleveland Herald,* March 20, 23*. *Cleveland Daily Plain Dealer,* March 24*.

March 23, 1854. Cleveland. Private. "Japan and the Japanese." *Cleveland Herald,* March 20, 24*. *Cleveland Daily Plain Dealer,* March 25*.

March 24, 1854. Mt. Vernon. Mt. Vernon Literary Association. "Japan and the Japanese." *Mt. Vernon Democratic Banner,* March 28. Mt. Vernon *Ohio State Times,* March 27.

March 25, 1854. Newark. Newark People's Lecture Association. "Japan and the Japanese." *Newark Advocate,* March 22, 29*.

March 27, 1854. Sandusky. C. L. Derby. "The Arabs." *Sandusky Daily Commercial Register,* March 27, 28, 29.

March 31, 1854. Zanesville. Zanesville Popular Lecture Association. "The Arabs." *Daily Zanesville Courier,* January 18; March 31; April 1.

April 1, 1854. Columbus. Columbus Atheneum. "The Arabs." Columbus *Daily Ohio State Journal,* March 30; April 2.

April 3, 1854. Chillicothe. Chillicothe Popular Lecture Association. "The Arabs." Fee: $50.00. Gross receipts: $125.00. Chillicothe *Daily Scioto Gazette,* April 3, 4*, 8.

April 4, 1854. Cincinnati. Cincinnati Young Men's Mercantile Library Association. "The Arabs." *Daily Cincinnati Gazette*, April 3, 5*.

April 5, 1854. Dayton. Dayton Lyceum. "The Arabs." *Dayton Journal and Advertiser*, April 11.

April 7, 1854. Chillicothe. Chillicothe Popular Lecture Association. "Japan and the Japanese." Fee: $50.00. Gross receipts: $79.90. Chillicothe *Daily Scioto Gazette*, April 7, 8*.

April 8, 1854. Columbus. Columbus Atheneum. "Japan and the Japanese." Columbus *Daily Ohio State Journal*, April 7, 10*.

April 10, 1854. Zanesville. Probably Zanesville Popular Lecture Association. "Japan and the Japanese." *Daily Zanesville Courier*, April 10, 11. *Zanesville Gazette*, April 18*.

April 26, 1854. Springfield. Probably private. "The Arabs." *Springfield Dollar Nonpareil*, April 27.

April 27, 1854. Circleville. Probably Pickaway Lyceum. "The Arabs." *Circleville Watchman*, April 27; May 4.

April 29, 1854. Newark. Newark People's Lecture Association. "The Arabs." *Newark Advocate*, April 19; May 3.

May 2, 1854†. Mansfield. Probably private. Probably "The Arabs." Ashland *Ohio Union*, April 26. *Sandusky Daily Commercial Register*, April 28.

May 3, 1854. Oberlin. Oberlin College Literary Societies. "The Arabs." *Oberlin Evangelist*, XI, No. 10 (May 10, 1854). *Sandusky Daily Commercial Register*, May 8*.

May 4, 1854. Akron. Akron Young Men's Lyceum. "The Arabs." Akron *Summit Beacon*, April 26; May 10*.

May 5, 1854. Painesville. Probably private. "Japan and the Japanese." *Painesville Telegraph*, May 3, 10.

January 4, 1855. Steubenville. Steubenville Atheneum. "India." *Steubenville American Union*, January 3, 10.

January 8, 1855. Newark. Probably Newark People's Lecture Association. "India." Chillicothe *Daily Scioto Gazette*, January 16. *Zanesville Gazette*, January 16.

January 13, 1855. Toledo. Toledo Young Men's Association. "India." *Daily Toledo Blade*, January 13, 15*.

January 15, 1855. Columbus. Columbus Atheneum. "The Philosophy of Travel." Columbus *Daily Ohio State Journal*, January 15. Columbus *Daily Capital City Fact*, January 16.

January 16, 1855. Cincinnati. Cincinnati Young Men's Mercantile Library Association. "India." *Daily Cincinnati Gazette*, January 17. *Cincinnati Daily Commercial*, January 16, 17.

January 18, 1855. Chillicothe. Chillicothe Popular Lecture Association. "India." Chillicothe *Daily Scioto Gazette*, January 18, 19.

January 19, 1855. Xenia. Xenia Lyceum. "Japan and the Japanese." *Xenia Torch-Light*, January 10, 24.

January 21, 1855. Yellow Springs. Antioch College. "Religions of the World." Horace Mann, Manuscript Letter to Bayard Taylor, July 1, 1854 (photostat in the Antioch College Library). Maria L. Moore, Manuscript Diary (Antioch College Library).

January 23, 1855. Cincinnati. Cincinnati Young Men's Mercantile Library Association. "The Philosophy of Travel." *Daily Cincinnati Gazette*, January 22, 24*. *Cincinnati Daily Commercial*, January 24*.

January 24, 1855. Zanesville. Probably Zanesville Astronomical Society. "The Philosophy of Travel." *Zanesville Gazette*, January 30.

February 1, 1855. Canton. Canton People's Lecture Association. "The Arabs." Fee: $50.00. Canton *Stark County Democrat*, January 24; February 7*.

February 3, 1855. Cleveland. Private. "India." *Cleveland Herald*, February 3, 5.

February 5, 1855. Cleveland. Private. "The Philosophy of Travel." *Cleveland Herald*, February 5, 7. *Cleveland Daily Plain Dealer*, February 6.

February 6, 1855. Cincinnati. Cincinnati Young Men's Mercantile Library Association. "The Animal Man." *Cincinnati Daily Enquirer*, February 6, 7*.

February 7, 1855. Wilmington. Probably private. "The Arabs." *Wilmington Independent*, February 9, 1855.

February 8, 1855. Chillicothe. Chillicothe Popular Lecture Association. "The Philosophy of Travel." Chillicothe *Daily Scioto Gazette*, February 8, 9.

February 10, 1855†. Columbus. Columbus Atheneum. "India." Columbus *Daily Ohio State Journal*, February 10.

February 12, 1855. Hamilton. Hamilton and Rossville Library Association. "India." *Hamilton Intelligencer*, February 8, 15.

April 24, 1855. Springfield. Private. "The Philosophy of Travel." *Springfield Weekly Republic*, April 27.

January 11, 1856. Cleveland. Cleveland Library Association. "The Animal Man." *Cleveland Herald*, January 11. Cleveland *Ohio Farmer*, January 26*. *Sandusky Daily Commercial Register*, January 17.

January 25, 1859. Cleveland. Cleveland Library Association. "Life in the North." *Cleveland Daily Herald*, January 25, 26. *Cleveland Daily Plain Dealer*, January 26*. *Cleveland Morning Leader*, January 26*.

January 31, 1859. Sandusky. Sandusky Young Men's Library Association. "Moscow." *Sandusky Daily Commercial Register*, January 31; February 1*.

February 2, 1859. Norwalk. Whittlesey Academy. "Life in the North." *Norwalk Reflector*, February 1, 8.

February 3, 1859. Cincinnati. Cincinnati Young Men's Mercantile Li-

brary Association. "Life in the North." Gross receipts: $433.00.
Cincinnati Daily Gazette, February 3, 4*, 7. *Cincinnati Daily Commercial*, February 4*. *Cincinnati Daily Enquirer*, February 4.

February 4, 1859. Delaware. Delaware Young Men's Lecture Association. "Life in the North." *Delaware Democratic Standard*, January 24; February 10.

February 4, 1859. Columbus. Congregational Church Lecture Association. "Life in the North." Columbus *Daily Ohio State Journal*, February 4, 5, 7*.

February 5, 1859. Yellow Springs. Antioch College. "Moscow." *Springfield Evening News and Journal*, February 8. *Xenia Torch-Light*, February 9.

February 7, 1859. Cincinnati. Cincinnati Young Men's Mercantile Library Association. "Moscow." Gross receipts: $470.00. *Cincinnati Daily Gazette*, February 8*, 11. *Cincinnati Daily Commercial*, February 9*. *Cincinnati Daily Enquirer*, February 8*.

February 8, 1859. Cleveland. Cleveland Young Men's Christian Association. "Moscow." *Cleveland Daily Herald,* February 8. *Cleveland Daily Plain Dealer*, February 9*. *Cleveland Morning Leader*, February 9*. Cleveland *Ohio Farmer*, February 19*. Fee: $100.00. *The Young Men's Christian Association of Cleveland* (Cleveland: J. B. Savage, 1900), p. 36.

February 9, 1859. Toledo. Toledo Young Men's Association. "Life in the North." Gross receipts: $125.00. *Daily Toledo Blade*, February 9, 10; January 26, 1860.

January 5, 1860. Cincinnati. Cincinnati Young Men's Mercantile Library Association. "Von Humboldt." *Cincinnati Daily Gazette,* January 5, 6. *Cincinnati Daily Commercial*, January 7*. *Cincinnati Daily Enquirer*, January 7*.

January 6, 1860. Cincinnati. Cincinnati Young Men's Mercantile Library Association. "Life in the Arctic Regions." *Cincinnati Daily Gazette*, January 6, 7*.

January 23, 1860. Norwalk. Whittlesey Academy. "Von Humboldt." *Norwalk Reflector*, January 31.

January 24, 1860. Toledo. Toledo Young Men's Association. "Moscow." Door receipts (exclusive of season tickets): $82.00. *Daily Toledo Blade*, January 24, 25, 26.

April 2, 1860. Cleveland. Cleveland Library Association. "Von Humboldt." *Daily Cleveland Herald*, April 2, 3. *Cleveland Daily Plain Dealer*, April 3. *Cleveland Morning Leader*, April 3*.

November 20, 1860. Cincinnati. Cincinnati Young Men's Mercantile Library Association. "Man and Climate." *Cincinnati Daily Gazette*, November 20, 21*. *Cincinnati Daily Commercial*, November 21*. *Cincinnati Daily Enquirer*, November 21.

November 21, 1860. Lebanon. Lebanon Congregational Society. "Man and Climate." Lebanon *Weekly Western Star*, November 29.

November 22, 1860. Cleveland. Cleveland Library Association. "Man
and Climate." *Daily Cleveland Herald*, November 22, 23. *Cleveland Daily Plain Dealer*, November 23*. *Cleveland Morning Leader*,
November 23*.

November 26, 1860. Springfield. Private. "Life in the Arctic Regions."
Springfield Daily News, November 27.

December 8, 1860. Oberlin. Oberlin Irving Lecture Association. "Man
and Climate." Oberlin *Lorain County News*, December 12*. *Oberlin Students' Monthly*, III (January, 1861), 92.

February 13, 1861. Ashtabula. Ashtabula Lecture Association. "Man
and Climate." *Ashtabula Telegraph*, February 9, 16.

February 14, 1861†. Berlin Heights. Sponsor not announced. "Man and
Climate." *Sandusky Daily Commercial Register*, February 6.

February 25, 1861†. Dayton. Dayton Young Men's Christian Association. "Life in the North." *Daily Dayton Journal*, February 24.

February 26, 1861. Cincinnati. Cincinnati Union Bethel. "Moscow and
the Russians." *Cincinnati Daily Gazette*, February 25, 27*. *Cincinnati Daily Enquirer*, February 27*.

February 27, 1861†. Wooster. Wooster Library Association. Subject
not announced. Wooster *Wayne County Democrat*, February 21.

March 22, 1861. Conneaut. Conneaut Literary Association. "Life in the
North." *Conneaut Reporter*, March 28*.

January 7, 1862. Zanesville. Zanesville Young Men's Literary Association. "The American People, Socially and Politically." *Daily
Zanesville Courier*, January 7, 8*.

January 8, 1862. Columbus. Columbus Atheneum. "American Civilization." Columbus *Daily Ohio State Journal*, January 8. Columbus
Daily Ohio Statesman, January 9. Columbus *Daily Capital City
Fact*, January 9.

January 9, 1862. Cleveland. Cleveland Library Association. "The American People, Socially and Politically." *Daily Cleveland Herald*,
January 9, 10. *Cleveland Morning Leader*, January 10*.

January 10, 1862. Cincinnati. Cincinnati Young Men's Mercantile
Library Association. "The American People, Socially and Politically." *Cincinnati Daily Gazette*, January 10, 11*. *Cincinnati Daily
Commercial*, January 11*.

December 3, 1863. Cleveland. Cleveland Library Association. "Russia
and Her People." *Daily Cleveland Herald*, December 3, 4. *Cleveland Daily Plain Dealer*, December 4. *Cleveland Morning Leader*,
December 4.

February 23, 1864. Warren. Warren Polemics Club. "Russia and Her
People." Warren *Western Reserve Chronicle*, February 17. *Warren
Constitution*, March 1.

February 24, 1864. Toledo. Toledo Young Men's Association. "Russia
and Her People." *Daily Toledo Blade*, February 24, 25*.

January 17, 1865. Cincinnati. Private. "Ourselves and Our Relations."
Cincinnati Daily Gazette, January 18, 1865.

November 9, 1865. Cincinnati. Private. "Russia and the Russians."
Cincinnati Daily Gazette, November 10*. *Cincinnati Daily Enquirer,* November 9, 10*.

January 15, 1867. Cleveland. Cleveland Library Association. "American
Life." *Cleveland Morning Herald,* January 15, 16*.

November 2, 1869. Cincinnati. Private. "Views of American Society."
Cincinnati Daily Gazette, November 2, 3*. *Cincinnati Daily Commercial,* November 3*. *Cincinnati Daily Enquirer,* November 3*.

December 11, 1869. Toledo. Private. "Life in Europe and America."
Daily Toledo Blade, December 11, 13*.

December 13, 1869. Cleveland. Private. "Life in Europe and America."
Cleveland Daily Plain Dealer, December 13, 14. *Cleveland Daily
Leader,* December 14*.

December 14, 1869. Massillon. Private. "Life in Europe and America."
Canton Repository and Republican, December 16.

December 15, 1869. Springfield. Private. "Life in Europe and America."
Springfield Daily Republic, December 15, 16*.

December 16, 1869. Columbus. Private. "Life in Europe and America."
Columbus *Daily Ohio State Journal,* December 16, 17*.

December 18, 1869. Chillicothe. Private. "Life in Europe and America."
Chillicothe *Scioto Gazette,* December 22.

EDWIN P. WHIPPLE

February 15, 1853. Cincinnati. Cincinnati Young Men's Mercantile
Library Association. "The American Mind." *Daily Cincinnati
Gazette,* February 15, 16.

February 17, 1853. Cincinnati. Cincinnati Young Men's Mercantile
Library Association. "The English Mind." *Daily Cincinnati Gazette,*
February 17, 18*.

February 19, 1853. Cleveland. Cleveland Library Association. "The
American Mind." *Cleveland Herald,* February 18, 21. *Cleveland
Daily Plain Dealer,* February 21. Cleveland *Morning Daily True
Democrat,* February 21.

February 21, 1853. Cleveland. Cleveland Library Association. "Heroism." *Cleveland Herald,* February 19, 22*. *Cleveland Daily Plain
Dealer,* February 22.

November 23, 1853†. Cleveland. Cleveland Library Association. "Eccentric Character." *Cleveland Herald,* November 21.

December 3, 1853. Toledo. Toledo Young Men's Association. "Eccentric Character." *Daily Toledo Blade,* December 2, 5*.

December 6, 1853†. Cincinnati. Cincinnati Young Men's Mercantile
Library Association. "Eccentric Character." *Daily Cincinnati
Gazette,* December 5.

December 7, 1853. Columbus. Columbus Atheneum. "Heroic Character." Columbus *Daily Ohio State Journal*, December 6, 9*. Columbus *Daily Ohio Statesman*, December 8.

December 8, 1853. Cincinnati. Cincinnati Young Men's Mercantile Library Association. "Heroism." *Daily Cincinnati Gazette*, December 8, 9.

December 9, 1853. Zanesville. Zanesville Popular Lecture Association. "Eccentric Character." *Daily Zanesville Courier*, December 9, 10.

December 14, 1855. Dayton. Dayton Library Association. "The History of Joan of Arc." Fee: $50.00. *Daily Dayton Journal*, December 14, 15; January 16, 1856. *Dayton Daily Gazette*, December 17.

December 14, 1857. Cleveland. Cleveland Library Association. "Young Men in History." *Daily Cleveland Herald*, December 14, 15*.

January 17, 1862. Cleveland. Cleveland Library Association. "Grit." *Daily Cleveland Herald*, January 17, 18. *Cleveland Daily Plain Dealer*, January 18. *Cleveland Morning Leader*, January 18.

February 10, 1868. Youngstown. Youngstown Library and Lecture Association. "Shoddy." Youngstown *Mahoning Register*, February 6, 13.

February 13, 1868. Cleveland. Cleveland Library Association. "Loafing and Laboring." *Morning Cleveland Herald*, February 13, 14.

February 14, 1868. Toledo. Toledo Library Association. "Loafing and Laboring." *Daily Toledo Blade*, February 15. *Toledo Daily Commercial*, February 14, 15.

INDEX